"ARTHUR, THE GREATEST KING"

GARLAND REFERENCE LIBRARY
OF THE HUMANITIES
(VOL. 830)

ing Arthur of Britain.

From *The Story of King Arthur and His Knights*,
written and illustrated by Howard Pyle.
New York: Scribner's, 1903.

"ARTHUR, THE GREATEST KING"

An Anthology of
Modern Arthurian Poems

edited by
ALAN LUPACK

foreword by
RAYMOND H. THOMPSON

GARLAND PUBLISHING, INC.
NEW YORK & LONDON
1988

LIBRARY OF CONGRESS CATALOGING-IN-PUBLICATION DATA

Arthur, the greatest king : an anthology of modern Arthurian poems/
edited by Alan Lupak ; foreword by Raymond H. Thompson.
   p. cm.– (Garland reference library of the humanities; vol.
830)
   ISBN 0-8240-5733-3 (alk. paper)
   1. Arthur, King–Poetry. 2. Middle Ages–Poetry. 3. Kings
and rulers–Poetry. 4. English poetry–19th century.
5. English poetry–20th century. 6. American poetry.
7. Arthurian romances.
I. Lupack, Alan. II. Series.
PR1195.A75A78   1988
821'.008'0351–dc19   88-6401

Cover illustration from *The Story of the Champions of the Round
Table,* written and illustrated by Howard Pyle. New York: Scribner's,
1905.

Printed on acid-free, 250-year-life paper

MANUFACTURED IN THE UNITED STATES OF AMERICA

As is everything,

for Barbara

Contents

Acknowledgments

Thomas Caldecot Chubb, "Merlin," reprinted from *The White God and Other Poems*, copyright 1920 by Yale University Press.

John Ciardi, "Launcelot in Hell," reprinted from *In the Stoneworks* (Rutgers University Press) by permission of Ms. Judith H. Ciardi.

Thom Gunn, "Merlin in the Cave: He Speculates Without a Book," reprinted by permission of Faber and Faber Ltd. from *The Sense of Movement* by Thom Gunn.

C. S. Lewis, "Launcelot," from *Narrative Poems* by C. S. Lewis, copyright © 1969 by The Trustees of the Estate of C. S. Lewis. Reprinted by permission of Harcourt Brace Jovanovich, Inc.

John Masefield, "The Sailing of Hell Race" and "The Fight at Camlan," reprinted with permission of Macmillan Publishing Company from *Midsummer Night and Other Tales in Verse* by John Masefield. Copyright 1928, and renewed 1956, by John Masefield. "The Ballad of Sir Bors," reprinted with permission of Macmillan Publishing Company from *Poems* by John Masefield (New York: Macmillan, 1953).

Edgar Lee Masters, "Ballad of Launcelot and Elaine" and "The Death of Sir Launcelot," from *Songs and Satires*, published by The Macmillan Company. Reprinted by permission of Ms. Ellen C. Masters.

Foreword

The vigor of Arthurian legend can sometimes surprise even its
most ardent admirers. We have pondered its origins, admired its
flowering in medieval romance, regretted its retreat into obscurity
with the waning of the Middle Ages, and rejoiced at its revival in the
nineteenth and twentieth centuries. Yet the extent of this revival still
has not been fully appreciated. The poems of Tennyson and a
handful of major poets on the one hand, and occasional novels by
popular authors like T. H. White and Mary Stewart on the other,
which is all that most readers ever discover, represent but the tip of
the iceberg as far as modern Arthurian literature is concerned.
Moreover, poetry and fiction are only two of many forms in which
Arthurian legend finds expression. They include plays and puppet
plays, films and television shows, operas and musicals, paintings and
carvings, comics and games—the list is as long as human ingenuity
can make it.

Yet of all the forms poetry retains pride of place, thanks to the
achievements of such medieval masters as Chrétien de Troyes,
Wolfram von Eschenbach, and the Gawain-poet. That the tradition
they built continues to flourish is demonstrated by this anthology
with its richly varied offerings. Alongside poets of the stature of
Wordsworth, Tennyson, and Arnold, we find some who today are
largely forgotten, as well as others who are still known but whose
Arthurian verse has attracted little notice.

Yet the poems of all, both the eminent and the obscure, remain valuable, both for their intrinsic merit and for their contribution to the vitality of Arthurian tradition. Great works do not arise out of a vacuum. Rather they stand out as the most notable among many that are significant, just as the deeds of Lancelot and Tristan, Gawain and Galahad overshadow those of their companions of the Round Table. Moreover, just as the deeds of all the knights, regardless of degree, are necessary to build and maintain the reputation of the Round Table, so the works of all the poets are necessary to build and maintain Arthurian tradition.

The fresh directions that this tradition is taking in the hands of modern poets is one measure of its vitality. Here I shall cite only two: the fascination with Merlin that is reflected in the number of poems about him; and the sensitive treatment of Arthurian women by female poets. An anthology like this allows us to appreciate such developments, even as we savor once again those familiar patterns that move us so deeply.

My one regret in perusing this anthology is that there was not room for more poems. Yet if omissions encourage us to reread old favorites, as the editor suggests, then that too will have served a valuable purpose.

Raymond H. Thompson
December, 1987

Introduction

Although almost everyone is familiar with some of the modern prose treatments of the Arthurian legends through the works of such popular writers as T. H. White, John Steinbeck, Mary Stewart, and Thomas Berger, modern (i.e., nineteenth- and twentieth-century) Arthurian poetry is generally less well known. For most people, Arthurian poetry means the romances of the Middle Ages. And, to be sure, works like Layamon's *Brut, Sir Gawain and the Green Knight,* and the *Alliterative Morte Arthure* remain highpoints of Arthurian literature. Perhaps the only widely known modern Arthurian poem is Tennyson's *Idylls of the King,* but there are many other fine examples.

Contemporary critics are often skeptical about or simply ignore Arthurian poems other than the early masterpieces and would probably agree that "the miraculous legend of Excalibur does not come very near to us, and, as reproduced by any modern writer, must be a mere ingenious exercise of fancy." This statement, made by a reviewer of Tennyson's *Poems,* published in 1842, was a comment on the "Morte d'Arthur," which was the seed from which the *Idylls* grew. Yet, despite critical suspicion of the Arthurian legends as a fit subject for modern poetry, poets have—as the contents of this anthology suggest—continued to find inspiration in the tales about the Once and Future King.

It is only to be expected that the rich suggestiveness of the Arthurian stories would inspire poets of different ages and temperaments. The mine of Arthurian symbol, allusion, character, and narrative is deep and nearly inexhaustible. It is, therefore, also understandable that these legends attract both beginning writers—like Sinclair Lewis, whose first published work is the short poem "Launcelot"—and more mature ones, whose Arthurian poems come at the height of their literary careers, as is the case with many of those represented in this collection.

This wealth of material is in large part responsible for the continuing tradition of Arthurian poetry from the Middle Ages to the present. Another factor is the variety of perspectives from which Arthur can be seen and the variety of settings into which he can be placed. The legendary hero surrounded by a band of faithful and not-so-faithful warriors and ladies, the historical king, and the savior who will return to aid his people in a time of need are all aspects of Arthur that have formed the basis for poems. The legendary subjects have, naturally, been the most often used by modern poets, primarily because of the large cast of characters and the many dramatic and symbolic incidents they provide. In fact, poems about Merlin and about the Holy Grail vie with those about the loves of Lancelot and Guinevere and of Tristan and Isolt for numerical superiority in the history of Arthurian poetry.

But it was the belief in the historical Arthur (or at least the promotion of his historicity for political purposes) combined with the legend of Arthur's return that kept Arthurian poetry alive when the renewed interest in the Classics changed the nature of the romance during the Renaissance. Henry VII's claim that as a Tudor he was descended from Arthur and that he restored the line of Arthur at a time of great need (the Wars of the Roses) was fostered by his descendants. When Polydore Vergil attacked Arthur's historicity, he was answered by the King's Antiquary, John Leland. Leland had been appointed by Henry VIII, who ruled because of the untimely death of Henry VII's first son, Arthur.

So when Edmund Spenser makes Prince Arthur the hero of *The Faerie Queene*, he has political as well as poetic motivation. The planned (though not actualized) uniting of Prince Arthur with Gloriana, who represents Elizabeth I, would have suggested that Elizabeth and the Tudor line she represents are at least the moral descendants of Arthur.

If Spenser's choice of Arthur as a hero for his epic is motivated largely by politics, it is nonetheless a significant development in Arthurian poetry. It showed that the Arthurian material could be adapted into an apparently alien framework, even into a Classical one, the framework both of the epic and of the Aristotelian virtues that play such an important role in *The Faerie Queene*. At the same time it provides an example for future poets by demonstrating that they need not be slaves to tradition. Thus Spenser is the first post-medieval poet to take seriously the Arthurian material and to adapt it to the concerns of his age.

The epic tradition continues into the seventeenth century. John Milton considered writing an Arthurian epic but abandoned the project for the loftier theme of *Paradise Lost.* It is understandable why a poet whose pamphlets document his Puritan and anti-royalist feelings would reject a theme that depends for its effect on present-ing a noble and sympathetic king and that shows the best of those who betrayed him repenting their actions. Perhaps also the sympa-thy that must be evoked for Lancelot and Guinevere was contrary to his moral inclinations.

The Arthurian epic in the seventeenth century was left to Sir Richard Blackmore to write. In fact, he wrote two: *Prince Arthur* (1695) and *King Arthur* (1697). His epics mix Geoffrey of Mon-mouth, Vergil, and Milton to tell, in the former work, of Arthur's coming to power as an allegory of the triumph of William of Orange and, in the latter, of the conquest of the Gauls by Arthur as an allegory of the defeat of Louis XIV by William. These works, though interesting historically, are not totally successful as poems and are perhaps most remembered because of Pope's reference in "The Dunciad" to "Blackmore's endless line."

The moral and political considerations that led Spenser and Blackmore to write Arthurian epics and Milton to reject the writing of one appear again in the nineteenth century in Bulwer-Lytton's *King Arthur* and Tennyson's *Idylls.* In the intervening period, the Age of Reason, no Arthurian epic and relatively few Arthurian poems of any length were written. And yet that century was crucial in the development of Arthurian poetry.

The rational side of the eighteenth-century mind rejected many of the fantastic events of medieval romance and looked instead to the Classics for models because Classical authors were believed to have captured universal truths. The epic, as produced by Homer and Vergil, was considered the highest and noblest form of poetry. But there was another side to the eighteenth century, a pre-romantic leaning toward the art of the Middle Ages and the emotion and inspiration that such art was thought to represent. There resulted an antiquarian movement that sought to preserve and to make available native romances and ballads. This movement was as important to the rediscovery of vernacular texts as Renaissance scholarship was to the rediscovery of the Classics.

One of the most influential works in this revival was Thomas Percy's *Reliques of Ancient English Poetry: Consisting of Old Heroic Ballads, Songs, and Other Pieces of Our Earlier Poets, (Chiefly of the Lyric Kind.) Together with Some Few of Later Date.* Published in 1765, this collection made available a wide range of material from the Middle Ages and the Renaissance. Included in its three volumes were six ballads that treated various aspects of the Arthurian legends, such as Lancelot's fight with Tarquin, King Ryence's demand that Arthur send his beard as a sign of submission, and Sir Gawain's marriage to a loathly lady who becomes fair. The focus on specific incidents rather than on the epic scope of the legend is a model for later poets.

But perhaps more significant than this approach is Percy's defense of medieval "romance" (a term he uses almost interchangeably with "ballad") in his introduction to the third volume of the collection. Percy says that though they are "full of the exploded fictions of Chivalry," the romances "frequently display great descriptive and inventive powers" and that "many of them exhibit no mean attempts at Epic Poetry" (p. viii). This linking of the romances— which Percy feels often contain the "rich ore of an Ariosto or a Tasso" buried "among the rubbish and dross of barbarous times" (p. ix)— with the epic is a way of using eighteenth-century critical standards to argue for the quality of the medieval material. His claim is that "Nature and common sense had supplied to these old simple bards the want of critical art, and taught them some of the most essential rules of Epic Poetry" (p. xii).

Percy goes so far as to summarize the Arthurian romance *Libius Disconius* (better known as *Libeaus Desconus*) to show the courage and nobility of Gawain's son. He concludes that the romance is "as regular in its conduct, as any of the finest poems of classical antiquity" (p. xvi).

Percy's defense was immediately more successful in stirring interest in the old romances than in inspiring the creation of new Arthurian poetry. In fact, even the romantic poets who, it seems, should have been drawn to this material produced very little Arthurian poetry. The only complete poem dedicated to the subject by a major British romantic poet is William Wordsworth's "The Egyptian Maid," which appeared in his collection *Yarrow Revisited and Other Poems* in 1835. (Sir Walter Scott devotes a portion of "The Bridal of Triermain" to an Arthurian story.) Perhaps this scarcity is a response to what every poet attempting to deal with any aspect of the legend must feel: the weight of the tradition. In writing about England's most famous king, the romantic inclination toward originality and individuality would have to yield at least a little to the powerful and well-known traditions that surround him.

Wordsworth asserts his originality by creating an incident not found in Malory or any other source and by taking certain liberties with the traditional characters. He indicates that for everything but the "Names and persons" in the poem, "the Author is answerable." His narrative tells of an Egyptian maiden who is coming to Arthur's court to marry one of his knights because of the assistance that Arthur had given the maiden's father. When Merlin's "freakish will" leads him to destroy her ship, he must be instructed by Nina, the Lady of the Lake, and then must correct the wrong done by his arbitrary use of power. The poem thus becomes a comment on the responsibility of those who wield power.

The liberties he took with tradition, the focus on a single (and original) incident, and the molding of the material to a particular theme make Wordsworth's modest poem a significant beginning for modern Arthurian poetry. At the same time, it is, like most of the best Arthurian poetry, very much a product of its age. Romantic elements abound: the exotic, the power of nature, the death of a beautiful woman, and others.

Still, it was not until the Victorian poets took up the legends that Arthurian themes flourished in modern British poetry. Tennyson's *Idylls* were, of course, seminal in this process. His influence can be seen clearly in an imitator like Thomas Westwood, who published in 1866 his poem *The Sword of Kingship*, which tells of Arthur's youth and his pulling the sword from the anvil. But even in this poem, whose verse imitates Tennyson's and whose plot is drawn largely from Malory, one sees some of the vast potential that modern poets have recognized in the Arthurian material. For, despite its general lack of originality, there are touches that make it distinctive and worthy of attention. Westwood, perhaps alone among Arthurian poets, captures in a few scenes some of the spirited enthusiasm of youth that seems natural to the character of Arthur. Although some superficial and heavy-handed references to Arthur's birth on Christmas day make the future king into a second Christ, Westwood still depicts Arthur and Key as making maidens blush with their "saucy smiles." Westwood's best scenes are those in which Arthur pulls the sword with youthful confidence and in which, "on a merry mischief bent," he taunts the monstrous giant Caradoc, who, despite pulling with a strength that would have torn an oak "from its seven centuries' hold beneath the rocks," is unable to budge the sword.

Another minor poet, Robert Stephen Hawker, wrote a poem on the Holy Grail, "The Quest of the Sangraal," in 1864. Hawker felt, with some justification, that Westwood borrowed from this poem in "The Quest of the Sancgreall," which the latter wrote in 1868. But Hawker's poem is noteworthy for reasons other than Westwood's borrowings. Tennyson visited Hawker in 1848, before either had written his poem on the Grail. The two poets ultimately treated the Grail theme in very different ways and for very different purposes. It is interesting, however, that in both versions it is Arthur's sense of duty that keeps him from undertaking the quest. (Hawker has his Arthur say, "The true shepherd must not shun the fold.")

Hawker is most concerned with the Grail as a mystical symbol. Thus he describes in some detail its spiritual history, going back to the time of Joseph of Arimathea when the Grail, "as though it clung to some ethereal chain,/Brought down high Heaven to earth at Arimathèe." Its significance to Arthur is also quite different in Hawker's poem. Whereas Tennyson's Arthur sees the quest as the beginning of the end of the fellowship of the Round Table, Hawker's Arthur, who has no children, feels that his name will live on if future generations can say that his knights "brought the Sangraal back by his command."

The poems of Westwood and Hawker, like the ballads and romances that became available in the latter part of the eighteenth and the early part of the nineteenth century, focused on specific incidents, as did most of the poems by Victorian authors. There was, however, a return to the epic tradition in Edward Bulwer-Lytton's *King Arthur* and in Tennyson's *Idylls*.

Bulwer-Lytton's epic, which appeared in 1848, is far less successful than Tennyson's in capturing the spirit of its age. It has, in fact, been called by James Merriman "the last of the eighteenth-century epics" (in "The Last Days of the Eighteenth-Century Epic: Bulwer-Lytton's Arthuriad," *Studies in Medievalism*, 2, no. 4 [Fall 1983], 16). Bulwer-Lytton created an episodic plot in twelve books, complete with most of the expected epic devices. His Arthur, who as a Welsh king would rather die than surrender his freedom, becomes symbolic of the love of freedom of the British people. While the theme is worthy of epic treatment, the vagaries of the plot frustrate the expectations created by the theme. Often—e.g., as when Arthur is led on his journey by a white dove that periodically perches on his helmet or when he does battle with walruses in the Arctic regions—it is difficult to take the story seriously, even allowing for the nineteenth century's somewhat distorted view of the Middle Ages. At times, elements of the plot seem closer to some of the absurdities of Gothic novels than to the true spirit of medieval romance.

Though he did manipulate his idylls so that they numbered twelve, Tennyson was less concerned with the mechanics of the epic. As the *Idylls* grew from the 1842 "Morte d'Arthur" to the completed collection, he maintained a thematic and structural consistency that is not only compelling in its own right but also seems to be a perfect reflection of the Victorian age. In addition to—and probably more essential than—his stated theme of soul at war with sense, Tennyson consistently balances "the true and the false" (which he initially intended to be a subtitle to the 1859 *Idylls*), appearance and reality; and he presents characters who must, like all of us, cope with the fact that things are sometimes better and often worse than they seem. The resulting tensions thus have a universal significance at the same time that they are the perfect metaphor for an age that was itself torn between faith and doubt, hope and despair.

The Victorian age saw in the very scientific, technological, and intellectual advances that brought hope of bettering the human condition a darker side, an undermining of faith (expressed so well in Arnold's poem "Dover Beach") and a potential for exploitation that called into question the notion of progress. This duality, which lasts even to the present day, is one of the most important reasons for the popularity of Arthurian material among modern poets. The Arthurian world, like the modern world, has great potential for improving the human lot; but it seems that such an ideal is always frustrated by the failings and imperfections that are inherent in the world and those who inhabit it.

Tennyson is the first poet to capture this duality and to express it in a form perfectly suited to the modern world; so he may be said to be the father of modern Arthurian poetry.

In addition to his epic, Tennyson is also the author of several shorter Arthurian poems, including both his earliest and his latest treatments of the legends. "Sir Launcelot and Queen Guinevere" was probably his first Arthurian effort (though not the first published—written, at least in part, in 1830, it was not published until 1842). The poem is fascinating because of its emphasis on Guinevere's beauty, which is so great that she "seem'd a part of joyous Spring" and which makes it worth sacrificing "all other bliss" for "one kiss/Upon her perfect lips." This attitude is vastly different from—or at least vastly simpler than—that found in the *Idylls*.

The first and the last published of Tennyson's Arthurian poems— "The Lady of Shalott" (1832, reprinted in a revised form in 1842) and

"Merlin and the Gleam" (1889)—are noteworthy, not only because of their Arthurian subject matter, but also because that material is used (as it is later on by Emerson) as a comment on the life of the artist. In the former, the Lady of Shalott represents the artist, destined to be lonely and unappreciated. In the latter, Merlin represents Tennyson himself and the Gleam he follows is the artist's imagination.

A lesser poet than Tennyson has written a variation on the theme of Merlin and the Gleam. Scottish poet John Veitch's "Merlin" treats, as his introductory note explains, "Merlin Caledonius, known also as Merlin Wylt and Silvestris," who is the earlier of the two Merlins from which the romancers formed "a third or legendary Merlin." The Merlin of the poem has lost his lord Gwenddoleu in battle, and so, when he is attacked by a band of rustics who consider him the devil's son, he has no protector. The rustics drown Merlin, but his former lover Hwimleian, "The Gleam," appears to him and their spirits are united with each other and with the natural world. Veitch's Gleam, who represents unity with the natural world, is a very different symbol from that employed by Tennyson, but one that works perfectly in a poem so rich in natural imagery.

Other Victorian poets treated the Arthurian material with a good deal of originality. One of the finest products of the age is William Morris's "The Defence of Guenevere," in which the Queen explains her actions from several perspectives that combine to reveal her character. She describes the beginning of the passionate attraction between herself and Launcelot and even reminds Gauwaine of his own mother's passion and its fatal results. In addition, Morris puts into her mouth a revealing metaphor early in the poem. The comparison of her decision to a choice offered by an angel between two cloths, one representing heaven and one hell, shows how difficult and arbitrary life's choices sometimes are and how momentous an apparently small decision can be. There is some doubt as to what Guenevere actually believes to be true and what she says for effect. What does she mean, for example, when she says that Gauwaine lies in his accusation? But despite some ambiguities, there is no doubt that the poem is one of the earliest attempts to have the reader consider the feelings and personality of Guenevere and so is a forerunner of many later works, novels as well as poems.

In "King Arthur's Tomb," Morris shows first Launcelot's and then Guenevere's perspective on their relationship before bringing them together for a final meeting at Arthur's tomb. In addition to the poignance attained in this last encounter, Morris uses imagery skillfully to convey meaning, as when he describes an arras on which "the wind set the silken kings a-sway," an image that recalls the instability and ultimate collapse of Arthur's realm.

Two of Morris's poems focus on a different side of the legends. "Sir Galahad, A Christmas Mystery" does for Galahad what "The Defence of Guenevere" does for the Queen. It makes him a real person, and it does so by the unconventional device of showing his loneliness and doubts. In "The Chapel in Lyonness," Galahad's devotion is rewarded when he is able to cure the suffering Sir Ozana.

Originality such as that shown by Morris in his depiction of Guenevere and Galahad—an originality that adds to the tradition without distorting it—is the hallmark of the best of modern Arthurian poetry. Matthew Arnold's *Tristram and Iseult* displays the same kind of originality. More important than his bringing together the lovers for a last meeting and joining them in death is the final section of the poem, "Iseult of Brittany." In this section Arnold portrays a saddened Iseult of Brittany who "seems one dying in a mask of youth." The picture of a woman who has grown old before her time is heightened by the fact that she watches over her own children, whose vitality has not yet been dried up by "the gradual furnace of the world." Another original touch is Arnold's ending the poem by having Iseult tell her children the story of Merlin and Vivian. There is an ironic appropriateness in this tale. It underscores the plight of Iseult, who wanted her lover beside her, by describing a Vivian who "grew passing weary of her love." Iseult is actually more like Merlin than Vivian. She is trapped in a life that holds little joy for her and that is very limited, trapped because she was rejected by a lover who did not desire her attentions.

Algernon Charles Swinburne also took up the Tristram legend in his very long poem "Tristram of Lyonesse," which focuses on the passion of the lovers. This poem is intended to offer a view of the Arthurian world that contrasts sharply with Tennyson's. It is rich in natural imagery that emphasizes the natural force of the love shared by Tristram and Iseult and presents a view of their love far different from that of Tennyson, who turns the great passion into a sordid affair.

As in Swinburne's retelling of the Tristram story, so too in his *Tale of Balen* is fate an overpowering force. The author did not have to alter Malory's version of Balin's story very much to show how destiny governs human lives. Even in Malory, Balin is buffeted by fortune as harshly and as clearly as Oedipus, and there is something of the feel of a Greek play about the tale. But whereas in Malory

Balin's story is preparatory for subtler tragedies that follow and dissipate its effect, in Swinburne's version this is not the case and the reader feels the full force of fate.

A fascinating shorter poem by Swinburne appeared posthumously in a privately printed edition in 1915. "King Ban" depicts a grief as passionate as the love of Tristram and Iseult. King Ban of Benwick, Lancelot's father, is overcome by this grief when his castle is betrayed by his own men to the invading Claudas of Gaul. Though the poem is unfinished, it would be hard to tell if it were not labeled a fragment, because it is complete in its presentation of the overwhelming force of sorrow.

Some Victorian poets less well known than Tennyson, Morris, Arnold, and Swinburne also produced excellent Arthurian poems. Perhaps the best of these is "The Last Ballad" by John Davidson. This poem portrays a Lancelot maddened by his unintentional betrayal of Guinevere, which led to the birth of Galahad. Apparently afflicted for years, he is cured finally by his son but remains torn between his love for the Queen and his desire to find the Grail. When he struggles to achieve "a vision of the cup," he only sees "a vision of the Queen." Despite his torment, the poem suggests, his love for Guinevere ennobles Lancelot. He shows mercy in battle to his foes because his love "had sealed" on the world "the look, the soul of Guinevere." Though the poem has been criticized as being overly romantic, it actually uses the background of Lancelot's undying love and his struggle against that love as a metaphor to suggest the human blindness that leads people to view as a flaw that which is actually their strength and to seek salvation in something other than that which truly provides it.

In the early part of the twentieth century, drama became the preferred form for treating the legends, but some writers, like Ernest Rhys and John Masefield, produced both plays and poems based on the story of Arthur. Rhys, who wrote the plays *Enid*, *Gwenevere*, and *The Masque of the Grail*, also wrote more than a score of Arthurian poems, some of them with unusual twists on the traditional material. In "Sir Launcelot and the Sancgreal," for example, Rhys seems to see the blast of divine light, which traditionally keeps Lancelot from reaching the Grail, as a kind of blessing: he appends a moral to his poem that advises sinners to "beat at the door, and cry, and enter in" in order that "you shall win the Grail, and see the Light." Never mind that, according to Malory, the Light saps Lancelot's strength so that for twenty-four days "he lay stylle as a dede man." Rhys also reflects a growing interest in the folklore surrounding the Arthurian legends in a poem like "King Arthur's Sleep," which is based on the legend that Arthur and his knights lie sleeping until Britain needs them again.

The title poem in Masefield's collection, *Midsummer Night and Other Tales in Verse*, draws on a part of the same legend, the notion that the sleepers wake on midsummer night. Masefield's collection is a strange and not entirely successful blend of the historical and the legendary, the traditional and the original. In many of his poems, Masefield tries to present a more realistic, more historical world than the magic realm of the romances. In "The Fight at Camlan," which tells of the beginning of the last battle, the fighting starts not because of an adder supplied by fate to bring about the destined end but when Kolgrim, one of the pirates Modred has allied himself with, decides it is folly to talk when Arthur is within bowshot and all that needs to be done is to "shoot the hound,/Crown Modred King and bring it to an end."

But not all of Masefield's poems display this kind of realism. One of the most compelling pieces in his collection gives an almost mythic picture of Arthur. In "The Sailing of Hell Race," Masefield sends Arthur down to the sea. This poem is not unflawed. Arthur's desire to sail west "to the wilderness of nothing sure" is clearly derivative from Tennyson's "Ulysses." And there are some infelicities of phrasing, as when Arthur's ship is called a "gleaming clipper" (not, by the way, the worst anachronism in the collection: in the poem "The Fight on the Wall," Modred's followers try to break in on the trapped Lancelot and Guinevere "as through the scrum a pack goes crashing/In football play"). Nevertheless, here perhaps more than in any of Masefield's poems Arthur approaches the stature of the legendary king. And though the poem borrows from Tennyson, Homer, and others, it is one of the few modern poems that has echoes—distant though they may be—of the mythic Arthur of early Celtic literature and even borrows some of its details from *The Spoils of Annwfn*. The Masefield of *Salt-Water Ballads* also shows through in some of the sea imagery, especially early in the poem.

Natural imagery plays a large part in modern Arthurian poetry. Perhaps this is a result of the romantic origins of the subject in the nineteenth century. Whatever its source, Masefield is only one of many poets to draw on the natural world. From Wordsworth's "Egyptian Maid" through Tennyson's and Swinburne's poems, there can be seen in Arthurian poetry a romantic interest in nature. This interest continues into the twentieth century and can be seen in Masefield's sea imagery and in a poem like Alfred Noyes's "The

Riddles of Merlin." In this poem, Merlin's "miracles" are used as a metaphor for the beauties of nature, which cannot be explained by science. (Edwin Muir's poem "Merlin," which gave Mary Stewart the title for her novel *The Crystal Cave*, also looks to Merlin for the answer to life's mysteries.) Noyes's poem captures a sense of wonder much like that evoked by the magical realm of Lyonnesse in Thomas Hardy's poem "When I Set Out for Lyonnesse."

The richness of the Arthurian material allows modern poets to treat the spiritual as well as the natural realm. Many of them have used Arthurian themes—most often the Grail quest—as a way of commenting on the condition of the modern world. This is what T. S. Eliot did in *The Waste Land* and what other modern poems do: from the fairly simple and direct homage to Perceval's spirituality in Jessie Weston's "Knights of King Arthur's Court" to the elaborately symbolic and complex poems of Charles Williams. (Of course, not only the Grail story is used for such comment. Martyn Skinner, who brings the tradition of Arthurian epic poetry into the twentieth century, uses the myth of Arthur's return to comment on the over-regulation and dehumanization of modern society in *The Return of Arthur*.)

Williams's concern with uniting the spiritual and the natural is reflected in the poem "The Crowning of Arthur." In *Arthurian Torso* (London: Oxford University Press, 1948, pp. 111-112), C. S. Lewis comments on this poem: "Externally all is well: nay, more than well, all is gorgeous. The poem is full of torch-light, flute music, heraldry. The heraldic beasts on the shields, conventionalized into symbols of honour and order, are an expression of the long desired union between Broceliande and Byzantium. . . . But the union is precarious." Merlin, seeing the events from the perspective of Byzantium, also sees—or rather he foresees—the destructive elements of Arthur's court, such as the affair between Lamorack and Morgause (which another poem in Williams's cycle, "Lamorack and the Queen Morgause of Orkney," depicts as lacking any element of true spiritual love) and the love of Lancelot and Guinevere. In "The Departure of Merlin," which comes later in the sequence of events of Williams's poems than Merlin's beguilement does in Malory, Arthur's advisor leaves the world "better and worse, more redeemed and more condemned," as Lewis says (p. 172) and as the images of the despairing sailor and of Galahad sitting in the Siege Perilous suggest.

Charles Williams's colleague, C. S. Lewis, who like Williams wrote a novel, *That Hideous Strength*, in which Arthurian themes are used in the context of a struggle between good and evil, also wrote an Arthurian poem centering on the quest for the Grail. Lewis's poem is fascinating in its account of the sense of loneliness and loss that hangs over Arthur's hall and of the effect of the quest on the knights who undertook it—things that are generally ignored by modern poets. Gawain, the first to return, is unlike the Gawain of old—"with eye/Unfrank, and voice ambiguous, and his answers short." When Launcelot, the focus of the poem, returns, he delays visiting the Queen; and when he finally does, he stares into the fire (perhaps a reminder of the eternal fires of hell) as he tells of his adventures. After hearing that he was not one of the three best knights of Christendom, Launcelot arrives at the dwelling of a lady who has prepared three coffins for the "three best knights of earth," Lamorake, Tristram, and Launcelot. This scene, in which the poem culminates, reads like an episode from a Gothic romance. (It is, in fact, strangely reminiscent of William Faulkner's "A Rose for Emily," which is so deeply embedded in the Gothic tradition.) The lady hopes to get the living knights to lie in the coffins, which are rigged with a device that will drop a "razor-keen" blade on their necks. After killing them she plans to "Keep those bright heads and comb their hair and make them lie/Between my breasts and worship them until I die." These chilling lines, the last in the poem, explain the change in Launcelot, who has been made to confront an extreme and perverted form of the worldliness he has been guilty of. Though the differences between his love for the Queen and the lady's desire to possess the three earthly knights are obvious, so too are the differences between the way chosen by the three best knights of Christendom and that chosen by Launcelot and the other "earthly knights."

Although the Arthurian legends are native to Britain and seem at odds with American ideals and values (as Twain's parody in *A Connecticut Yankee in King Arthur's Court* implies), a surprising number of American poets of the nineteenth and twentieth centuries have dealt with the legends. These versions are often marked by originality in the treatment of the Arthurian material, and some of the best of them adapt the traditional material to an American perspective.

Like the poems of Lewis and Williams, the earliest American Arthurian poem centers on the story of the Grail. James Russell Lowell's *The Vision of Sir Launfal* (1848) combines the romantic use of natural imagery and the spiritual message of the Grail story in a distincitve way. The poem is often criticized for being poorly structured. This is largely because the prelude to the first part, with its lengthy description of the beauties of nature, is longer than that part itself. (Nor is the poem helped by the fact that the line summing up nature's beauties—"And what is so rare as a day in June?"—has been too often quoted.) But the description here is balanced nicely by the winter scene that forms the prelude to the second part. And the nature description is an important (if admittedly too long) comment on the poem itself. For, as Lowell observes in the prelude to the first part, Sir Launfal remembered to keep his vow to seek the Grail in the summer when it is "easy now for the heart to be true." Launfal's problem is that he will do the easy thing. In the dream vision, which makes up most of the poem, he leaves his proud hall, which opens its gates only to the nobility. To a leper begging at the gate, he tosses "a piece of gold in scorn." Saying he prefers "the poor man's crust," the beggar refuses the gold.

After searching around the world for the Grail (still in the dream vision), Launfal returns during the cold of winter, which reflects the winter that had been in his soul. But now, having experienced poverty and suffering himself, he gives the leper a crust of bread and a drink of water from a wooden bowl. At this, the leper is glorified, showing that he is Christ himself; and he tells Launfal that the Grail is the wooden cup in which he offered the water—that is, the Grail is the heartfelt charity that one man offers to another; thus it is something that comes from within and is not found by searching the world over. The implication is that achieving the Grail is not something that is only possible for one or a very few knights but that it is possible for anyone who loves and respects his fellow man.

When he wakes from this vision, Launfal has learned his lesson. His blindness has turned to kindness. He opens the gates of his castle to all, so that "there's no poor man in the North Countree/But is lord of the earldom as much as he."

Because of its democratic treatment of the Grail theme, its experimentation with the medieval dream vision, and its sometimes exceptional imagery, *The Vision of Sir Launfal* is a noteworthy poem and one whose merits outweigh its structural weakness.

Launfal's dream vision might be seen as symbolic of a person's ability to learn through the imagination. The power of the imagination is also a central element in Ralph Waldo Emerson's portrayal of Merlin. For him, Merlin is a bard and a prophet, a seer whose song seems at times to "convey" or reflect the secrets of the universe, at other times almost to control or direct them. In "Merlin II," for example, Emerson writes of the "subtle rhymes with ruin rife." (Emerson's Merlin contrasts with Thomas Caldecot Chubb's. Both Merlins are seers, but Chubb's character's vision is more mystic and passive.) Emerson clearly prefers the bardic Merlin to the Merlin of the romances because the latter surrendered himself (or, one might say, his self-reliance) to Nimue and thus became a prisoner of Nature rather than one who was "in tune with" it, as the bardic Merlin is.

Just as Lowell was not the only American author of an Arthurian poem to treat the power of the imagination, so too was he not the only one to experiment with a medieval form. A much less significant writer, John Leslie Hall, produced an imitation of the alliterative verse of the Anglo-Saxons in "Cerdic and Arthur." The verse is appropriate since the poem focuses more on the Saxon invaders than on Arthur, who, though like Beowulf "eager for glory," dies halfway through the poem. It is then the Saxon Cerdic who founds a kingdom that becomes the "bulwark of freedom."

Though poets like Eugene Field, Richard Hovey (better known for his sequence of Arthurian plays, collectively called *Launcelot and Guenevere: A Poem in Dramas*, than for his Arthurian poems), Sara Teasdale, and others treat Arthurian themes in short and often finely crafted poems, it is not until Edwin Arlington Robinson writes about Broceliande and Camelot that there is another major Arthurian poem by an American author.

Robinson's three book-length Arthurian poems—*Merlin* (1917), *Lancelot* (1920), and *Tristram* (1927)—are obviously influenced by the tendency of his time to treat Arthurian themes in plays. All the poems are dramatic, the highpoints usually coming in dialogues between the principal characters. It is also clear that the poems are, on one level, very much a product of their times. In one of his letters, Robinson said that "there is a certain amount [of symbolic significance] in *Merlin* and *Lancelot*, which were suggested by the world war—Camelot representing in a way the going of a world that is now pretty much gone."

Of the three, *Tristram* was the most popular. This poem demonstrates Robinson's skill at characterization, particularly through his depiction of the quiet strength and unwavering love of Isolt of Brittany. But the poem is overall not as good as *Merlin*. In both poems, there is the tragedy of the loss of an idyllic world that the characters can imagine but not obtain for more than a brief moment. In *Merlin* there is a double loss, as Merlin's conscience forces him to leave the Edenic world of Broceliande that he shares, willingly, with Vivian and to return to Camelot, which he knows he cannot save from its impending doom. Robinson's Merlin becomes a type of American Adam, who is prevented by historical forces from being successful in creating either of the two Edens he envisions.

Robinson's *Lancelot* follows Malory fairly closely as it chronicles the destructive results of the fatal love between Arthur's queen and his greatest knight. But it is more than a verse retelling because of its treatment of the psychological motivation and responses of the characters involved.

Robinson deleted from his original version of *Lancelot* a section that was published in 1929 as *Modred* in a limited edition of two hundred and fifty copies. Beverly Taylor and Elisabeth Brewer (in *The Return of King Arthur* [Cambridge: D. S. Brewer, 1983], p. 187) claim that Robinson made the change because he thought the publishers felt the poem was too long but that it "proved fortunate, for Modred, who never appears in the poem, remains horrifying as a disembodied force of evil."

Whatever the advantages for *Lancelot*, *Modred* is itself well crafted. It is a fine dramatic scene in which Modred manipulates Colgrevance so he will help with the unsavory work of trapping Lancelot and Guinevere. Modred's understanding of Colgrevance and his ability to use the basically noble man's virtues, his fearlessness and his sense of duty, against him make Modred a fascinatingly dangerous and despicable villain. This small piece is indicative of the quality of Robinson's Arthurian works, which are among the finest modern Arthurian poems.

In the early part of this century, a number of female poets produced poems that focus on Arthurian women, something that foreshadows the focus on these women by contemporary novelists.

Sara Teasdale's "Guenevere" is a monologue in the tradition of Morris's "Defence of Guenevere." The Queen complains of being "branded for a single fault." Her vivid description of her meeting with Lancelot reveals the deep emotion that caused her to frustrate the expectations of those who wanted her to play a particular role, to "be right fair,/A little kind, and gownèd wondrously." In fact, the poem might be read as a woman's complaint that she is expected to conform to the standards of others who frown on her having deep emotions.

Edna St. Vincent Millay's "Elaine" is also a monologue by an Arthurian woman. It is notable less for its picture of Elaine's devoted love than for revealing the desperation of that love, which makes its way through Elaine's studied composure, and for the way it hints at her impending tragic end.

Though Dorothy Parker's Iseult of Brittany is a victim like Millay's Elaine, Parker's poem "Guinevere at Her Fireside" presents a very different kind of woman. Her more cynical queen respects the king but is not happy that her bed has become just "a thing to kneel beside." So she turns to Lancelot because "Tristram was busied otherwhere."

Other twentieth-century authors have found inspiration in the legends in a variety of ways. Some poets treat them with somber intensity, as Sinclair Lewis does in his poem "Launcelot" (which first appeared in the *Yale Literary Magazine* in 1904). Others treat the Arthurian material with farcical humor, as does Christopher Ward, who in his poem "King Arthur" ascribes Guinevere's dissatisfaction with her husband to his accepting as a gift from her father the Round Table, which is so large that they don't have enough silverware to set it or enough money to pay the butcher for meat for the hundred and fifty knights it seats.

Sometimes modern poets build on or reinterpret earlier traditions and sometimes they are startlingly original in their use of Arthurian material. Edgar Lee Masters, for example, returns to the ballad form that helped to initiate the modern interest in Arthurian poetry. In his "Ballad of Launcelot and Elaine," he retells the story of the begetting of Galahad and in "The Death of Sir Launcelot" tells of that knight's final days and holy death. These poems contain touches that are worthy of the form they imitate. The former says of Elaine's maid that "Dame Brisen was the subtlest witch/That was that time in life;/She was as if Beelzebub/Had taken her to wife." And in the latter, after Launcelot takes up the holy life, there is an evocative description of his armor: "His shield went clattering on the wall/To a dolorous wail or wind;/His casque was rust, his mantle dust/With spider webs entwined." Similarly, Yvor Winters's poem "Sir Gawaine and the Green Knight" depends on its source for narrative background, its originality lying in the compacting of the story and in the handling of the natural imagery that runs through it (and that is so appropriate in a reinterpretation of the medieval poem).

In sharp contrast to such treatments of the Arthurian material is a poem like Jack Spicer's "The Holy Grail." The unusual form and content of this poem at first seem at odds with the traditional Arthurian characters. But the contrast is intentional in a poem that explores the nature of poetry itself, the clash between the real and the ideal, and the real quest that people must undertake and that a poem can help them understand—if not achieve—better than the Grail can. Spicer comments that "the grail is the opposite of poetry/Fills us up instead of using us as a cup the dead drink from." Of the relationship between poem and Grail, he says, "The poem. Opposite. Us. Unfulfilled."

Another poem, "Launcelot in Hell," by John Ciardi is untraditional in its treatment of the love between Launcelot and Guinevere and of the final days of Camelot. Ciardi deromanticizes the events. His Launcelot has killed Arthur in the final battle and then thrown his sword into a swamp where "no fairy arm reached out of the muck to catch it." Worst of all, from the romantic perspective, is Launcelot's attitude toward the Queen. He refers to her as a "mare" that he mounted and is disgusted by her turning to religion. This harshly realistic view of the bitter end of the Arthurian realm seems to justify Launcelot's statement that "there is no moral," and yet the title provides an ironic comment on this statement that shows that Ciardi's Launcelot does not fully comprehend, or at least does not fully explain, the events even in their demystified form.

Two other poems, one by a British poet and one by an American, that show the originality that modern authors can bring to the traditional material are Thom Gunn's "Merlin in the Cave: He Speculates Without a Book" and Richard Wilbur's "Merlin Enthralled." Both treat the same incident from the legends: they show Merlin after he has been beguiled and trapped in the cave or the tree; but they treat this material in very different ways. Gunn's Merlin sees, now that he is trapped in the cave without a book, that there is more to the world than the absolute that he challenged. There is the real world of change, the world of the bee and the rook. In the cave, he watches "the flux I never guessed" and realizes that the world of the absolute is "very cold." In the end, he determines that the meaning of life is "in each movement that I take" and that the rook and the bee "are the whole and not a part." In short, he realizes that meaning must be found in each event, in each individual thing in the world and not in some static theory of the absolute.

Thus, in Gunn, Merlin's entrapment is for him "another start." In Wilbur, on the other hand, Merlin's entrapment symbolizes a necessary end. In a poem that exemplifies Wilbur's typically brilliant use of language and imagery, he shows us that though "Fate would be fated" and "Dreams desire to sleep," the "forsaken will not understand" their loss. So the king and the knights go in quest of Merlin. They go out "aimlessly riding," but not with the Providence-directed aimlessness of the traditional quest. And they leave "their drained cups on the table round," a wonderful phrase that suggests on the one hand a striking contrast to the ever-full cup of the Grail and on the other the lack of order that negates the wholeness and purpose of the Round Table. The body of the poem develops a pattern of water imagery, which culminates when Niniane receives

Merlin "as the sea receives a stream." The flow of the water is perfectly appropriate to the flow of events that results in the passing of the glory of Camelot. The poem ends in an image that sums up and concretizes the passing: the mail of the questing knights "grew quainter as they clopped along./The sky became a still and woven blue." The word "clopped" turns the warhorses of the knights into tired nags; and as the sky becomes a "still and woven blue," the heroes become figures in a tapestry.

These two works by Gunn and Wilbur are excellent poems. The qualifier "Arthurian" is not needed. Though, as many of the poems in this volume indicate, to be an excellent Arthurian poem is to be in good company. Throughout the nineteenth and twentieth centuries, some of the most important writers—and many minor writers—have found the Arthurian legends to be a vital source of inspiration and have achieved a balance between the weight of the tradition and the originality that modern poets strive for. These works have now become part of the continuing line of Arthurian poetry and will help to show to future poets that the legends of Camelot are not just "medieval" stories but are always potential sources of material because they are timeless in their insights into human nature and the human condition.

*　*　*

I have based the selection of poems for inclusion in this anthology on several principles that, I trust, will lead to a good sampling of the Arthurian poetry written in the nineteenth and twentieth centuries. Many readers will have favorite poems of their own that they would have liked to have seen included; and I am aware that another volume of equal length could have been filled without exhausting the Arthurian poetry that is good, important, or interesting for one reason or another.

My first principle has been to include only poems that can be printed in their entirety. Thus I have opted not to include, for example, selections from Tennyson's *Idylls* or Robinson's *Tristram*, as significant as these poems may be. I have decided instead to include poems such as Robinson's *Modred*, which is virtually unavailable, and Tennyson's "Sir Launcelot and Queen Guenevere" and "The Lady of Shalott," which are not as well known as they should be. Many of the long Arthurian poems are readily available, and one can only hope that those which are not will be reprinted whole (or in part in another context). At any rate, it is always easier to track down one long poem than to find the dozen or so shorter pieces that might be displaced by selections from a couple of longer ones.

I have also tried to represent as widely as possible writers who are considered important by literary scholars and historians. I have, however, included works by poets who are clearly not major authors when I found their Arthurian poems to be quite good or interesting in their own right.

Perhaps the most difficult choices have been those made from a book of Arthurian poems by a single author. In selecting a few poems from the collections of John Masefield and Charles Williams, I have tried to choose poems that are indicative of the best that their volumes have to offer—though here, as elsewhere, I realize that other readers might have made different choices.

In the final analysis, every anthology is, by its very nature, incomplete. And one who compiles an anthology can only hope that those who read it will delight in some previously unknown works, renew their familiarity with works unread for a long time, or perhaps even return to a favorite text that has been omitted, if only to convince themselves that the anthologist has erred in not including it.

The Anthology

The Egyptian Maid
Or
The Romance of the Water Lily

William Wordsworth

[For the names and persons in the following poem, see the "History of the renowned Prince Arthur and his Knights of the Round Table;" for the rest the Author is answerable; only it may be proper to add, that the Lotus, with the bust of the goddess apppearing to rise out of the full-blown flower, was suggested by the beautiful work of ancient art, once included among the Townley Marbles, and now in the British Museum.]

> While Merlin paced the Cornish sands,
> Forth-looking toward the Rocks of Scilly,
> The pleased Enchanter was aware
> Of a bright Ship that seemed to hang in air,
> Yet was she work of mortal hands,
> And took from men her name—THE WATER LILY.

> Soft was the wind, that landward blew;
> And, as the Moon, o'er some dark hill ascendant,
> Grows from a little edge of light
> To a full orb, this Pinnace bright,
> As nearer to the Coast she drew,
> Appeared more glorious, with spread sail and pendant.

Upon this winged Shape so fair
Sage Merlin gazed with admiration:
Her lineaments, thought he, surpass
Aught that was ever shown in magic glass;
In patience built with subtle care;
Or, at a touch, set forth with wondrous transformation.

Now, though a Mechanist, whose skill
Shames the degenerate grasp of modern science,
Grave Merlin (and belike the more
For practising occult and perilous lore)
Was subject to a freakish will
That sapped good thoughts, or scared them with defiance.

Provoked to envious spleen, he cast
An altered look upon the advancing Stranger
Whom he had hailed with joy, and cried,
"My Art shall help to tame her pride—"
Anon the breeze became a blast,
And the waves rose, and sky portended danger.

With thrilling word, and potent sign
Traced on the beach, his work the Sorcerer urges;
The clouds in blacker clouds are lost,
Like spiteful Fiends that vanish, crossed
By Fiends of aspect more malign;
And the winds roused the Deep with fiercer scourges.

But worthy of the name she bore
Was this Sea-flower, this buoyant Galley;
Supreme in loveliness and grace
Of motion, whether in the embrace
Of trusty anchorage, or scudding o'er
The main flood roughened into hill and valley.

Behold, how wantonly she laves
Her sides, the Wizard's craft confounding;
Like something out of Ocean sprung
To be for ever fresh and young,
Breasts the sea-flashes, and huge waves
Top-gallant high, rebounding and rebounding!

But Ocean under magic heaves,
And cannot spare the Thing he cherished:
Ah! what avails that She was fair,
Luminous, blithe, and debonair?
The storm has stripped her of her leaves;
The Lily floats no longer!—She hath perished.

Grieve for her,—She deserves no less;
So like, yet so unlike, a living Creature!
No heart had she, no busy brain;
Though loved, she could not love again;
Though pitied, *feel* her own distress;
Nor aught that troubles us, the fools of Nature.

Yet is there cause for gushing tears;
So richly was this Galley laden;
A fairer than Herself she bore,
And, in her struggles, cast ashore;
A lovely One, who nothing hears
Of wind or wave—a meek and guileless Maiden.

Into a cave had Merlin fled
From mischief, caused by spells himself had muttered;
And, while repentant all too late,
In moody posture there he sate,
He heard a voice, and saw, with half-raised head,
A Visitant by whom these words were uttered:

"On Christian service this frail Bark
Sailed" (hear me, Merlin!) "under high protection,
Though on her prow a sign of heathen power
Was carved—a Goddess with a Lily flower,
The old Egyptian's emblematic mark
Of joy immortal and of pure affection.

"Her course was for the British strand,
Her freight it was a Damsel peerless;
God reigns above, and Spirits strong
May gather to avenge this wrong
Done to the Princess, and her Land
Which she in duty left, though sad not cheerless.

"And to Caerleon's loftiest tower
Soon will the Knights of Arthur's Table
A cry of lamentation send;
And all will weep who there attend,
To grace that Stranger's bridal hour,
For whom the sea was made unnavigable.

"Shame! should a Child of Royal Line
Die through the blindness of thy malice:"
Thus to the Necromancer spake
Nina, the Lady of the Lake,
A gentle Sorceress, and benign,
Who ne'er embittered any good man's chalice.

"What boots," continued she, "to mourn?
To expiate thy sin endeavour!
From the bleak isle where she is laid,
Fetched by our art, the Egyptian Maid
May yet to Arthur's court be borne
Cold as she is, ere life be fled for ever.

"My pearly Boat, a shining Light,
That brought me down that sunless river,
Will bear me on from wave to wave,
And back with her to this sea-cave;
Then Merlin! for a rapid flight
Through air to thee my charge will I deliver.

"The very swiftest of thy Cars
Must, when my part is done, be ready;
Meanwhile, for further guidance, look
Into thy own prophetic book;
And, if that fail, consult the Stars
To learn thy course; farewell! be prompt and steady."

This scarcely spoken, she again
Was seated in her gleaming Shallop,
That, o'er the yet-distempered Deep,
Pursued its way with bird-like sweep,
Or like a steed, without a rein,
Urged o'er the wilderness in sportive gallop.

6

Soon did the gentle Nina reach
That Isle without a house or haven;
Landing, she found not what she sought,
Nor saw of wreck or ruin aught
But a carved Lotus cast upon the shore
By the fierce waves, a flower in marble graven.

Sad relique, but how fair the while!
For gently each from each retreating
With backward curve, the leaves revealed
The bosom half, and half concealed,
Of a Divinity, that seemed to smile
On Nina as she passed, with hopeful greeting.

No quest was hers of vague desire,
Of tortured hope and purpose shaken;
Following the margin of a bay,
She spied the lonely Cast-away,
Unmarred, unstripped of her attire,
But with closed eyes,—of breath and bloom forsaken.

Then Nina, stooping down, embraced,
With tenderness and mild emotion,
The Damsel, in that trance embound;
And, while she raised her from the ground,
And in the pearly shallop placed,
Sleep fell upon the air, and stilled the ocean.

The turmoil hushed, celestial springs
Of music opened, and there came a blending
Of fragrance, underived from earth,
With gleams that owed not to the Sun their birth,
And that soft rustling of invisible wings
Which Angels make, on works of love descending.

And Nina heard a sweeter voice
Than if the Goddess of the Flower had spoken:
"Thou hast achieved, fair Dame! what none
Less pure in spirit could have done;
Go, in thy enterprise rejoice!
Air, earth, sea, sky, and heaven, success betoken."

So cheered she left that Island bleak,
A bare rock of the Scilly cluster;
And, as they traversed the smooth brine,
The self-illumined Brigantine
Shed, on the Slumberer's cold wan cheek
And pallid brow, a melancholy lustre.

Fleet was their course, and when they came
To the dim cavern, whence the river
Issued into the salt-sea flood,
Merlin, as fixed in thought he stood,
Was thus accosted by the Dame:
"Behold to thee my Charge I now deliver!

"But where attends thy chariot—where?"
Quoth Merlin, "Even as I was bidden,
So have I done; as trusty as thy barge
My vehicle shall prove—O precious Charge!
If this be sleep, how soft! if death, how fair!
Much have my books disclosed, but the end is hidden."

He spake, and gliding into view
Forth from the grotto's dimmest chamber
Came two mute Swans, whose plumes of dusky white
Changed, as the pair approached the light,
Drawing an ebon car, their hue
(Like clouds of sunset) into lucid amber.

Once more did gentle Nina lift
The Princess, passive to all changes:
The car received her; then up-went
Into the ethereal element
The Birds with progress smooth and swift
As thought, when through bright regions memory ranges.

Sage Merlin, at the Slumberer's side,
Instructs the Swans their way to measure;
And soon Caerleon's towers appeared,
And notes of minstrelsy were heard
From rich pavilions spreading wide,
For some high day of long-expected pleasure.

Awe-stricken stood both Knights and Dames
Ere on firm ground the car alighted;
Eftsoons astonishment was past,
For in that face they saw the last
Last lingering look of clay, that tames
All pride, by which all happiness is blighted.

Said Merlin, "Mighty King, fair Lords,
Away with feast and tilt and tourney!
Ye saw, throughout this Royal House,
Ye heard, a rocking marvellous
Of turrets, and a clash of swords
Self-shaken, as I closed my airy journey.

"Lo! by a destiny well known
To mortals, joy is turned to sorrow;
This is the wished-for Bride, the Maid
Of Egypt, from a rock conveyed
Where she by shipwreck had been thrown;
Ill sight! but grief may vanish ere the morrow."

"Though vast thy power, thy words are weak,"
Exclaimed the King, "a mockery hateful;
Dutiful Child! her lot how hard!
Is this her piety's reward?
Those watery locks, that bloodless cheek!
O winds without remorse! O shore ungrateful!

"Rich robes are fretted by the moth;
Towers, temples, fall by stroke of thunder;
Will that, or deeper thoughts, abate
A Father's sorrow for her fate?
He will repent him of his troth;
His brain will burn, his stout heart split asunder.

"Alas! and I have caused this woe;
For, when my prowess from invading Neighbours
Had freed his Realm, he plighted word
That he would turn to Christ our Lord,
And his dear Daughter on a Knight bestow
Whom I should choose for love and matchless labours.

9

"Her birth was heathen, but a fence
Of holy Angels round her hovered;
A Lady added to my court
So fair, of such divine report
And worship, seemed a recompence
For fifty kingdoms by my sword recovered.

"Ask not for whom, O champions true!
She was reserved by me her life's betrayer;
She who was meant to be a bride
Is now a corse; then put aside
Vain thoughts, and speed ye, with observance due
Of Christian rites, in Christian ground to lay her."

"The tomb," said Merlin, "may not close
Upon her yet, earth hide her beauty;
Not froward to thy sovereign will
Esteem me, Liege! if I, whose skill
Wafted her hither, interpose
To check this pious haste of erring duty.

"My books command me to lay bare
The secret thou art bent on keeping;
Here must a high attest be given,
What Bridegroom was for her ordained by Heaven;
And in my glass significants there are
Of things that may to gladness turn this weeping.

"For this, approaching, One by One,
Thy Knights must touch the cold hand of the Virgin;
So, for the favoured One, the Flower may bloom
Once more; but, if unchangeagble her doom,
If life departed be for ever gone,
Some blest assurance, from this cloud emerging,

May teach him to bewail his loss;
Not with a grief that, like a vapour, rises
And melts; but grief devout that shall endure
And a perpetual growth secure
Of purposes which no false thought shall cross
A harvest of high hopes and noble enterprises."

"So be it," said the King;—"anon,
Here, where the Princess lies, begin the trial;
Knights each in order as ye stand
Step forth."—To touch the pallid hand
Sir Agravaine advanced; no sign he won
From Heaven or Earth;—Sir Kaye had like denial.

Abashed, Sir Dinas turned away;
Even for Sir Percival was no disclosure;
Though he, devoutest of all Champions, ere
He reached that ebon car, the bier
Whereon diffused like snow the Damsel lay,
Full thrice had crossed himself in meek composure.

Imagine (but ye Saints! who can?)
How in still air the balance trembled;
The wishes, peradventure the despites
That overcame some not ungenerous Knights;
And all the thoughts that lengthened out a span
Of time to Lords and Ladies thus assembled.

What patient confidence was here!
And there how many bosoms panted!
While drawing toward the Car Sir Gawaine, mailed
For tournament, his Beaver vailed,
And softly touched; but, to his princely cheer
And high expectancy, no sign was granted.

Next, disencumbered of his harp,
Sir Tristram, dear to thousands as a brother,
Came to the proof, nor grieved that there ensued
No change;—the fair Izonda he had wooed
With love too true, a love with pangs too sharp,
From hope too distant, not to dread another.

Not so Sir Launcelot;—from Heaven's grace
A sign he craved, tired slave of vain contrition;
The royal Guinever looked passing glad
When his touch failed.—Next came Sir Galahad;
He paused, and stood entranced by that still face
Whose features he had seen in noontide vision.

11

For late, as near a murmuring stream
He rested 'mid an arbour green and shady,
Nina, the good Enchantress, shed
A light around his mossy bed;
And, at her call, a waking dream
Prefigured to his sense the Egyptian Lady.

Now, while the bright-haired front he bowed,
And stood, far-kenned by mantle furred with ermine,
As o'er the insensate Body hung
The enrapt, the beautiful, the young,
Belief sank deep into the crowd
That he the solemn issue would determine.

Nor deem it strange; the Youth had worn
That very mantle on a day of glory,
The day when he achieved that matchless feat,
The marvel of the PERILOUS SEAT,
Which whosoe'er approached of strength was shorn,
Though King or Knight the most renowned in story.

He touched with hesitating hand,
And lo! those Birds, far-famed through Love's dominions,
The Swans, in triumph clap their wings;
And their necks play, involved in rings,
Like sinless snakes in Eden's happy land;—
"Mine is she," cried the Knight;—again they clapped their pinions.

"Mine was she—mine she is, though dead,
And to her name my soul shall cleave in sorrow;"
Whereat, a tender twilight streak
Of colour dawned upon the Damsel's cheek;
And her lips, quickening with uncertain red,
Seemed from each other a faint warmth to borrow.

Deep was the awe, the rapture high,
Of love emboldened, hope with dread entwining,
When, to the mouth, relenting Death
Allowed a soft and flower-like breath,
Precursor to a timid sigh,
To lifted eyelids, and a doubtful shining.

In silence did King Arthur gaze
Upon the signs that pass away or tarry;
In silence watched the gentle strife
Of Nature leading back to life;
Then eased his Soul at length by praise
Of God, and Heaven's pure Queen—the blissful Mary.

Then said he, "Take her to thy heart
Sir Galahad! a treasure that God giveth
Bound by indissoluble ties to thee
Through mortal change and immortality;
Be happy and unenvied, thou who art
A goodly Knight that hath no Peer that liveth!"

Not long the Nuptials were delayed;
And sage tradition still rehearses
The pomp the glory of that hour
When toward the Altar from her bower
King Arthur led the Egyptian Maid,
And Angels carolled these far-echoed verses;—

Who shrinks not from alliance
Of evil with good Powers,
To God proclaims defiance,
And mocks whom he adores.

A Ship to Christ devoted
From the Land of Nile did go;
Alas! the bright Ship floated,
An Idol at her Prow.

By magic domination,
The Heaven-permitted vent
Of purblind mortal passion,
Was wrought her punishment.

The Flower, the Form within it,
What served they in her need?
Her port she could not win it,
Nor from mishap be freed.

The tempest overcame her,
And she was seen no more;
But gently gently blame her,
She cast a Pearl ashore.

The Maid to Jesu hearkened,
And kept to him her faith,
Till sense in death was darkened,
Or sleep akin to death.

But Angels round her pillow
Kept watch, a viewless band;
And, billow favouring billow,
She reached the destined strand.

Blest Pair! whate'er befall you,
Your faith in Him approve
Who from frail earth can call you,
To bowers of endless love!

The Sword of Kingship

THOMAS WESTWOOD

At Christmas-tide, while wassail mirth ran high,
To royal Uther, by his queen Igrayne,
Was born a son; whom, wrapp'd in swaddling clothes
Of cloth of gold, the monarch took, and charged
Two knights and two fair maids to bear away,
Adown the castle stair and through the night,
To one that waited by the postern door.
No question to be ask'd, no word be said.

Blank faces wore the knights, and puzzled looks
And dazed the damsels, but the king's command
Was peremptory; so adown the stair,
Close-clasp'd and warm, their precious freight they bore,
Across the courtyard, underneath the stars.
Beside the door stood Merlin, who the babe
Took in his arms, and, without word or sign,
Departed. Like a wraith beyond the moat
He stole, and vanish'd on the windy wold;
And as he vanish'd, lo! a luminous star
Rose in the heaven, and brighten'd as it rose,
And broaden'd till the land was full of light.
And one fair maid,—of sixteen summers she,—
Lifting her lily face in white amaze,
Thought, "Sure our blessed Lord is born again!"

IVRE REX BRITANNIÆ

HOW ARTHVR DREW THE SWORD

From *The Book of Romance*,
by Andrew Lang, illustrated by Henry Ford.
London: Longmans, Green and Co., 1902.

Athwart the wold, and o'er th' untrodden snow,
Pass'd Merlin, a wierd shadow, without pause.
Around him, as he went, the wind, with sound
Of viols sweet and low, sang lullaby.
Above him, in its orbit, moved the star,
To marshal him the way that he should go.

It led him to a donjon, perch'd aloft,
Like falcon's eyrie, on a spire of crag—
Black chasms in front, and at its base the sea—
Sir Ector's donjon, in the western wilds.
Beside his yule-fire sate that peerless knight,
And read, from monkish page, the legend old
Of the Nativity—the Orient Star,
The mystic Magi, with their gift of myrrh,
The God-child in the manger. Dame Iseult,
His spouse, with awe-dilated eyes, drank in
The wondrous story. At their feet lay stretch'd
A shaggy wolf-hound, huge of jaw and limb;
And nestling in the savage creature's fur,
Round-cheek'd and ruddy, slept their latest born.

No footfall—but, instinctive, both were 'ware
Of an unwonted presence in the hall—
Merlin's, whose ghostly shadow blurr'd the light.
To good Sir Ector salutation brief
The wizard gave—then with obeisance laid
His burden on the noble lady's knees,
Who call'd upon her saints. The bands unswathed,
Behold, the babe lay, like a folded rose,
In slumber; but anon, roused by the glare,
First crow'd, then whimper'd, till the pitying dame
Broke out in yearnings as of mother-love,
And caught him to her breast, and gave him suck,
And cherish'd him thenceforth as her own son.
And soon a priestly man, by Merlin sent,
Baptized the boy, and ARTHUR was his name.

Ere long the King fell sick, and while he lay,
Sore-stricken, a marauding host o'er-ran
His borders, and waged battle with his knights
At vantage, and his subjects vex'd and slew.

Then up spake Merlin: "King, no longer bide
Prone on thy couch, but to the strife of spears
Wend forth, in litter borne, if such must be,
High on the backs of men; for if thy foes
But see thee in the van, the day is thine!"

So was it done as Merlin had devised.
They bore the King in litter to the field—
A royal presence, with a deathly face—
And by St. Alban's, on a wild March morn,
'Mid road and river, met a mighty horde
Of Norsemen, and that day Sir Ulfius hight,
And stout Sir Brastias, did grand feats of arms;
And in the Northern battle Uther's men
Fought and o'ercame, and all his foemen fled.

And straight the King to London hied, and made
Much joy of his success; but, smitten anew
With mortal fever, three whole nights and days
Speechless he lay, and sore his barons grieved,
And help besought of Merlin in their need.

Quoth Merlin, "Help is none—Heaven's will be done!
But take this counsel,—at to-morrow's dawn
Seek the King's presence, and, with God's good grace,
His tongue shall be unloosed, and he shall speak."
And on the morrow, when the rising sun
Redden'd the east, and from the sloping hills
Roll'd the mists upward, knights and barons went
With Merlin to the King, and Merlin spake:—

"By Christ, and the thrice-blessed Trinity,
King, I adjure thee, make thy purpose clear!
Shall Arthur, thy true son, when thou art gone,
Rule o'er thy realm and sit upon thy throne?
Before thy lieges all, and before God,
Speak, my Lord Uther, let thy will be known!"

And Utherpendragon turn'd him on his bed,
And moan'd, and raised a ghastly face at length,
In the blear light, and cross'd himself, and said:—
"Before my lieges all, and before God,

18

I bless my son! God's blessing and the saints'
Befall him! He is king. My work is done.
But if he claim not this my crown and realm,
Or make not good his claim, with knightly feats,
And kingly wisdom, as befits my son,
Perish my blessing—it is none of his!"

Then suddenly Utherpendragon dropp'd
Dead on his couch, as drops a canker'd pine
When the bolt cleaves it, and all heads were bow'd,
And all hearts sorrow'd; and with regal pomp,
And long procession down cathedral aisles,
'Neath pall, and floating plume, and level shield,
They bore him to his rest. And Igrayne wept.

Then year on year in grievous jeopardy
The realm remain'd. For prince and paladin
Made trial of their might, in deadly feuds,
With plot and counterplot, through covert hope
Of kingship; and the sea grew black with barks
Of Vikings, that like kestrels round the coast
Hover'd, and froze the people's hearts with fear.
At dead of night the hills broke out ablaze
With beacon-fires—wild Norsemen scour'd the plains,
And drove the herds—and wives, that sat at home,
Wept wearily for those that came no more.

But, when the gloom was deepest, Merlin pray'd,
Th' Archbishop Engelbert, who held his court
At Canterbury, in his diocese,
To issue edicts, bidding all true knights
Repair to London, at the time of Yule,
On pain of penance and anathema.
"For peradventure, on that day," quoth he,
"On which our Saviour Lord from heaven came down,
God may vouchsafe a miracle, and show
Whose head shall wear the crown." The Primate did
As Merlin counsell'd, and the barons came,
Obedient, to the tryst. The frosty roads
Rang with the dint of hoofs. Long trains of knights,
Pages, and dames in litters, silken-draped,
And pursuivants, in brilliant tabards, wound,

Like party-colour'd serpents o'er the meads,
And through the snowy passes of the hills.

On Christmas-eve, at nightfall, a great host
Encamp'd about the minster, and a troop
Of holy men from tent to tent pass'd round,
And shrived the knights, and left them pure of sin,
And ready for the chrism, and for the crown.

In clouds the Christmas morning dimly dawn'd;—
Grey gloom'd the minster aisles; but ere the mass
Was ended, an effulgent sunshine broke
Through the east oriel, and all men were 'ware
That by the altar stood a snow-white stone,
Four-square, and on its summit, in the midst,
An anvil, holding in its iron bulk
A naked sword, along whose edges ran
This legend: "**Whoso plucks me from my place
Is England's rightful king. Amen. Amen.**"
Then shook the multitude with sudden stir
Of passion, as the woodland summits shake,
When, swooping from a cloud, Euroclydon
The storm-wind strikes them; but the Primate knelt,
And quell'd the growing tumult with his prayer,
And, after, preach'd of peace and pure intents.

The benediction utter'd, one by one,
Princes and paladins he bade approach,
And try their prowess on the magic sword.
Then were gaunt arms of Titan strength outstretch'd,
To which the sinews clung, like knotted cords;—
Then was the sword clutch'd by as gnarlèd fists,
As his that slew the Hydra. Faces flush'd
Purple, and foreheads became ridged, like backs
Of Berkshire wolds; broad shoulders stoop'd and rose;
Oaths, fierce as thunder-claps, were smother'd back
'Twixt gnashing teeth—in vain, in vain, in vain!
Immoveable within its sheath the sword
Stood, its gold legend glittering in the sun.

Then spake the Primate: "God's Elect is not
Amongst you here this day. Now note my will.

20

Let ten true knights be chosen, of noble strain,
And constant, day and night, keep watch and ward,
Beside the stone and the miraculous sword,
Till he shall come, who is ordain'd of Heaven."

So said, so done. Ten knights of noble strain
Were chosen, five by five, to keep the watch.
And the suns rose, and set, and rose again,
And down the frozen aisles the winter's wind
Blew shrilly, and the winter moon shone cold.
And not a knight in Christendom but tried
To win the sword . . . except the Elect of God.

It chanced, on New Year's Day, a joust was given
With open lists; and to the tournay came
Sir Ector, with his handsome son, Sir Key,
Just dubb'd a knight, and Sir Key's brother-in-arms,
Arthur, a stalwart youth, straight as a pine;
With eyes as blue and bland as the June heaven,
Broad brow set round with curls, and royal mouth,
Firm-shut, and strong. These twain rode side by side,
Scanning the silken litters as they pass'd,
And chuckling, when the rose on maiden's cheek
Deepen'd to damask at their saucy smiles;
But near the lists, the scatter-brain'd Sir Key
Bethought him he had left his sword at home,
And pray'd young Arthur to ride back at speed,
In quest of it. This did he; but arrived
Before the mansion, every door was shut,
And window barr'd; Sir Ector's dame had gone
To see the jousts with her bower-maidens all.
Then Arthur stamp'd a hasty foot, and vow'd
That not for want of glaive Sir Key should miss
His jousting. "To the church I'll hie, and snatch
The sword they prate of from the wizard stone!"
Wide open stood the minster doors, and deep
The sacred silence; of the watching knights
No vestige; tournay sports had lured them thence.
Straight up the aisle young Arthur strode, and bent
A reverent knee beside the altar step,
And breathed a prayer; then pluck'd the magic sword
Out of the anvil, brandish'd it aloft,

And, without further tarrying, hurried back,
Alert, to find Sir Key. But he with awe
Gazed at the golden legend on the blade,
And call'd his sire, and cried aloud: "This brand
Is mine, and mine, too, England's realm and crown!"
Much marvell'd good Sir Ector; but in doubt
Of what was best, to the Lord Primate went,
And told his tale; who, when the jousts were o'er,
Bade all the knights and nobles meet anew,
Within the minster walls. There question'd he
By what strange sleight Sir Key had won the sword?
Sir Key, with pucker'd lips and stammering speech,
The truth avow'd. "Youth," said the Primate then,
Turning to Arthur, "since the skill was thine
To take the sword, say, canst thou thrust it back
Into its iron sheath?" "Small feat were that!"
Quoth Arthur, with a smile; and, stepping up,
Into the anvil thrust the naked blade.
"Now pluck it forth, Sir Key!" the Primate urged,
"And prove thy right." And bold Sir Key began
To tug, to haul—and tugging, hauling still,
The sweat-drops roll'd in rivers down his cheeks,
And angry flashes glinted from his eyes.
Then Arthur jeer'd him: "Nay, hast lost thy wits,
Good gossip mine? See, 'tis no more than this!"
And, with the slightest twitch of fingers twain,
Out came the sword, and a wild sunbeam ran
Along the steel and lit the legend up,
In diamond sparkles. Then Sir Ector knelt
At Arthur's feet, and hail'd him Lord and King,
While bold Sir Key stood blushing, half in wrath,
And half compunction. But the assembled peers
Look'd on, with lowering brows and sullen lips,
Or mutter'd: "It were shame this nameless boy
Should sit on Uther's throne and wear his crown!"
And soon a conflict rose, and swords were bared
In menace, till the Primate spake, and bade
Young Arthur thrust the sword into its place,
And tarry further ordeal, at the feast
Of Candlemas ensuing—the ten knights,
Meanwhile, to keep impregnable watch and ward.

This did they, five by five, as at the first.
And the suns rose, and set, and rose again;
And down the frozen aisles the winter's wind
Sang shrilly, and the winter moon shone cold.
But as at Christmas, so at Candlemas;
Save Arthur's only, not an arm was found
To wield the sword, though from the Cornish hills
Came Caradoc, a caitiff knight, of frame
Like to Goliath's; heavy was his spear,
As any weaver's beam—his stature huge,
His rigid chest, a rock—on either fist
Six fingers—on each monstrous foot six toes.
This giant, with a thunderous laugh, that woke
The echoes of the hills ten leagues away,
Thrust back to right and left the puny crowd,
As sheers a ship its course through summer seas,
And, to the altar stalking, clutch'd the sword
Contemptuous, as it were a baby's toy,
And pull'd. Loud laugh'd the multitude, to see
The tawny Cyclops foaming at the mouth,
Furious, because no whit the blade would budge.
He pull'd with strength that would have torn an oak
From its seven centuries' hold beneath the rocks—
He pull'd till, spent and breathless, his eyes stood
Out of his head, with wonder and despite.
But Arthur, on a merry mischief bent,
Pluck'd forth the glaive, and springing down the steps,
Fenced at Goliath for a minute's space,
With rapid cut and thrust, achieving thus
The giant's downfall and discomfiture;
For gibes and jeers, like whistling arrow-flights,
Hail'd on him; till, with buffetings of all
That cross'd his path, out of the doors he dash'd,
Half mad, and like an evil hurricane,
Rush'd howling homeward to his Cornish hills.

But vain these portents of the Elect of God.
The peers, obdurate, claim'd a new delay
Till Easter, and the Primate, moved with hope
By sage concessions to enforce Heaven's will,
Ordain'd fresh trial on that holy day.

And still the knights kept watch beside the stone,
With pacings to and fro, till through the pane
A blander moon shed silver on the sword,
And the wind, wandering 'mid the pillars, brought
Odours and omens of the coming Spring.

But as at Candlemas, at Easter too,
One issue, one resolve,—defeat, delay,—
With strife amongst the noblest—gauntlets flung
And lifted, ay, and knightly battle waged
"A outrance," in the lists. The Archbishop then
Convoked the estates of Britain for the eve
Of Pentecost, in ultimate ordeal;—
Too long, he said, had England's realm remain'd
Kingless, with peril gathering round the throne.

So the suns rose, and set, and rose again,
In slow succession, till the season turn'd,
And to the knights in vigil came the scent
Of beanflowers, and the smell of growing corn.

*   *   *   *   *

Over the pleasant meads, at Pentecost,
The minster bells rang out a merry chime,—
Over the bean-tufts, with their brindled bloom,
Over the corn-fields, with their waving corn;
No cloud in Heaven, and the long-harass'd earth
Calm, with the foretaste of a rest to come.

At gloaming, back the minster portals roll'd,
And knights and nobles, in a stormy throng,
Choked nave and chancel. Vespers o'er, at once
The Primate summon'd whoso dared resist
God's judgment, thrice made manifest, to brave
The final ordeal. Then upsprang a band
Of paladins, such as the world ne'er saw,
Fit framers of the famous Table Round,
Heroic shapes, that with untoward fate
Strove, as the demi-gods of heathen tale,
Strove in their war with Heaven—like them to fall.
For vain their chivalry and pure intents—

Vain strength of soul and strength of arm—all vain!
Immoveable within its sheath the sword
Stood, its strange legend burning like a flame.

Then Arthur, at the Primate's bidding, came,—
A youth as fair as he, who in the vale
Of Elah, with a sling and with a stone,
The champion of the Philistines o'erthrew,
Before the hosts of Israel. Meek, he knelt
Beside the altar, while the priestly palms
Were laid, in blessing, on his comely head,
All cluster'd over with thick golden curls.
"King Arthur, God's Elect, draw forth the sword!"
And lightly stepp'd he, lightly drew the sword,
And having drawn it, lo! a luminous star
Rose in the heaven, and brighten'd as it rose,
And broaden'd, till the fane was full of light.
And in that sudden glory men were 'ware
That, from their station by the altar side,
Anvil and stone had vanish'd like a dream.
Then swift emotion shook the hearts of all,
Half awe and half remorse; and with a sound
Of seas that surge, and sweep o'er shingly shores,
A tumult grew and spread, and broke at length
Into a vehement shout, "Long live the King!
Long live King Arthur!" from ten thousand throats,
Not one dissentient. Through the minster doors
The uproar burst, and fill'd the streets, and ran
Like wild-fire through the town—beyond the town—
For as the lightning speeds from cloud to cloud,
So sped the gladness through the length and breadth
Of England, till its every corner rang
With universal shouts of jubilee.
And the wind swept the shoutings out to sea,
And paled the Vikings' ruddy cheeks with fear,
And drove their black barks from the British main.

So Arthur won King Uther's crown and throne!
And when his seat was sure, and not a knight—
Save caitiff Caradoc, the Cornish bear—
But had sworn fealty, wizard Merlin told
To him and to Igrayne his wondrous tale.

Great joy had Queen Igrayne; her widow'd heart
Wax'd warm with household cheer; but evermore
To good Sir Ector and his dame the King,
From old respect and dear familiar use,
Clung, with the love and duty of a son.
Sir Ector, his high chancellor he made,
Sir Key, his seneschal; and when the dame
To Camelot in early summer came,
He saw, and ran to meet her from afar,
And kiss'd her mouth, and kiss'd her wrinkled cheeks,
And knelt before her, as had been his wont,
For daily blessing in the years that were.

Here ends the story of the magic sword
Of Arthur, Builder of the Table Round.

The Quest of the Sangraal

ROBERT S. HAWKER

The name Sangraal is derived from *San*, the breviate of *Sanctus* or
Saint, *Holy*, and *Graal*, the Keltic word for Vessel or Vase. All that is
known of the Origin and History of this mysterious Relique will be
rehearsed in the Poem itself. As in the title, so in the Knightly Names,
I have preferred the Keltic to other sources of spelling and sound.—
R.S.H.

Ho! for the Sangraal! vanish'd Vase of Heaven!
That held, like Christ's own heart, an hin[1] of blood!
Ho! for the Sangraal! . . .
               How the merry shout
Of reckless riders on their rushing steeds,
Smote the loose echo from the drowsy rock
Of grim Dundagel, thron'd along the sea!

"Unclean! unclean! ten cubits and a span,[2]
Keep from the wholesome touch of human-kind:
Stand at the gate, and beat the leper's bell,
But stretch not forth the hand for holy thing,—
Unclean, as Egypt at the ebb of Nile!"
Thus said the monk, a lean and gnarlèd man;

27

From *King Arthur and His Knights,*
by Maude Radford Warren, illustrated by Walter J. Enright.
New York: Rand McNally, 1905 (copyright).

His couch was on the rock, by that wild stream
That floods, in cataract, Saint Nectan's Kieve:[3]
One of the choir, whose life is Orison.
They had their lodges in the wilderness,
Or built them cells beside the shadowy sea,
And there they dwelt with angels, like a dream:
So they unroll'd the volume of the Book,
And fill'd the fields of the Evangelist
With antique thoughts, that breath'd of Paradise.

Uprose they for the Quest—the bounding men
Of the siege perilous, and the granite ring—
They gathered at the rock, yon ruddy tor;[4]
The stony depth where lurked the demon-god,
Till Christ, the mighty Master, drave him forth.

There stood the knights, stately, and stern, and tall;
Tristan, and Perceval, Sir Galahad,
And he, the sad Sir Lancelot of the lay:
Ah me! that logan[5] of the rocky hills,
Pillar'd in storm, calm in the rush of war,
Shook, at the light touch of his lady's hand!

See! where they move, a battle-shouldering kind!
Massive in mould, but graceful: thorough men:
Built in the mystic measure of the Cross:—
Their lifted arms the transome: and their bulk,
The Tree, where Jesu stately stood to die—
Thence came their mastery in the field of war:—
Ha! one might drive battalions—one, alone!

See! now, they pause; for in their midst, the King,
Arthur, the Son of Uter, and the Night,
Helm'd with Pendragon, with the crested Crown,
And belted with the sheath'd Excalibur,[6]
That gnash'd his iron teeth, and yearn'd for war!
Stern was that look (high natures seldom smile)
And in those pulses beat a thousand kings.
A glance! and they were husht: a lifted hand!
And his eye ruled them like a throne of light.
Then, with a voice that rang along the moor,
Like the Archangel's trumpet for the dead,
He spake—while Tamar sounded to the sea.

29

"Comrades in arms! Mates of The Table Round!
Fair Sirs, my fellows in the bannered ring,
Ours is a lofty tryst! this day we meet,
Not under shield, with scarf and knightly gage,
To quench our thirst of love in ladies' eyes:
We shall not mount to-day that goodly throne,
The conscious steed, with thunder in his loins,
To launch along the field the arrowy spear:
Nay, but a holier theme, a mightier Quest—
'Ho! for the Sangraal, vanish'd Vase of God!'

"Ye know that in old days, that yellow Jew,
Accursèd Herod; and the earth-wide judge,
Pilate the Roman—doomster for all lands,
Or else the Judgment had not been for all,—
Bound Jesu-Master to the world's tall tree,
Slowly to die. . . .
        Ha! Sirs, had we been there,
They durst not have assayed their felon deed,
Excalibur had cleft them to the spine!

Slowly He died, a world in every pang,
Until the hard centurion's cruel spear
Smote His high heart: and from that severed side,
Rush'd the red stream that quencht the wrath of Heaven!

"Then came Sir Joseph, hight of Arimathèe,
Bearing that awful Vase, the Sangraal!
The Vessel of the Pasch, Shere Thursday night,
The selfsame Cup, wherein the faithful Wine
Heard God, and was obedient unto Blood.
Therewith he knelt and gathered blessèd drops
From his dear Master's Side that sadly fell,
The ruddy dews from the great tree of life:
Sweet Lord! what treasures! like the priceless gems
Hid in the tawny casket of a king,—
A ransom for an army, one by one!

"That wealth he cherisht long: his very soul
Around his ark: bent as before a shrine!

"He dwelt in Orient Syria: God's own land:
The ladder foot of heaven—where shadowy shapes
In white appparel glided up and down.
His home was like a garner, full of corn,
And wine and oil; a granary of God!
Young men, that no one knew, went in and out,
With a far look in their eternal eyes!
All things were strange and rare: the Sangraal,
As though it clung to some ethereal chain,
Brought down high Heaven to earth at Arimathèe.

"He lived long centuries and prophesied.
A girded pilgrim ever and anon,
Cross-staff in hand, and, folded at his side,
The mystic marvel of the feast of blood!
Once, in old time, he stood in this dear land,
Enthrall'd—for lo! a sign! his grounded staff
Took root, and branch'd, and bloom'd, like Aaron's rod:
Thence came the shrine, the cell; therefore he dwelt,
The vassal of the Vase, at Avalon!

"This could not last, for evil days came on,
And evil men: the garbage of their sin
Tainted this land, and all things holy fled.
The Sangraal was not: on a summer eve,
The silence of the sky brake up in sound!
The tree of Joseph glowed with ruddy light:
A harmless fire, curved like a molten vase,
Around the bush, and from the midst, a voice:
Thus hewn by Merlin on a runic stone:—
Kirioth : el : Zannah : aulohee : pedah   :

"Then said the shuddering seer—he heard and knew
The unutterable words that glide in Heaven,
Without a breath or tongue, from soul to soul—

"'The land is lonely now: Anathema!
The link that bound it to the silent grasp
Of thrilling worlds is gathered up and gone:
The glory is departed; and the disk
So full of radiance from the touch of God!
This orb is darkened to the distant watch

Of Saturn and his reapers, when they pause,
Amid their sheaves, to count the nightly stars.

"'All gone! but not for ever: on a day
There shall rise a king from Keltic loins,
Of mystic birth and name, tender and true;
His vassals shall be noble, to a man:
Knights strong in battle till the war is won:
Then while the land is husht on Tamar side,
So that the warder upon Carradon
Shall hear at once the river and the sea—
That king shall call a Quest: a kindling cry:
'Ho! for the Sangraal! vanish'd Vase of God!'

"'Yea! and it shall be won! A chosen knight,
The ninth from Joseph in the line of blood,
Clean as a maid from guile and fleshly sin—
He with the shield of Sarras;[7] and the lance,
Ruddy and moisten'd with a freshening stain,
As from a sever'd wound of yesterday—
He shall achieve the Graal: he alone!'"

"Thus wrote Bard Merlin on the Runic hide
Of a slain deer: rolled in an aumry chest.

"And now, fair Sirs, your voices: who will gird
His belt for travel in the perilous ways?
This thing must be fulfilled:—in vain our land
Of noble name, high deed, and famous men;
Vain the proud homage of our thrall, the sea,
If we be shorn of God. Ah! loathsome shame!
To hurl in battle for the pride of arms:
To ride in native tournay, foreign war:
To count the stars; to ponder pictured runes,
And grasp great knowledge, as the demons do,
If we be shorn of God:—we must assay
The myth and meaning of this marvellous bowl:
It shall be sought and found:—"
                              Thus said the King.

Then rose a storm of voices; like the sea,
When Ocean, bounding, shouts with all his waves.

High-hearted men! the purpose and the theme,
Smote the fine chord that thrills the warrior's soul
With touch and impulse for a deed of fame.

Then spake Sir Gauvain, counsellor of the King,
A man of Pentecost for words that burn:—

"Sirs! we are soldiers of the rock and ring:
Our Table Round is earth's most honoured stone;
Thereon two worlds of life and glory blend,
The boss upon the shield of many a land,
The midway link with the light beyond the stars!
This is our fount of fame! Let us arise,
And cleave the earth like rivers; like the streams
That win from Paradise their immortal name:
To the four winds of God, casting the lot.
So shall we share the regions, and unfold
The shrouded mystery of those fields of air.

"Eastward! the source and spring of life and light!
Thence came, and thither went, the rush of worlds,
When the great cone of space[8] was sown with stars.
There rolled the gateway of the double dawn,
When the mere God shone down, a breathing man.
There, up from Bethany, the Syrian Twelve
Watched their dear Master darken into day.
Thence, too, will gleam the Cross, the arisen wood:[9]
Ah, shuddering sign, one day, of terrible doom!
Therefore the Orient is the home of God.

"The West! a Galilee: the shore of men;
The symbol and the scene of populous life:
Full Japhet journeyed thither, Noe's son,
The prophecy of increase in his loins.
Westward[10] Lord Jesu looked His latest love,
His yearning Cross along the peopled sea,
The innumerable nations in His soul.
Thus came that type and token of our kind,
The realm and region of the set of sun,
The wide, wide West; the imaged zone of man.

"The North! the lair of demons, where they coil,
And bound, and glide, and travel to and fro:
Their gulph, the underworld, this hollow orb,
Where vaulted columns curve beneath the hills,
And shoulder us on their arches: there they throng;
The portal of their pit, the polar gate,
Their fiery dungeon mocked with northern snow:
There, doom and demon haunt a native land,
Where dreamy thunder mutters in the cloud,
Storm broods, and battle breathes, and baleful fires
Shed a fierce horror o'er the shuddering North.

"But thou! O South Wind, breathe thy fragrant sigh!
We follow on thy perfume, breath of heaven!
Myriads, in girded albs, for ever young,
Their stately semblance of embodied air,
Troop round the footstool of the Southern Cross,
That pentacle of stars: the very sign
That led the Wise Men towards the Awful Child,
Then came and stood to rule the peaceful sea.
So, too, Lord Jesu from His mighty tomb[11]
Cast the dear shadow of his red right hand,
To soothe the happy South—the angels' home.

"Then let us search the regions, one by one,
And pluck this Sangraal from its cloudy cave."

So Merlin brought the arrows: graven lots,
Shrouded from sight within a quiver'd sheath,
For choice and guidance in the perilous path,
That so the travellers might divide the lands.
They met at Lauds, in good Saint Nectan's cell,
For fast, and vigil, and their knightly vow:
Then knelt, and prayed, and all received their God.

"Now for the silvery arrows! Grasp and hold!"

Sir Lancelot drew the North: that fell domain,
Where fleshly man must brook the airy fiend—
His battle-foe, the demon—ghastly War!
Ho! stout Saint Michael shield them, knight and knave!

The South fell softly to Sir Perceval's hand:
Some shadowy angel breathed a silent sign,
That so that blameless man, that courteous knight,
Might mount and mingle with the happy host
Of God's white army in their native land.
Yea! they shall woo and soothe him, like the dove.

But hark! the greeting—"Tristan for the West!"
Among the multitudes, his watchful way,
The billowy hordes beside the seething sea;
But will the glory gleam in loathsome lands?
Will the lost pearl shine out among the swine?
Woe, father Adam, to thy loins and thee!

Sir Galahad holds the Orient arrow's name:
His chosen hand unbars the gate of day;
There glows that heart, fill'd with his mother's blood,
That rules in every pulse, the world of man;
Link of the awful Three, with many a star.
O! blessèd East! 'mid visions such as thine,
'Twere well to grasp the Sangraal, and die.

Now feast and festival in Arthur's hall:
Hark! stern Dundagel softens into song!
They meet for solemn severance, knight and king,
Where gate and bulwark darken o'er the sea.
Strong men for meat, and warriors at the wine,
They wreak the wrath of hunger on the beeves,
They rend rich morsels from the savoury deer,
And quench the flagon like Brun-guillie[12] dew!
Hear! how the minstrels prophesy in sound,
Shout the King's Waes-hael, and Drink-hael the Queen!
Then said Sir Kay, he of the arrowy tongue,
"Joseph and Pharaoh! how they build their bones!
Happier the boar were quick than dead to-day."

The Queen! the Queen! how haughty on the dais!
The sunset tangled in her golden hair:
A dove amid the eagles—Gwennivar!
Aishah! what might is in that glorious eye!

See their tamed lion[13] from Brocelian's glade,
Couched on the granite like a captive king!
A word—a gesture—or a mute caress—
How fiercely fond he droops his billowy mane,
And wooes, with tawny lip, his lady's hand!

The dawn is deep; the mountains yearn for day;
The hooting cairn[14] is husht—that fiendish noise,
Yelled from the utterance of the rending rock,
When the fierce dog of Cain barks from the moon.[15]

The bird of judgment chants the doom of night,
The billows laugh a welcome to the day,
And Camlan ripples, seaward, with a smile.

Down with the eastern bridge! the warriors ride,
And thou, Sir Herald, blazon as they pass!
Foremost sad Lancelot, throned upon his steed,
His yellow banner, northward, lapping light:
The crest, a lily, with a broken stem,
The legend, **Stately once and ever fair;**
It hath a meaning, seek it not, O King!

A quaint embroidery Sir Perceval wore;
A turbaned Syrian, underneath a palm,
Wrestled for mastery with a stately foe,
Robed in a Levite's raiment, white as wool:
His touch o'erwhelmed the Hebrew, and his word,
Whoso is strong with God shall conquer man,
Coil'd in rich tracery round the knightly shield.
Did Ysolt's delicate fingers weave the web,
That gleamed in silken radiance o'er her lord?
A molten rainbow, bent, that arch in heaven,
Which leads straightway to Paradise and God;
Beneath, came up a gloved and sigilled hand,
Amid this cunning needlework of words,
When toil and tears have worn the westering day,
Behold the smile of fame! so brief: so bright.
A vast archangel floods Sir Galahad's shield:
Mid-breast, and lifted high, an Orient cruse,
Full filled, and running o'er with Numynous[16] light,
As though it held and shed the visible God;

36

Then shone this utterance as in graven fire,
I thirst! O Jesu! let me drink and die!

So forth they fare, King Arthur and his men,
Like stout quaternions of the Maccabee:
They halt, and form at craggy Carradon;
Fit scene for haughty hope and stern farewell.
Lo! the rude altar, and the rough-hewn rock,
The grim and ghastly semblance of the fiend,
His haunt and coil within that pillar'd home.
Hark! the wild echo! Did the demon breathe
That yell of vengeance from the conscious stone?

There the brown barrow curves its sullen breast,
Above the bones of some dead Gentile's soul:
All husht—and calm—and cold—until anon
Gleams the old dawn—the well-remembered day—
Then may you hear, beneath that hollow cairn,
The clash of arms: the muffled shout of war;
Blent with the rustle of the kindling dead!

They stand—and hush their hearts to hear the King.
Then said he, like a prince of Tamar-land—
Around his soul, Dundagel and the sea—

"Ha! Sirs—ye seek a noble crest to-day,
To win and wear the starry Sangraal,
The link that binds to God a lonely land.
Would that my arm went with you, like my heart!
But the true shepherd must not shun the fold:
For in this flock are crouching grievous wolves,
And chief among them all, my own false kin.
Therefore I tarry by the cruel sea,
To hear at eve the treacherous mermaid's song,
And watch the wallowing monsters of the wave,—
'Mid all things fierce, and wild, and strange, alone!

"Ay! all beside can win companionship:
The churl may clip his mate beneath the thatch,
While his brown urchins nestle at his knees:
The soldier give and grasp a mutual palm,
Knit to his flesh in sinewy bonds of war:

The knight may seek at eve his castle-gate,
Mount the old stair, and lift the accustom'd latch,
To find, for throbbing brow and weary limb,
That paradise of pillows, one true breast:
But he, the lofty ruler of the land,
Like yonder Tor, first greeted by the dawn,
And wooed the latest by the lingering day,
With happy homes and hearths beneath his breast,
Must soar and gleam in solitary snow.
The lonely one is, evermore, the King.
So now farewell, my lieges, fare ye well,
And God's sweet Mother be your benison!
Since by grey Merlin's gloss, this wondrous cup
Is, like the golden vase in Aaron's ark,
A fount of manha for a yearning world,
As full as it can hold of God and heaven,
Search the four winds until the balsam breathe,
Then grasp, and fold it in your very soul!

"I have no son, no daughter of my loins,
To breathe, 'mid future men, their father's name:
My blood will perish when these veins are dry;
Yet am I fain some deeds of mine should live—
I would not be forgotten in this land:
I yearn that men I know not, men unborn,
Should find, amid these fields, King Arthur's fame!
Here let them say, by proud Dundagel's walls—
'They brought the Sangraal back by his command,
They touched these rugged rocks with hues of God:'
So shall my name have worship, and my land.

"Ah! native Cornwall! throned upon the hills,
Thy moorland pathways worn by Angel feet,
Thy streams that march in music to the sea
'Mid Ocean's merry noise, his billowy laugh!
Ah me! a gloom falls heavy on my soul—
The birds that sung to me in youth are dead;
I think, in dreamy vigils of the night,
It may be God is angry with my land,
Too much athirst for fame, too fond of blood;
And all for earth, for shadows, and the dream
To glean an echo from the winds of song!

38

"But now, let hearts be high! the Archangel held
A tournay with the fiend on Abarim,
And good Saint Michael won his dragon-crest!

"Be this our cry! the battle is for God!
If bevies of foul fiends withstand your path,
Nay! if strong angels hold the watch and ward,
Plunge in their midst, and shout, 'A Sangraal!'"

He ceased; the warriors bent a knightly knee,
And touched, with kiss and sign, Excalibur;
Then turned, and mounted for their perilous way!

That night Dundagel shuddered into storm—
The deep foundations shook beneath the sea:
Yet there they stood, beneath the murky moon,
Above the bastion, Merlin and the King.
Thrice waved the sage his staff, and thrice they saw
A peopled vision throng the rocky moor.

First fell a gloom, thick as a thousand nights,
A pall that hid whole armies; and beneath
Stormed the wild tide of war; until on high
Gleamed red the dragon, and the Keltic glaive
Smote the loose battle of the roving Dane!
Then yelled a fiercer fight: for brother blood
Rushed mingling, and twin dragons fought the field!
The grisly shadows of his faithful knights
Perplext their lord: and in their midst, behold!
His own stern semblance waved a phantom brand,
Drooped, and went down the war. Then cried the King,
"Ho! Arthur to the rescue!" and half drew
Excalibur; but sank, and fell entranced.

A touch aroused the monarch: and there stood
He, of the billowy beard and awful eye,
The ashes of whole ages on his brow—
Merlin the bard, son of a demon-sire!
High, like Ben Amram at the thirsty rock,
He raised his prophet staff: that runic rod,
The stem of Igdrasil[17]—the crutch of Raun—
And wrote strange words along the conscious air.

39

Forth gleamed the east, and yet it was not day!
A white and glowing horse outrode the dawn;
A youthful rider ruled the bounding rein,
And he, in semblance of Sir Galahad shone:
A vase he held on high; one molten gem,
Like massive ruby or the chrysolite:
Thence gushed the light in flakes; and flowing, fell
As though the pavement of the sky brake up,
And stars were shed to sojourn on the hills,
From grey Morwenna's stone to Michael's tor,
Until the rocky land was like a heaven.

Then saw they that the mighty Quest was won!
The Sangraal swoon'd along the golden air:
The sea breathed balsam, like Gennesaret:
The streams were touched with supernatural light:
And fonts of Saxon rock, stood, full of God!
Altars arose, each like a kingly throne,
Where the royal chalice, with its lineal blood,
The Glory of the Presence, ruled and reigned.
This lasted long: until the white horse fled,
The fierce fangs of the libbard in his loins:
Whole ages glided in that blink of time,
While Merlin and the King, looked, wondering, on.

But see! once more the wizard-wand arise,
To cleave the air with signals, and a scene.

Troops of the demon-north, in yellow garb,
The sickly hue of vile Iscariot's hair,
Mingle with men, in unseen multitudes!
Unscared, they throng the valley and the hill;
The shrines were darkened and the chalice void:
That which held God was gone: Maran-atha!
The awful shadows of the Sangraal, fled!
Yet giant-men arose, that seemed as gods,
Such might they gathered from the swarthy kind:
The myths were rendered up: and one by one,
The Fire—the Light—the Air—were tamed and bound
Like votive vassals at their chariot-wheel.
Then learnt they War: yet not that noble wrath,
That brings the generous champion face to face

With equal shield, and with a measured brand,
To peril life for life, and do or die;
But the false valour of the lurking fiend
To hurl a distant death from some deep den:
To wing with flame the metal of the mine:
And, so they rend God's image, reck not who!

"Ah! haughty England! lady of the wave!"
Thus said pale Merlin to the listening King,
"What is thy glory in the world of stars?
To scorch and slay: to win demoniac fame,
In arts and arms; and then to flash and die!
Thou art the diamond of the demon-crown,
Smitten by Michael upon Abarim,
That fell; and glared, an island of the sea.
Ah! native England! wake thine ancient cry;
Ho! for the Sangraal! vanish'd Vase of Heaven,
That held, like Christ's own heart, an hin of blood!"

He ceased; and all around was dreamy night:
There stood Dundagel, throned: and the great sea
Lay, a strong vassal at his master's gate,
And, like a drunken giant, sobb'd in sleep!

Author's Notes

[1]The hin was a Hebrew measure, used for the wine of the sacrifice.
[2]The distance at which a leper was commanded to keep from every healthy
person.
[3]Or cauldron.
[4]Routor, the red hill, so named from the heath which blossoms on the hill-
side.
[5]Logan, or shuddering stone. A rock of augury found in all lands, a relic of
the patriarchal era of belief. A child or an innocent person could move
it, as Pliny records, with a stalk of asphodel; but a strong man, if guilty,
could not shake it with all his force.
[6]A Hebrew name, signifying "champer of the steel."
[7]The city of "Sarras in the spiritual place" is the scene of many a legend of
mediaeval times. In all likelihood it was identical with Charras or
Charran of Holy Writ. There was treasured up the shield, the sure
shelter of the Knight of the Quest. The lance which pierced our blessed
Saviour's side was also there preserved.

[8]Space is a created thing, material and defined. As time is *mensura motus*, so is space *mensura loci*; and it signifies that part of God's presence which is measured out to enfold the planetary universe. The tracery of its outline is a cone. Every path of a planet is a curve of that conic figure: and as motion is the life of matter, the whirl of space in its allotted courses is the cause of that visible movement of the sun and the solar system towards the star Alcyone as the fixed centre in the cone of space.

[9]The "Sign of the Son of Man," the signal of the last day, was understood, in the early ages, to denote the actual Cross of Calvary; which was to be miraculously recalled into existence, and, angel-borne, to announce the advent of the Lord in the sky.

[10]Our Lord was crucified with His back towards the east: His face therefore was turned towards the west, which is always, in sacred symbolism, the region of the people.

[11]Our Lord was laid in His sepulchre with His head towards the west: His right hand therefore gave symbolic greeting to the region of the south; as His left hand reproached and gave a fatal aspect to the north.

[12]The golden-hill, from *brun*, "a hill" and *guillie*, "golden:" so called from the yellow gorse with which it is clothed.

[13]This appropriate fondling of the knights of Dundagel moves Villemarque to write, "qui me plaise et me charme quand je le trouve couché aux pieds d'Ivan, le mufle allongé sur ses deux pattes croisées, les yeux à demi-ouvert et revant."

[14]See Borlase, bk. iii, ch. iii for "Karn-idzek:" touched by the moon at some weird hour of the night, it hooted with oracular sound.

[15]Cain and his dog: Dante's version of the man in the moon was a thought of the old simplicity of primeval days.

[16]When the cone of space had been traced out and defined, the next act of creation was to replenish it with that first and supernatural element which I have named 'Numyne.' The forefathers called it the spiritual or ethereal element, *coelum*; from Genesis i. 2. Within its texture the other and grosser elements of light and air ebb and flow, cling and glide. Therein dwell the forces, and thereof Angels and all spiritual things receive their substance and form.

[17]Igdrasil, the mystic tree, the ash of the Keltic ritual. The Raun or Rowan is also the ash of the mountain, another magic wood of the northern nations.

Sir Launcelot and Queen Guinevere
A Fragment

ALFRED, LORD TENNYSON

Like souls that balance joy and pain,
With tears and smiles from heaven again
The maiden Spring upon the plain
Came in a sunlit fall of rain.
    In crystal vapor everywhere
Blue isles of heaven laugh'd between,
And far, in forest-deeps unseen,
The topmost elm-tree gather'd green
    From draughts of balmy air.

Sometimes the linnet piped his song;
Sometimes the throstle whistled strong;
Sometimes the sparhawk, wheel'd along,
Hush'd all the groves from fear of wrong;
    By grassy capes with fuller sound
In curves the yellowing river ran,
And drooping chestnut-buds began
To spread into the perfect fan,
    Above the teeming ground.

Then, in the boyhood of the year,
Sir Launcelot and Queen Guinevere

Rode thro' the coverts of the deer,
With blissful treble ringing clear.
    She seem'd a part of joyous Spring;
A gown of grass-green silk she wore,
Buckled with golden clasps before;
A light-green tuft of plumes she bore
    Closed in a golden ring.

Now on some twisted ivy-net,
Now by some tinkling rivulet,
In mosses mixt with violet
Her cream-white mule his pastern set;
    And fleeter now she skimm'd the plains
Than she whose elfin prancer springs
By night to eery warblings,
When all the glimmering moorland rings
    With jingling bridle-reins.

As she fled fast thro' sun and shade,
The happy winds upon her play'd,
Blowing the ringlet from the braid.
She look'd so lovely, as she sway'd
    The rein with dainty finger-tips,
A man had given all other bliss,
And all his worldly worth for this,
To waste his whole heart in one kiss
    Upon her perfect lips.

The Lady of Shalott

ALFRED, LORD TENNYSON

Part I

On either side the river lie
Long fields of barley and of rye,
That clothe the wold and meet the sky;
And thro' the field the road runs by
　　To many-tower'd Camelot;
And up and down the people go,
Gazing where the lilies blow
Round an island there below,
　　The island of Shalott.

Willows whiten, aspens quiver,
Little breezes dusk and shiver
Thro' the wave that runs for ever
By the island in the river
　　Flowing down to Camelot.
Four gray walls, and four gray towers,
Overlook a space of flowers,
And the silent isle imbowers
　　The Lady of Shalott.

By the margin, willow-veil'd
Slide the heavy barges trail'd

By slow horses; and unhail'd
The shallop flitteth silken-sail'd
     Skimming down to Camelot:
But who hath seen her wave her hand?
Or at the casement seen her stand?
Or is she known in all the land,
     The Lady of Shalott?

Only reapers, reaping early
In among the bearded barley,
Hear a song that echoes cheerly
From the river winding clearly,
     Down to tower'd Camelot;
And by the moon the reaper weary,
Piling sheaves in uplands airy,
Listening, whispers " 'T is the fairy
     Lady of Shalott."

Part II

There she weaves by night and day
A magic web with colors gay.
She has heard a whisper say
A curse is on her if she stay
     To look down to Camelot.
She knows not what the curse may be,
And so she weaveth steadily,
And little other care hath she,
     The Lady of Shalott.

And moving thro' a mirror clear
That hangs before her all the year,
Shadows of the world appear.
There she sees the highway near
     Winding down to Camelot;
There the river eddy whirls,
And there the surly village-churls,
And the red cloaks of market girls,
     Pass onward from Shalott.

Sometimes a troop of damsels glad,
An abbot on an ambling pad,
Sometimes a curly shepherd-lad,
Or long-hair'd page in crimson clad,
    Goes by to tower'd Camelot;
And sometimes thro' the mirror blue
The knights come riding two by two:
She hath no loyal knight and true,
    The Lady of Shalott.

But in her web she still delights
To weave the mirror's magic sights,
For often thro' the silent nights
A funeral, with plumes and lights
    And music, went to Camelot;
Or when the moon was overhead,
Came two young lovers lately wed:
"I am half sick of shadows," said
    The Lady of Shalott.

            Part III

A bow-shot from her bower-eaves,
He rode between the barley-sheaves.
The sun came dazzling thro' the leaves,
And flamed upon the brazen greaves
    Of bold Sir Lancelot.
A red-cross knight for ever kneel'd
To a lady in his shield,
That sparkled on the yellow field,
    Beside remote Shalott.

The gemmy bridle glitter'd free,
Like to some branch of stars we see
Hung in the golden Galaxy.
The bridle bells rang merrily
    As he rode down to Camelot;
And from his blazon'd baldric slung
A mighty silver bugle hung,
And as he rode his armor rung,
    Beside remote Shalott.

All in the blue unclouded weather
Thick-jewell'd shone the saddle-leather,
The helmet and the helmet-feather
Burn'd like one burning flame together,
    As he rode down to Camelot;
As often thro' the purple night,
Below the starry clusters bright,
Some bearded meteor, trailing light,
    Moves over still Shalott.

His broad clear brow in sunlight glow'd;
On burnish'd hooves his war-horse trode;
From underneath his helmet flow'd
His coal-black curls as on he rode,
    As he rode down to Camelot.
From the bank and from the river
He flash'd into the crystal mirror,
"Tirra lirra," by the river
    Sang Sir Lancelot.

She left the web, she left the loom,
She made three paces thro' the room,
She saw the water-lily bloom,
She saw the helmet and the plume,
    She look'd down to Camelot.
Out flew the web and floated wide;
The mirror crack'd from side to side;
"The curse is come upon me," cried
    The Lady of Shalott.

Part IV

In the stormy east-wind straining,
The pale yellow woods were waning,
The broad stream in his banks complaining,
Heavily the low sky raining
    Over tower'd Camelot;
Down she came and found a boat
Beneath a willow left afloat
And round about the prow she wrote
    The Lady of Shalott.

And down the river's dim expanse
Like some bold seër in a trance,
Seeing all his own mischance—
With a glassy countenance
    Did she look to Camelot.
And at the closing of the day
She loosed the chain, and down she lay;
The broad stream bore her far away,
    The Lady of Shalott.

Lying, robed in snowy white
That loosely flew to left and right—
The leaves upon her falling light—
Thro' the noises of the night
    She floated down to Camelot;
And as the boat-head wound along
The willowy hills and fields among,
They heard her singing her last song,
    The Lady of Shalott.

Heard a carol, mournful, holy,
Chanted loudly, chanted lowly,
Till her blood was frozen slowly,
And her eyes were darken'd wholly,
    Turn'd to tower'd Camelot.
For ere she reach'd upon the tide
The first house by the water-side,
Singing in her song she died,
    The Lady of Shalott.

Under tower and balcony,
By garden-wall and gallery,
A gleaming shape she floated by,
Dead-pale between the houses high,
    Silent into Camelot.
Out upon the wharfs they came,
Knight and burgher, lord and dame,
And round the prow they read her name,
    The Lady of Shalott.

Who is this? and what is here?
And in the lighted palace near

Died the sound of royal cheer;
And they cross'd themselves for fear,
     All the knights at Camelot:
But Lancelot mused a little space;
He said, "She has a lovely face;
God in his mercy lend her grace,
     The Lady of Shalott."

Merlin and the Gleam

ALFRED, LORD TENNYSON

I

O young Mariner,
You from the haven
Under the sea-cliff,
You that are watching
The gray Magician
With eyes of wonder,
I am Merlin,
And *I* am dying,
I am Merlin
Who follow The Gleam.

II

Mighty the Wizard
Who found me at sunrise
Sleeping, and woke me
And learn'd me Magic!
Great the Master,
And sweet the Magic,
When over the valley,
In early summers,
Over the mountain,

On human faces,
And all around me,
Moving to melody,
Floated The Gleam.

III

Once at the croak of a Raven who crost it,
A barbarous people,
Blind to the magic,
And deaf to the melody,
Snarl'd at and cursed me.
A demon vext me,
The light retreated,
The landskip darken'd,
The melody deaden'd,
The Master whisper'd
"Follow The Gleam."

IV

Then to the melody,
Over a wilderness
Gliding, and glancing at
Elf of the woodland,
Gnome of the cavern,
Griffin and Giant,
And dancing of Fairies
In desolate hollows,
And wraiths of the mountain,
And rolling of dragons
By warble of water,
Or cataract music
Of falling torrents,
Flitted The Gleam.

V

Down from the mountain
And over the level,
And streaming and shining on
Silent river,

Silvery willow,
Pasture and plowland,
Horses and oxen,
Innocent maidens,
Garrulous children,
Homestead and harvest,
Reaper and gleaner,
And rough-ruddy faces
Of lowly labour,
Slided The Gleam.—

VI

Then, with a melody
Stronger and statelier,
Led me at length
To the city and palace
Of Arthur the king;
Touch'd at the golden
Cross of the churches,
Flash'd on the Tournament,
Flicker'd and bicker'd
From helmet to helmet,
And last on the forehead
Of Arthur the blameless
Rested The Gleam.

VII

Clouds and darkness
Closed upon Camelot;
Arthur had vanish'd
I knew not whither,
The king who loved me,
And cannot die;
For out of the darkness
Silent and slowly
The Gleam, that had waned to a wintry glimmer
On icy fallow
And faded forest,
Drew to the valley
Named to the shadow,

And slowly brightening
Out of the glimmer,
And slowly moving again to a melody
Yearningly tender,
Fell on the shadow,
No longer a shadow,
But clothed with The Gleam.

VIII

And broader and brighter
The Gleam flying onward,
Wed to the melody,
Sang thro' the world;
And slower and fainter,
Old and weary,
But eager to follow,
I saw, whenever
In passing it glanced upon
Hamlet or city,
That under the Crosses
The dead man's garden,
The mortal hillock,
Would break into blossom;
And so to the land's
Last limit I came—
And can no longer,
But die rejoicing,
For thro' the Magic
Of Him the Mighty,
Who taught me in childhood,
There on the border
Of boundless Ocean,
And all but in Heaven
Hovers The Gleam.

IX

Not of the sunlight,
Not of the moonlight,
Not of the starlight!
O young Mariner,

Down to the haven,
Call your companions,
Launch your vessel,
And crowd your canvas,
And, ere it vanishes
Over the margin,
After it, follow it,
Follow The Gleam.

The Defence of Guenevere

WILLIAM MORRIS

But, knowing now that they would have her speak,
She threw her wet hair backward from her brow,
Her hand close to her mouth touching her cheek,

As though she had had there a shameful blow,
And feeling it shameful to feel ought but shame
All through her heart, yet felt her cheek burned so,

She must a little touch it; like one lame
She walked away from Gauwaine, with her head
Still lifted up; and on her cheek of flame

The tears dried quick; she stopped at last and said:
"O knights and lords, it seems but little skill
To talk of well-known things past now and dead.

"God wot I ought to say, I have done ill,
And pray you all forgiveness heartily!
Because you must be right, such great lords; still

"Listen, suppose your time were come to die,
And you were quite alone and very weak;
Yea, laid a dying while very mightily

"The wind was ruffling up the narrow streak
Of river through your broad lands running well:
Suppose a hush should come, then some one speak:

"'One of these cloths is heaven, and one is hell,
Now choose one cloth for ever; which they be,
I will not tell you, you must somehow tell

"'Of your own strength and mightiness; here, see!'
Yea, yea, my lord, and you to ope your eyes,
At foot of your familiar bed to see

"A great God's angel standing, with such dyes,
Not known on earth, on his great wings, and hands,
Held out two ways, light from the inner skies

"Showing him well, and making his commands
Seem to be God's commands, moreover, too,
Holding within his hands the cloths on wands;

"And one of these strange choosing cloths was blue,
Wavy and long, and one cut short and red;
No man could tell the better of the two.

"After a shivering half-hour you said:
'God help! heaven's colour, the blue;' and he said, 'hell.'
Perhaps you then would roll upon your bed,

"And cry to all good men that loved you well,
'Ah Christ! if only I had known, known, known;'
Launcelot went away, then I could tell,

"Like wisest man how all things would be, moan,
And roll and hurt myself, and long to die,
And yet fear much to die for what was sown.

"Nevertheless you, O Sir Gauwaine, lie,
Whatever may have happened through these years,
God knows I speak truth, saying that you lie."

Her voice was low at first, being full of tears,
But as it cleared, it grew full loud and shrill,
Growing a windy shriek in all men's ears,

A ringing in their startled brains, until
She said that Gauwaine lied, then her voice sunk,
And her great eyes began again to fill,

Though still she stood right up, and never shrunk,
But spoke on bravely, glorious lady fair!
Whatever tears her full lips may have drunk,

She stood, and seemed to think, and wrung her hair,
Spoke out at last with no more trace of shame,
With passionate twisting of her body there:

"It chanced upon a day that Launcelot came
To dwell at Arthur's court: at Christmas-time
This happened; when the heralds sung his name,

"Son of King Ban of Benwick, seemed to chime
Along with all the bells that rang that day,
O'er the white roofs, with little change of rhyme.

"Christmas and whitened winter passed away,
And over me the April sunshine came,
Made very awful with black hail-clouds, yea

"And in the Summer I grew white with flame,
And bowed my head down: Autumn, and the sick
Sure knowledge things would never be the same,

"However often Spring might be most thick
Of blossoms and buds, smote on me, and I grew
Careless of most things, let the clock tick, tick,

"To my unhappy pulse, that beat right through
My eager body; while I laughed out loud,
And let my lips curl up at false or true,

"Seemed cold and shallow without any cloud.
Behold my judges, then the cloths were brought;
While I was dizzied thus, old thoughts would crowd,

"Belonging to the time ere I was bought
By Arthur's great name and his little love;
Must I give up for ever then, I thought,

"That which I deemed would ever round me move
Glorifying all things; for a little word,
Scarce ever meant at all, must I now prove

"Stone-cold for ever? Pray you, does the Lord
Will that all folks should be quite happy and good?
I love God now a little, if this cord

"Were broken, once for all what striving could
Make me love anything in earth or heaven?
So day by day it grew, as if one should

"Slip slowly down some path worn smooth and even,
Down to a cool sea on a summer day;
Yet still in slipping there was some small leaven

"Of stretched hands catching small stones by the way,
Until one surely reached the sea at last,
And felt strange new joy as the worn head lay

"Back, with the hair like sea-weed; yea all past
Sweat of the forehead, dryness of the lips,
Washed utterly out by the dear waves o'ercast,

"In the lone sea, far off from any ships!
Do I not know now of a day in Spring?
No minute of the wild day ever slips

"From out my memory; I hear thrushes sing,
And wheresoever I may be, straightway
Thoughts of it all come up with most fresh sting:

"I was half mad with beauty on that day,
And went without my ladies all alone,
In a quiet garden walled round every way;

"I was right joyful of that wall of stone,
That shut the flowers and trees up with the sky,
And trebled all the beauty: to the bone,

"Yea right through to my heart, grown very shy
With weary thoughts, it pierced, and made me glad;
Exceedingly glad, and I knew verily,

"A little thing just then had made me mad;
I dared not think, as I was wont to do,
Sometimes, upon my beauty; if I had

"Held out my long hand up against the blue,
And, looking on the tenderly darken'd fingers,
Thought that by rights one ought to see quite through,

"There, see you, where the soft still light yet lingers,
Round by the edges; what should I have done,
If this had joined with yellow spotted singers,

"And startling green drawn upward by the sun?
But shouting, loosed out, see now! all my hair,
And trancedly stood watching the west wind run

"With faintest half-heard breathing sound: why there
I lose my head e'en now in doing this;
But shortly listen: In that garden fair

"Came Launcelot walking; this is true, the kiss
Wherewith we kissed in meeting that spring day,
I scarce dare talk of the remember'd bliss,

"When both our mouths went wandering in one way,
And aching sorely, met among the leaves;
Our hands being left behind strained far away.

"Never within a yard of my bright sleeves
Had Launcelot come before: and now so nigh!
After that day why is it Guenevere grieves?

"Nevertheless you, O Sir Gauwaine, lie,
Whatever happened on through all those years,
God knows I speak truth, saying that you lie.

"Being such a lady could I weep these tears
If this were true? A great queen such as I
Having sinn'd this way, straight her conscience sears;

"And afterwards she liveth hatefully,
Slaying and poisoning, certes never weeps:
Gauwaine be friends now, speak me lovingly.

"Do I not see how God's dear pity creeps
All through your frame, and trembles in your mouth?
Remember in what grave your mother sleeps,

"Buried in some place far down in the south,
Men are forgetting as I speak to you;
By her head sever'd in that awful drouth

"Of pity that drew Agravaine's fell blow,
I pray you pity! let me not scream out
For ever after, when the shrill winds blow

"Through half your castle-locks! let me not shout
For ever after in the winter night
When you ride out alone! in battle-rout

"Let not my rusting tears make your sword light!
Ah! God of mercy, how he turns away!
So, ever must I dress me to the fight,

"So: let God's justice work! Gauwaine, I say,
See me hew down your proofs: yea all men know
Even as you said how Mellyagraunce one day,

"One bitter day in *la Fausse Garde*, for so
All good knights held it after, saw:
Yea, sirs, by cursed unknightly outrage; though

"You, Gauwaine, held his word without a flaw,
This Mellyagraunce saw blood upon my bed:
Whose blood then pray you? is there any law

"To make a queen say why some spots of red
Lie on her coverlet? or will you say:
'Your hands are white, lady, as when you wed,

"'Where did you bleed?' and must I stammer out, 'Nay,
I blush indeed, fair lord, only to rend
My sleeve up to my shoulder, where there lay

"'A knife-point last night': so must I defend
The honour of the Lady Guenevere?
Not so, fair lords, even if the world should end

"This very day, and you were judges here
Instead of God. Did you see Mellyagraunce
When Launcelot stood by him? what white fear

"Curdled his blood, and how his teeth did dance,
His side sink in? as my knight cried and said:
'Slayer of unarm'd men, here is a chance!

"'Setter of traps, I pray you guard your head,
By God I am so glad to fight with you,
Stripper of ladies, that my hand feels lead

"'For driving weight; hurrah now! draw and do,
For all my wounds are moving in my breast,
And I am getting mad with waiting so.'

"He struck his hands together o'er the beast,
Who fell down flat, and grovell'd at his feet,
And groan'd at being slain so young: 'At least,'

"My knight said, 'rise you, sir, who are so fleet
At catching ladies, half-arm'd will I fight,
My left side all uncovered!' then I weet,

"Up sprang Sir Mellyagraunce with great delight
Upon his knave's face; not until just then
Did I quite hate him, as I saw my knight

"Along the lists look to my stake and pen
With such a joyous smile, it made me sigh
From agony beneath my waist-chain, when

"The fight began, and to me they drew nigh;
Ever Sir Launcelot kept him on the right,
And traversed warily, and ever high

"And fast leapt caitiff's sword, until my knight
Sudden threw up his sword to his left hand,
Caught it, and swung it; that was all the fight,

"Except a spout of blood on the hot land;
For it was hottest summer; and I know
I wonder'd how the fire, while I should stand,

"And burn, against the heat, would quiver so,
Yards above my head; thus these matters went;
Which things were only warnings of the woe

"That fell on me. Yet Mellyagraunce was shent,
For Mellyagraunce had fought against the Lord;
Therefore, my lords, take heed lest you be blent

"With all this wickedness; say no rash word
Against me, being so beautiful; my eyes,
Wept all away to grey, may bring some sword

"To drown you in your blood; see my breast rise,
Like waves of purple sea, as here I stand;
And how my arms are moved in wonderful wise,

"Yea also at my full heart's strong command,
See through my long throat how the words go up
In ripples to my mouth; how in my hand

"The shadow lies like wine within a cup
Of marvellously colour'd gold; yea now
This little wind is rising, look you up,

"And wonder how the light is falling so
Within my moving tresses: will you dare,
When you have looked a little on my brow,

"To say this thing is vile? or will you care
For any plausible lies of cunning woof,
When you can see my face with no lie there

"For ever? am I not a gracious proof:
'But in your chamber Launcelot was found':
Is there a good knight then would stand aloof,

"When a queen says with gentle queenly sound:
'O true as steel come now and talk with me,
I love to see your step upon the ground

"'Unwavering, also well I love to see
That gracious smile light up your face, and hear
Your wonderful words, that all mean verily

"'The thing they seem to mean: good friend, so dear
To me in everything, come here to-night,
Or else the hours will pass most dull and drear;

"'If you come not, I fear this time I might
Get thinking over much of times gone by,
When I was young, and green hope was in sight:

"'For no man cares now to know why I sigh;
And no man comes to sing me pleasant songs,
Nor any brings me the sweet flowers that lie

"'So thick in the gardens; therefore one so longs
To see you, Launcelot; that we may be
Like children once again, free from all wrongs

"'Just for one night.' Did he not come to me?
What thing could keep true Launcelot away
If I said, 'Come'? there was one less than three

"In my quiet room that night, and we were gay;
Till sudden I rose up, weak, pale, and sick,
Because a bawling broke our dream up, yea

"I looked at Launcelot's face and could not speak,
For he looked helpless too, for a little while;
Then I remember how I tried to shriek,

"And could not, but fell down; from tile to tile
The stones they threw up rattled o'er my head
And made me dizzier; till within a while

"My maids were all about me, and my head
On Launcelot's breast was being soothed away
From its white chattering, until Launcelot said:

"By God! I will not tell you more to-day,
Judge any way you will: what matters it?
You know quite well the story of that fray,

"How Launcelot still'd their bawling, the mad fit
That caught up Gauwaine: all, all, verily,
But just that which would save me; these things flit.

64

"Nevertheless you, O Sir Gauwaine, lie,
Whatever may have happen'd these long years,
God knows I speak truth, saying that you lie!

"All I have said is truth, by Christ's dear tears."
She would not speak another word, but stood
Turn'd sideways; listening, like a man who hears

His brother's trumpet sounding through the wood
Of his foes' lances. She lean'd eagerly,
And gave a slight spring sometimes, as she could

At last hear something really; joyfully
Her cheek grew crimson, as the headlong speed
Of the roan charger drew all men to see,
The knight who came was Launcelot at good need.

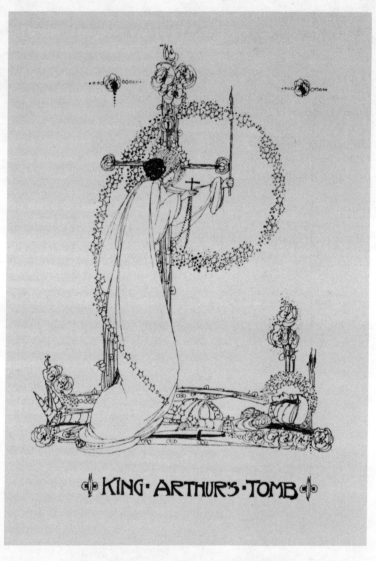

✤ KING · ARTHUR'S · TOMB ✤

From *The Defence of Guinevere and Other Poems,*
by William Morris, illustrated by Jessie King.
London and New York: John Lane, 1904.

King Arthur's Tomb

WILLIAM MORRIS

Hot August noon: already on that day
    Since sunrise through the Wiltshire downs, most sad
Of mouth and eye, he had gone leagues of way;
    Ay and by night, till whether good or bad

He was, he knew not, though he knew perchance
    That he was Launcelot, the bravest knight
Of all who since the world was, have borne lance,
    Or swung their swords in wrong cause or in right.

Nay, he knew nothing now, except that where
    The Glastonbury gilded towers shine,
A lady dwelt, whose name was Guenevere;
    This he knew also; that some fingers twine,

Not only in a man's hair, even his heart,
    (Making him good or bad I mean,) but in his life,
Skies, earth, men's looks and deeds, all that has part,
    Not being ourselves, in that half-sleep, half-strife,

(Strange sleep, strange strife,) that men call living; so
    Was Launcelot most glad when the moon rose,
Because it brought new memories of her. "Lo,
    Between the trees a large moon, the wind lows

"Not loud, but as a cow begins to low,
　　Wishing for strength to make the herdsman hear:
The ripe corn gathereth dew; yea, long ago,
　　In the old garden life, my Guenevere

"Loved to sit still among the flowers, till night
　　Had quite come on, hair loosen'd, for she said,
Smiling like heaven, that its fairness might
　　Draw up the wind sooner to cool her head.

"Now while I ride how quick the moon gets small,
　　As it did then: I tell myself a tale
That will not last beyond the whitewashed wall,
　　Thoughts of some joust must help me through the vale,

"Keep this till after: How Sir Gareth ran
　　A good course that day under my Queen's eyes,
And how she sway'd laughing at Dinadan.
　　No. Back again, the other thoughts will rise,

"And yet I think so fast 'twill end right soon:
　　Verily then I think, that Guenevere,
Made sad by dew and wind, and tree-barred moon,
　　Did love me more than ever, was more dear

"To me than ever, she would let me lie
　　And kiss her feet, or, if I sat behind,
Would drop her hand and arm most tenderly,
　　And touch my mouth. And she would let me wind

"Her hair around my neck, so that it fell
　　Upon my red robe, strange in the twilight
With many unnamed colours, till the bell
　　Of her mouth on my cheek sent a delight

"Through all my ways of being; like the stroke
　　Wherewith God threw all men upon the face
When he took Enoch, and when Enoch woke
　　With a changed body in the happy place.

"Once, I remember, as I sat beside,
　　She turn'd a little, and laid back her head,

And slept upon my breast; I almost died
  In those night-watches with my love and dread.

"There lily-like she bow'd her head and slept,
  And I breathed low, and did not dare to move,
But sat and quiver'd inwardly, thoughts crept,
  And frighten'd me with pulses of my Love.

"The stars shone out above the doubtful green
  Of her bodice, in the green sky overhead;
Pale in the green sky were the stars I ween,
  Because the moon shone like a star she shed

"When she dwelt up in heaven a while ago,
  And ruled all things but God: the night went on,
The wind grew cold, and the white moon grew low,
  One hand had fallen down, and now lay on

"My cold stiff palm; there were no colours then
  For near an hour, and I fell asleep
In spite of all my striving, even when
  I held her whose name-letters make me leap.

"I did not sleep long, feeling that in sleep
  I did some loved one wrong, so that the sun
Had only just arisen from the deep
  Still land of colours, when before me one

"Stood whom I knew, but scarcely dared to touch,
  She seemed to have changed so in the night;
Moreover she held scarlet lilies, such
  As Maiden Margaret bears upon the light

"Of the great church walls, natheless did I walk
  Through the fresh wet woods, and the wheat that morn,
Touching her hair and hand and mouth, and talk
  Of love we held, nigh hid among the corn.

"Back to the palace, ere the sun grew high,
  We went, and in a cool green room all day
I gazed upon the arras giddily,
  Where the wind set the silken kings a-sway.

"I could not hold her hand, or see her face;
	For which may God forgive me! but I think,
Howsoever, that she was not in that place."
	These memories Launcelot was quick to drink;

And when these fell, some paces past the wall,
	There rose yet others, but they wearied more,
And tasted not so sweet; they did not fall
	So soon, but vaguely wrenched his strained heart sore

In shadowy slipping from his grasp: these gone,
	A longing followed; if he might but touch
That Guenevere at once! Still night, the lone
	Grey horse's head before him vex'd him much,

In steady nodding over the grey road:
	Still night, and night, and night, and emptied heart
Of any stories; what a dismal load
	Time grew at last, yea, when the night did part,

And let the sun flame over all, still there
	The horse's grey ears turn'd this way and that,
And still he watch'd them twitching in the glare
	Of the morning sun, behind them still he sat,

Quite wearied out with all the wretched night,
	Until about the dustiest of the day,
On the last down's brow he drew his rein in sight
	Of the Glastonbury roofs that choke the way.

And he was now quite giddy as before,
	When she slept by him, tired out, and her hair
Was mingled with the rushes on the floor,
	And he, being tired too, was scarce aware

Of her presence; yet as he sat and gazed,
	A shiver ran throughout him, and his breath
Came slower, he seem'd suddenly amazed,
	As though he had not heard of Arthur's death.

This for a moment only, presently
	He rode on giddy still, until he reach'd

A place of apple-trees, by the thorn-tree
    Wherefrom St. Joseph in the days past preached.

Dazed there he laid his head upon a tomb,
    Not knowing it was Arthur's, at which sight
One of her maidens told her, "He is come,"
    And she went forth to meet him; yet a blight

Had settled on her, all her robes were black,
    With a long white veil only; she went slow,
As one walks to be slain, her eyes did lack
    Half her old glory, yea, alas! the glow

Had left her face and hands; this was because
    As she lay last night on her purple bed,
Wishing for morning, grudging every pause
    Of the palace clocks, until that Launcelot's head

Should lie on her breast, with all her golden hair
    Each side: when suddenly the thing grew drear,
In morning twilight, when the grey downs bare
    Grew into lumps of sin to Guenevere.

At first she said no word, but lay quite still,
    Only her mouth was open, and her eyes
Gazed wretchedly about from hill to hill;
    As though she asked, not with so much surprise

As tired disgust, what made them stand up there
    So cold and grey. After, a spasm took
Her face, and all her frame, she caught her hair,
    All her hair, in both hands, terribly she shook,

And rose till she was sitting in the bed,
    Set her teeth hard, and shut her eyes and seem'd
As though she would have torn it from her head,
    Natheless she dropp'd it, lay down, as she deem'd

It matter'd not whatever she might do:
    O Lord Christ! pity on her ghastly face!
Those dismal hours while the cloudless blue
    Drew the sun higher: He did give her grace;

71

Because at last she rose up from her bed,
    And put her raiment on, and knelt before
The blessed rood, and with her dry lips said,
    Muttering the words against the marble floor:

"Unless you pardon, what shall I do, Lord,
    But go to hell? and there see day by day
Foul deed on deed, hear foulest word on word,
    For ever and ever, such as on the way

"To Camelot I heard once from a churl,
    That curled me up upon my jennet's neck
With bitter shame; how then, Lord, should I curl
    For ages and for ages? dost thou reck

"That I am beautiful, Lord, even as you
    And your dear mother? why did I forget
You were so beautiful, and good, and true,
    That you loved me so, Guenevere? O yet

"If even I go to hell, I cannot choose
    But love you, Christ, yea, though I cannot keep
From loving Launcelot; O Christ! must I lose
    My own heart's love? see, though I cannot weep,

"Yet am I very sorry for my sin;
    Moreover, Christ, I cannot bear that hell,
I am most fain to love you, and to win
    A place in heaven some time: I cannot tell:

"Speak to me, Christ! I kiss, kiss, kiss your feet;
    Ah! now I weep!" The maid said, "By the tomb
He waiteth for you, lady," coming fleet,
    Not knowing what woe filled up all the room.

So Guenevere rose and went to meet him there,
    He did not hear her coming, as he lay
On Arthur's head, till some of her long hair
    Brush'd on the new-cut stone: "Well done! to pray

"For Arthur, my dear Lord, the greatest king
    That ever lived." "Guenevere! Guenevere!

Do you not know me, are you gone mad? fling
    Your arms and hair about me, lest I fear

"You are not Guenevere, but some other thing."
    "Pray you forgive me, fair lord Launcelot!
I am not mad, but I am sick; they cling,
    God's curses, unto such as I am; not

"Ever again shall we twine arms and lips."
    "Yea, she is mad: thy heavy law, O Lord,
Is very tight about her now, and grips
    Her poor heart, so that no right word

"Can reach her mouth; so, Lord, forgive her now,
    That she not knowing what she does, being mad,
Kills me in this way: Guenevere, bend low
    And kiss me once! for God's love kiss me! sad

"Though your face is, you look much kinder now;
    Yea once, once for the last time kiss me, lest I die."
"Christ! my hot lips are very near his brow,
    Help me to save his soul! Yea, verily,

"Across my husband's head, fair Launcelot!
    Fair serpent mark'd with V upon the head!
This thing we did while yet he was alive,
    Why not, O twisting knight, now he is dead?

"Yea, shake! shake now and shiver! if you can
    Remember anything for agony,
Pray you remember how when the wind ran
    One cool spring evening through fair aspen-tree,

"And elm and oak about the palace there
    The king came back from battle, and I stood
To meet him, with my ladies, on the stair,
    My face made beautiful with my young blood."

"Will she lie now, Lord God?" "Remember too,
    Wrung heart, how first before the knights there came
A royal bier, hung round with green and blue,
    About it shone great tapers with sick flame.

"And thereupon Lucius, the Emperor,
    Lay royal-robed, but stone-cold now and dead,
Not able to hold sword or sceptre more,
    But not quite grim; because his cloven head

"Bore no marks now of Launcelot's bitter sword,
    Being by embalmers deftly solder'd up;
So still it seem'd the face of a great lord,
    Being mended as a craftsman mends a cup.

"Also the heralds sung rejoicingly
    To their long trumpets; 'Fallen under shield,
Here lieth Lucius, King of Italy,
    Slain by Lord Launcelot in open field.'

"Thereat the people shouted: 'Launcelot!'
    And through the spears I saw you drawing nigh,
You and Lord Arthur: nay, I saw you not,
    But rather Arthur, God would not let die,

"I hoped, these many years; he should grow great,
    And in his great arms still encircle me,
Kissing my face, half blinded with the heat
    Of king's love for the queen I used to be.

"Launcelot, Launcelot, why did he take your hand,
    When he had kissed me in his kingly way?
Saying: 'This is the knight whom all the land
    Calls Arthur's banner, sword, and shield to-day;

"'Cherish him, love.' Why did your long lips cleave
    In such strange way unto my fingers then?
So eagerly glad to kiss, so loath to leave
    When you rose up? Why among helmed men

"Could I always tell you by your long strong arms,
    And sway like an angel's in your saddle there?
Why sicken'd I so often with alarms
    Over the tilt-yard? Why were you more fair

"Than aspens in the autumn at their best?
    Why did you fill all lands with your great fame,

So that Breuse even, as he rode, fear'd lest
    At turning of the way your shield should flame?

"Was it nought then, my agony and strife?
    When as day passed by day, year after year,
I found I could not live a righteous life!
    Didst ever think queens held their truth for dear?

"O, but your lips say: 'Yea, but she was cold
    Sometimes, always uncertain as the spring;
When I was sad she would be overbold,
    Longing for kisses. When war-bells did ring,

"'The back-toll'd bells of noisy Camelot.'"
    "Now, Lord God, listen! listen, Guenevere,
Though I am weak just now, I think there's not
    A man who dares to say: 'You hated her,

"'And left her moaning while you fought your fill
    In the daisied meadows!' lo you her thin hand,
That on the carven stone can not keep still,
    Because she loves me against God's command,

"Has often been quite wet with tear on tear,
    Tears Launcelot keeps somewhere, surely not
In his own heart, perhaps in Heaven, where
    He will not be these ages." "Launcelot!

"Loud lips, wrung heart! I say when the bells rang,
    The noisy back-toll'd bells of Camelot,
There were two spots on earth, the thrushes sang
    In the lonely gardens where my love was not,

"Where I was almost weeping; I dared not
    Weep quite in those days, lest one maid should say,
In tittering whispers: 'Where is Launcelot
    To wipe with some kerchief those tears away?'

"Another answer sharply with brows knit,
    And warning hand up, scarcely lower though:
'You speak too loud, see you, she heareth it,
    This tigress fair has claws, as I well know,

"'As Launcelot knows too, the poor knight! well-a-day!
    Why met he not with Iseult from the West,
Or better still, Iseult of Brittany?
    Perchance indeed quite ladyless were best.'

"Alas, my maids, you loved not overmuch
    Queen Guenevere, uncertain as sunshine
In March; forgive me! for my sin being such,
    About my whole life, all my deeds did twine,

"Made me quite wicked; as I found out then,
    I think; in the lonely palace where each morn
We went, my maids and I, to say prayers when
    They sang mass in the chapel on the lawn.

"And every morn I scarce could pray at all,
    For Launcelot's red-golden hair would play,
Instead of sunlight, on the painted wall,
    Mingled with dreams of what the priest did say;

"Grim curses out of Peter and of Paul;
    Judging of strange sins in Leviticus;
Another sort of writing on the wall,
    Scored deep across the painted heads of us.

"Christ sitting with the woman at the well,
    And Mary Magdalen repenting there,
Her dimmed eyes scorch'd and red at sight of hell
    So hardly 'scaped, no gold light on her hair.

"And if the priest said anything that seemed
    To touch upon the sin they said we did,
(This in their teeth) they looked as if they deem'd
    That I was spying what thoughts might be hid

"Under green-cover'd bosoms, heaving quick
    Beneath quick thoughts; while they grew red with shame,
And gazed down at their feet: while I felt sick,
    And almost shriek'd if one should call my name.

"The thrushes sang in the lone garden there:
    But where you were the birds were scared I trow:

Clanging of arms about pavilions fair,
  Mixed with the knights' laughs; there, as I well know,

"Rode Launcelot, the king of all the band,
  And scowling Gauwaine, like the night in day,
And handsome Gareth, with his great white hand
  Curl'd round the helm-crest, ere he join'd the fray;

"And merry Dinadan with sharp dark face,
  All true knights loved to see; and in the fight
Great Tristram, and though helmed you could trace
  In all his bearing the frank noble knight;

"And by him Palomydes, helmet off,
  He fought, his face brush'd by his hair,
Red heavy swinging hair; he fear'd a scoff
  So overmuch, though what true knight would dare

"To mock that face, fretted with useless care,
  And bitter useless striving after love?
O Palomydes, with much honour bear
  Beast Glatysaunt upon your shield, above

"Your helm that hides the swinging of your hair,
  And think of Iseult, as your sword drives through
Much mail and plate: O God, let me be there
  A little time, as I was long ago!

"Because stout Gareth lets his spear fall low,
  Gauwaine and Launcelot, and Dinadan
Are helm'd and waiting; let the trumpets go!
  Bend over, ladies, to see all you can!

"Clench teeth, dames, yea, clasp hands, for Gareth's spear
  Throws Kay from out his saddle, like a stone
From a castle-window when the foe draws near:
  'Iseult!' Sir Dinadan rolleth overthrown.

"'Iseult!' again: the pieces of each spear
  Fly fathoms up, and both the great steeds reel;
'Tristram for Iseult!' 'Iseult!' and 'Guenevere!'
  The ladies' names bite verily like steel.

"They bite: bite me, Lord God! I shall go mad,
    Or else die kissing him, he is so pale,
He thinks me mad already, O bad! bad!
    Let me lie down a little while and wail."

"No longer so, rise up, I pray you, love,
    And slay me really, then we shall be heal'd,
Perchance, in the aftertime by God above."
    "Banner of Arthur, with black-bended shield

"Sinister-wise across the fair gold ground!
    Here let me tell you what a knight you are,
O sword and shield of Arthur! you are found
    A crooked sword, I think, that leaves a scar

"On the bearer's arm, so be he thinks it straight,
    Twisted Malay's crease beautiful blue-grey,
Poison'd with sweet fruit; as he found too late,
    My husband Arthur, on some bitter day!

"O sickle cutting hemlock the day long!
    That the husbandman across his shoulder hangs,
And, going homeward about evensong,
    Dies the next morning, struck through by the fangs!

"Banner, and sword, and shield, you dare not die,
    Lest you meet Arthur in the other world,
And, knowing who you are, he pass you by,
    Taking short turns that he may watch you curl'd,

"Body and face and limbs in agony,
    Lest he weep presently and go away,
Saying: 'I loved him once,' with a sad sigh,
    Now I have slain him, Lord, let me go too, I pray.
                [Launcelot *falls.*

"Alas! alas! I know not what to do,
    If I run fast it is perchance that I
May fall and stun myself, much better so,
    Never, never again! not even when I die."

[LAUNCELOT, *on awaking.*
"I stretch'd my hands towards her and fell down,
    How long I lay in swoon I cannot tell:
My head and hands were bleeding from the stone,
    When I rose up, also I heard a bell."

Sir Galahad, A Christmas Mystery

WILLIAM MORRIS

It is the longest night in all the year,
    Near on the day when the Lord Christ was born;
Six hours ago I came and sat down here,
    And ponder'd sadly, wearied and forlorn.

The winter wind that pass'd the chapel door,
    Sang out a moody tune, that went right well
With mine own thoughts: I look'd down on the floor,
    Between my feet, until I heard a bell

Sound a long way off through the forest deep,
    And toll on steadily; a drowsiness
Came on me, so that I fell half asleep,
    As I sat there not moving: less and less

I saw the melted snow that hung in beads
    Upon my steel-shoes; less and less I saw
Between the tiles the bunches of small weeds:
    Heartless and stupid, with no touch of awe

Upon me, half-shut eyes upon the ground,
    I thought: O Galahad! the days go by,
Stop and cast up now that which you have found,
    So sorely you have wrought and painfully.

Night after night your horse treads down alone
    The sere damp fern, night after night you sit
Holding the bridle like a man of stone,
    Dismal, unfriended: what thing comes of it?

And what if Palomydes also ride,
    And over many a mountain and bare heath
Follow the questing beast with none beside?
    Is he not able still to hold his breath

With thoughts of Iseult? doth he not grow pale
    With weary striving, to seem best of all
To her, "as she is best," he saith? to fail
    Is nothing to him, he can never fall.

For unto such a man love-sorrow is
    So dear a thing unto his constant heart,
That even if he never win one kiss,
    Or touch from Iseult, it will never part.

And he will never know her to be worse
    Than in his happiest dreams he thinks she is:
Good knight, and faithful, you have 'scaped the curse
    In wonderful-wise; you have great store of bliss.

Yea, what if Father Launcelot ride out,
    Can he not think of Guenevere's arms, round
Warm and lithe, about his neck, and shout
    Till all the place grows joyful with the sound?

And when he lists can often see her face,
    And think, "Next month I kiss you, or next week,
And still you think of me": therefore the place
    Grows very pleasant, whatsoever he seek.

But me, who ride alone, some carle shall find
    Dead in my arms in the half-melted snow,
When all unkindly with the shifting wind,
    The thaw comes on at Candlemas: I know

Indeed that they will say: "This Galahad
    If he had lived had been a right good knight;

Ah! poor chaste body!" but they will be glad,
　　Not most alone, but all, when in their sight

That very evening in their scarlet sleeves
　　The gay-dress'd minstrels sing; no maid will talk
Of sitting on my tomb, until the leaves,
　　Grown big upon the bushes of the walk,

East of the Palace-pleasaunce, make it hard
　　To see the minster therefrom: well-a-day!
Before the trees by autumn were well bared,
　　I saw a damozel with gentle play,

Within that very walk say last farewell
　　To her dear knight, just riding out to find
(Why should I choke to say it?) the Sangreal,
　　And their last kisses sunk into my mind,

Yea, for she stood lean'd forward on his breast,
　　Rather, scarce stood; the back of one dear hand,
That it might well be kiss'd, she held and press'd
　　Against his lips; long time they stood there, fann'd

By gentle gusts of quiet frosty wind,
　　Till Mador de la porte a-going by,
And my own horsehoofs roused them; they untwined,
　　And parted like a dream. In this way I,

With sleepy face bent to the chapel floor,
　　Kept musing half asleep, till suddenly
A sharp bell rang from close beside the door,
　　And I leapt up when something pass'd me by,

Shrill ringing going with it, still half blind
　　I stagger'd after, a great sense of awe
At every step kept gathering on my mind,
　　Thereat I have no marvel, for I saw

One sitting on the altar as a throne,
　　Whose face no man could say he did not know,
And though the bell still rang, he sat alone,
　　With raiment half blood-red, half white as snow.

Right so I fell upon the floor and knelt,
　　Not as one kneels in church when mass is said,
But in a heap, quite nerveless, for I felt
　　The first time what a thing was perfect dread.

But mightily the gentle voice came down:
　　"Rise up, and look and listen, Galahad,
Good knight of God, for you will see no frown
　　Upon my face; I come to make you glad.

"For that you say that you are all alone,
　　I will be with you always, and fear not
You are uncared for, though no maiden moan
　　Above your empty tomb; for Launcelot,

"He in good time shall be my servant too,
　　Meantime, take note whose sword first made him knight,
And who has loved him alway, yea, and who
　　Still trusts him alway, though in all men's sight,

"He is just what you know, O Galahad,
　　This love is happy even as you say,
But would you for a little time be glad,
　　To make ME sorry long, day after day?

"Her warm arms round his neck half throttle ME,
　　The hot love-tears burn deep like spots of lead,
Yea, and the years pass quick: right dismally
　　Will Launcelot at one time hang his head;

"Yea, old and shrivell'd he shall win my love.
　　Poor Palomydes fretting out his soul!
Not always is he able, son, to move
　　His love, and do it honour: needs must roll

"The proudest destrier sometimes in the dust,
　　And then 'tis weary work; he strives beside
Seem better than he is, so that his trust
　　Is always on what chances may betide;

"And so he wears away, my servant, too,
　　When all these things are gone, and wretchedly

He sits and longs to moan for Iseult, who
    Is no care now to Palomydes: see,

"O good son, Galahad, upon this day,
    Now even, all these things are on your side,
But these you fight not for; look up, I say,
    And see how I can love you, for no pride

"Closes your eyes, no vain lust keeps them down.
    See now you have ME always; following
That holy vision, Galahad, go on,
    Until at last you come to ME to sing

"In Heaven always, and to walk around
    The garden where I am." He ceased, my face
And wretched body fell upon the ground;
    And when I look'd again, the holy place

Was empty; but right so the bell again
    Came to the chapel-door, there entered
Two angels first, in white, without a stain,
    And scarlet wings, then, after them, a bed

Four ladies bore, and set it down beneath
    The very altar-step, and while for fear
I scarcely dared to move or draw my breath,
    Those holy ladies gently came a-near,

And quite unarm'd me, saying: "Galahad,
    Rest here awhile and sleep, and take no thought
Of any other thing than being glad;
    Hither the Sangreal will be shortly brought,

"Yet must you sleep the while it stayeth here."
    Right so they went away, and I, being weary,
Slept long and dream'd of Heaven: the bell comes near,
    I doubt it grows to morning. Miserere!

Enter Two Angels in white, with scarlet wings; also, Four Ladies in gowns of
red and green; also an Angel, bearing in his hands a surcoat of white, with
a red cross.

An Angel.

O servant of the high God, Galahad!
    Rise and be arm'd: the Sangreal is gone forth
Through the great forest, and you must be had
    Unto the sea that lieth on the north:

There shall you find the wondrous ship wherein
    The spindles of King Solomon are laid,
And the sword that no man draweth without sin,
    But if he be most pure: and there is stay'd,

Hard by, Sir Launcelot, whom you will meet
    In some short space upon that ship: first, though,
Will come here presently that lady sweet,
    Sister of Percival, whom you well know,

And with her Bors and Percival: stand now,
    These ladies will to arm you.
FIRST LADY, *putting on the hauberk.*
                         Galahad,
That I may stand so close beneath your brow,
    I, Margaret of Antioch, am glad.

SECOND LADY, *girding him with the sword.*
That I may stand and touch you with my hand,
    O Galahad, I, Cecily, am glad.
THIRD LADY, *buckling on the spurs.*
That I may kneel while up above you stand,
    And gaze at me, O holy Galahad,

I, Lucy, am most glad.
FOURTH LADY, *putting on the basnet.*
                    O gentle knight,
That you bow down to us in reverence,
We are most glad, I, Katherine, with delight
    Must needs fall trembling.
ANGEL, *putting on the crossed surcoat.*
                    Galahad, we go hence,

For here, amid the straying of the snow,
    Come Percival's sister, Bors, and Percival.

*[The Four Ladies carry out the bed,
and all go but* Galahad.

GALAHAD.

How still and quiet everything seems now:
    They come, too, for I hear the horsehoofs fall.

Enter Sir Bors, Sir Percival *and* his Sister.

Fair friends and gentle lady, God you save!
    A many marvels have been here to-night;
Tell me what news of Launcelot you have,
    And has God's body ever been in sight?

SIR BORS.

Why, as for seeing that same holy thing,
    As we were riding slowly side by side,
An hour ago, we heard a sweet voice sing,
    And through the bare twigs saw a great light glide,

With many-colour'd raiment, but far off;
    And so pass'd quickly: from the court nought good;
Poor merry Dinadan, that with jape and scoff
    Kept us all merry, in a little wood

Was found all hack'd and dead: Sir Lionel
    And Gauwaine have come back from the great quest,
Just merely shamed; and Lauvaine, who loved well
    Your father Launcelot, at the king's behest

Went out to seek him, but was almost slain,
    Perhaps is dead now; everywhere
The knights come foil'd from the great quest, in vain;
    In vain they struggle for the vision fair.

86

The Chapel in Lyoness

WILLIAM MORRIS

Sir Ozana le cure Hardy.   Sir Galahad.

Sir Bors de Ganys.

Sir Ozana.

All day long and every day,
From Christmas-Eve to Whit-Sunday,
Within that Chapel-aisle I lay,
     And no man came a-near.

Naked to the waist was I,
And deep within my breast did lie,
Though no man any blood could spy,
     The truncheon of a spear.

No meat did ever pass my lips
Those days. Alas! the sunlight slips
From off the gilded parclose, dips,
     And night comes on apace.

My arms lay back behind my head;
Over my raised-up knees was spread
A samite cloth of white and red;
     A rose lay on my face.

Many a time I tried to shout;
But as in dream of battle-rout,
My frozen speech would not well out;
    I could not even weep.

With inward sigh I see the sun
Fade off the pillars one by one,
My heart faints when the day is done,
    Because I cannot sleep.

Sometimes strange thoughts pass through my head;
Not like a tomb is this my bed,
Yet oft I think that I am dead;
    That round my tomb is writ,

"Ozana of the hardy heart,
    Knight of the Table Round,
Pray for his soul, lords, of your part;
    A true knight he was found."

Ah! me, I cannot fathom it.   [*He sleeps.*

SIR GALAHAD.

All day long and every day,
Till his madness pass'd away,
I watch'd Ozana as he lay
    Within the gilded screen.

All my singing moved him not;
As I sung my heart grew hot,
With the thought of Launcelot
    Far away, I ween.

So I went a little space
From out the chapel, bathed my face
In the stream that runs apace
    By the churchyard wall.

There I pluck'd a faint wild rose,
Hard by where the linden grows,

Sighing over silver rows
  Of the lilies tall.

I laid the flower across his mouth;
The sparkling drops seem'd good for drouth;
He smiled, turn'd round towards the south,
  Held up a golden tress.

The light smote on it from the west;
He drew the covering from his breast,
Against his heart that hair he prest;
  Death him soon will bless.

SIR BORS.

I enter'd by the western door;
  I saw a knight's helm lying there:
I raised my eyes from off the floor,
  And caught the gleaming of his hair.

I stept full softly up to him;
  I laid my chin upon his head;
I felt him smile; my eyes did swim,
  I was so glad he was not dead.

I heard Ozana murmur low,
  "There comes no sleep nor any love."
But Galahad stoop'd and kiss'd his brow:
  He shiver'd; I saw his pale lips move.

SIR OZANA.

There comes no sleep nor any love;
  Ah me! I shiver with delight.
I am so weak I cannot move;
  God move me to thee, dear, to-night!
Christ help! I have but little wit:
My life went wrong; I see it writ,

"Ozana of the hardy heart,
    Knight of the Table Round,
Pray for his soul, lords, on your part;
    A good knight he was found."

Now I begin to fathom it.   [*He dies.*

SIR BORS.

Galahad sits dreamily;
What strange things may his eyes see,
Great blue eyes fix'd full on me?
On his soul, Lord, have mercy.

SIR GALAHAD.

Ozana, shall I pray for thee?
    Her cheek is laid to thine;
No long time hence, also I see
    Thy wasted fingers twine

Within the tresses of her hair
    That shineth gloriously,
Thinly outspread in the clear air
    Against the jasper sea.

Tristram and Iseult

MATTHEW ARNOLD

I

TRISTRAM

Tristram

Is she not come? The messenger was sure.
Prop me upon the pillows once again—
Raise me, my page! this cannot long endure.
—Christ, what a night! how the sleet whips the pane!
What lights will those out to the northward be?

The Page

The lanterns of the fishing-boats at sea.

Tristram

Soft—who is that, stands by the dying fire?

The Page

Iseult.

HOW SIR TRISTRAM
DRANK OF THE
LOVE DRINK

From Aubrey Beardsley's illustrations to
Le Morte DArthur.
London: Dent, 1893–94.

Tristram

Ah! not the Iseult I desire.

*   *   *   *

What Knight is this so weak and pale,
Though the locks are yet brown on his noble head,
Propt on pillows in his bed,
Gazing seaward for the light
Of some ship that fights the gale
On this wild December night?
Over the sick man's feet is spread
A dark green forest-dress;
A gold harp leans against the bed,
Ruddy in the fire's light.
I know him by his harp of gold,
Famous in Arthur's court of old;
I know him by his forest-dress—
The peerless hunter, harper, knight,
Tristram of Lyoness.

What Lady is this, whose silk attire
Gleams so rich in the light of the fire?
The ringlets on her shoulders lying
In their flitting lustre vying
With the clasp of burnish'd gold
Which her heavy robe doth hold.
Her looks are mild, her fingers slight
As the driven snow are white;
But her cheeks are sunk and pale.
Is it that the bleak sea-gale
Beating from the Atlantic sea
On this coast of Brittany,
Nips too keenly the sweet flower?
Is it that a deep fatigue
Hath come on her, a chilly fear,
Passing all her youthful hour
Spinning with her maidens here,
Listlessly through the window-bars
Gazing seawards many a league,
From her lonely shore-built tower,

While the knights are at the wars?
Or, perhaps, has her young heart
Felt already some deeper smart,
Of those that in secret the heart-strings rive,
Leaving her sunk and pale, though fair?
Who is this snowdrop by the sea?—
I know her by her mildness rare,
Her snow-white hands, her golden hair;
I know her by her rich silk dress,
And her fragile loveliness—
The sweetest Christian soul alive,
Iseult of Brittany.

Iseult of Brittany?—but where
Is that other Iseult fair,
That proud, first Iseult, Cornwall's queen?
She, whom Tristram's ship of yore
From Ireland to Cornwall bore,
To Tyntagel, to the side
Of King Marc, to be his bride?
She who, as they voyaged, quaff'd
With Tristram that spiced magic draught,
Which since then for ever rolls
Through their blood, and binds their souls,
Working love, but working teen?—
There were two Iseults who did sway
Each her hour of Tristram's day;
But one possess'd his waning time,
The other his resplendent prime.
Behold her here, the patient flower,
Who possess'd his darker hour!
Iseult of the Snow-White Hand
Watches pale by Tristram's bed.
She is here who had his gloom,
Where art thou who hadst his bloom?
One such kiss as those of yore
Might thy dying knight restore!
Does the love-draught work no more?
Art thou cold, or false, or dead,
Iseult of Ireland?

*   *   *   *

Loud howls the wind, sharp patters the rain,
And the knight sinks back on his pillows again.
He is weak with fever and pain,
And his spirit is not clear.
Hark! he mutters in his sleep,
As he wanders far from here,
Changes place and time of year,
And his closéd eye doth sweep
O'er some fair unwintry sea,
Not this fierce Atlantic deep,
While he mutters brokenly:—

Tristram

The calm sea shines, loose hang the vessel's sails;
Before us are the sweet green fields of Wales,
And overhead the cloudless sky of May.—
"Ah, would I were in those green fields at play,
Not pent on ship-board this delicious day!
Tristram, I pray thee, of thy courtesy,
Reach me my golden phial stands by thee,
But pledge me in it first for courtesy.—"
Ha! dost thou start? are thy lips blanch'd like mine?
Child, 'tis no true draught this, 'tis poison'd wine!
Iseult! . . . .

*   *   *   *

Ah, sweet angels, let him dream!
Keep his eyelids! let him seem
Not this fever-wasted wight
Thinn'd and paled before his time,
But the brilliant youthful knight
In the glory of his prime,
Sitting in the gilded barge,
At thy side, thou lovely charge,
Bending gaily o'er thy hand,
Iseult of Ireland!

And she too, that princess fair,
If her bloom be now less rare,
Let her have her youth again—
Let her be as she was then!
Let her have her proud dark eyes,
And her petulant quick replies—
Let her sweep her dazzling hand
With its gesture of command,
And shake back her raven hair
With the old imperious air!
As of old, so let her be,
That first Iseult, princess bright,
Chatting with her youthful knight
As he steers her o'er the sea,
Quitting at her father's will
The green isle where she was bred,
And her bower in Ireland,
For the surge-beat Cornish strand;
Where the prince whom she must wed
Dwells on loud Tyntagel's hill
High above the sounding sea.
And that potion rare her mother
Gave her, that her future lord,
Gave her, that King Marc and she,
Might drink it on their marriage-day,
And for ever love each other—
Let her, as she sits on board,
Ah, sweet saints, unwittingly!
See it shine, and take it up,
And to Tristram laughing say:
"Sir Tristram, of thy courtesy,
Pledge me in my golden cup!"
Let them drink it—let their hands
Tremble, and their cheeks be flame,
As they feel the fatal bands
Of a love they dare not name,
With a wild delicious pain,
Twine about their hearts again!
Let the early summer be
Once more round them, and the sea

Blue, and o'er its mirror kind
Let the breath of the May-wind,
Wandering through their drooping sails,
Die on the green fields of Wales!
Let a dream like this restore
What his eye must see no more!

Tristram

Chill blows the wind, the pleasaunce-walks are drear—
Madcap, what jest was this, to meet me here?
Were feet like those made for so wild a way?
The southern winter-parlour, by my fay,
Had been the likeliest trysting-place to-day!
"Tristram!—nay, nay—thou must not take my hand!—
Tristram!—sweet love!—we are betray'd—out-plann'd.
Fly—save thyself—save me!—I dare not stay."—
One last kiss first!—" 'Tis vain—to horse—away!"

    *   *   *   *

Ah! sweet saints, his dream doth move
Faster surely than it should,
From the fever in his blood!
All the spring-time of his love
Is already gone and past,
And instead thereof is seen
Its winter, which endureth still—
Tyntagel on its surge-beat hill,
The pleasaunce-walks, the weeping queen,
The flying leaves, the straining blast,
And that long, wild kiss—their last.
And this rough December-night,
And his burning fever-pain,
Mingle with his hurrying dream,
Till they rule it, till he seem
The press'd fugitive again,
The love-desperate banish'd knight
With a fire in his brain
Flying o'er the stormy main.

—Whither does he wander now?
Haply in his dreams the wind
Wafts him here, and lets him find
The lovely orphan child again
In her castle by the coast;
The youngest, fairest chatelaine,
Whom this realm of France can boast,
Our snowdrop by the Atlantic sea,
Iseult of Brittany.
And—for through the haggard air,
The stain'd arms, the matted hair
Of that stranger-knight ill-starr'd,
There gleam'd something, which recall'd
The Tristram who in better days
Was Launcelot's guest at Joyous Gard—
Welcomed here, and here install'd,
Tended of his fever here,
Haply he seems again to move
His young guardian's heart with love;
In his exiled loneliness,
In his stately, deep distress,
Without a word, without a tear.
—Ah! 'tis well he should retrace
His tranquil life in this lone place;
His gentle bearing at the side
Of his timid youthful bride;
His long rambles by the shore
On winter-evenings, when the roar
Of the near waves came, sadly grand,
Through the dark, up the drown'd sand,
Or his endless reveries
In the woods, where the gleams play
On the grass under the trees,
Passing the long summer's day
Idle as a mossy stone
In the forest-depths alone,
The chase neglected, and his hound
Couch'd beside him on the ground.
—Ah! what trouble's on his brow?
Hither let him wander now;

Hither, to the quiet hours
Pass'd among these heaths of ours
By the grey Atlantic sea;
Hours, if not of ecstasy,
From violent anguish surely free!

Tristram

All red with blood the whirling river flows,
The wide plain rings, the dazed air throbs with blows.
Upon us are the chivalry of Rome—
Their spears are down, their steeds are bathed in foam.
"Up, Tristram, up," men cry, "thou moonstruck knight!
What foul fiend rides thee? On into the fight!"
—Above the din her voice is in my ears;
I see her form glide through the crossing spears.—
Iseult! . . . .

       *   *   *   *

Ah! he wanders forth again;
We cannot keep him; now, as then,
There's a secret in his breast
Which will never let him rest.
These musing fits in the green wood
They cloud the brain, they dull the blood!
—His sword is sharp, his horse is good;
Beyond the mountains will he see
The famous towns of Italy,
And label with the blessed sign
The heathen Saxons on the Rhine.
At Arthur's side he fights once more
With the Roman Emperor.
There's many a gay knight where he goes
Will help him to forget his care;
The march, the leaguer, Heaven's blithe air,
The neighing steeds, the ringing blows—
Sick pining comes not where these are.
Ah! what boots it, that the jest
Lightens every other brow,

What, that every other breast
Dances as the trumpets blow,
If one's own heart beats not light
On the waves of the toss'd fight,
If oneself cannot get free
From the clog of misery?
Thy lovely youthful wife grows pale
Watching by the salt sea-tide
With her children at her side
For the gleam of thy white sail.
Home, Tristram, to thy halls again!
To our lonely sea complain,
To our forests tell thy pain!

Tristram

All round the forest sweeps off, black in shade,
But it is moonlight in the open glade;
And in the bottom of the glade shine clear
The forest-chapel and the fountain near.
—I think, I have a fever in my blood;
Come, let me leave the shadow of this wood,
Ride down, and bathe my hot brow in the flood.
—Mild shines the cold spring in the moon's clear light;
God! 'tis *her* face plays in the waters bright.
"Fair love," she says, "canst thou forget so soon,
At this soft hour, under this sweet moon?"—
Iseult! . . . .

*　*　*　*

Ah, poor soul! if this be so,
Only death can balm thy woe.
The solitudes of the green wood
Had no medicine for thy mood;
The rushing battle clear'd thy blood
As little as did solitude.
—Ah! his eyelids slowly break
Their hot seals, and let him wake;
What new change shall we now see?
A happier? Worse it cannot be.

Is my page here? Come, turn me to the fire!
Upon the window-panes the moon shines bright;
The wind is down—but she'll not come to-night.
Ah no! she is asleep in Cornwall now,
Far hence; her dreams are fair—smooth is her brow.
Of me she recks not, nor my vain desire.
—I have had dreams, I have had dreams, my page,
Would take a score years from a strong man's age;
And with a blood like mine, will leave, I fear,
Scant leisure for a second messenger.
—My princess, art thou there? Sweet, do not wait!
To bed, and sleep! my fever is gone by;
To-night my page shall keep me company.
Where do the children sleep? kiss them for me!
Poor child, thou art almost as pale as I;
This comes of nursing long and watching late.
To bed—good night!

*   *   *   *

She left the gleam-lit fireplace,
She came to the bed-side;
She took his hands in hers—her tears
Down on his wasted fingers rain'd.
She raised her eyes upon his face—
Not with a look of wounded pride,
A look as if the heart complained—
Her look was like a sad embrace;
The gaze of one who can divine
A grief, and sympathise.
Sweet flower! thy children's eyes
Are not more innocent than thine.
— But they sleep in shelter'd rest,
Like helpless birds in the warm nest,
On the castle's southern side;
Where feebly comes the mournful roar
Of buffeting wind and surging tide
Through many a room and corridor.
—Full on their window the moon's ray

Makes their chamber as bright as day.
It shines upon the blank white walls,
And on the snowy pillow falls,
And on two angel-heads doth play
Turn'd to each other—the eyes closed,
The lashes on the cheeks reposed.
Round each sweet brow the cap close-set
Hardly lets peep the golden hair;
Through the soft-open'd lips the air
Scarcely moves the coverlet.
One little wandering arm is thrown
At random on the counterpane,
And often the fingers close in haste
As if their baby-owner chased
The butterflies again.
This stir they have, and this alone;
But else they are so still!
—Ah, tired madcaps! you lie still;
But were you at the window now,
To look forth on the fairy sight
Of your illumined haunts by night,
To see the park-glades where you play
Far lovelier than they are by day,
To see the sparkle on the eaves,
And upon every giant-bough
Of those old oaks, whose wet red leaves
Are jewell'd with bright drops of rain—
How would your voices run again!
And far beyond the sparkling trees
Of the castle-park one sees
The bare heaths spreading, clear as day,
Moor behind moor, far, far away,
Into the heart of Brittany.
And here and there, lock'd by the land,
Long inlets of smooth glittering sea,
And many a stretch of watery sand
All shining in the white moon-beams—
But you see fairer in your dreams!

What voices are these on the clear night-air?
What lights in the court—what steps on the stair?

II

ISEULT OF IRELAND

Tristram

Raise the light, my page! that I may see her.—
    Thou art come at last, then, haughty Queen!
Long I've waited, long I've fought my fever;
    Late thou comest, cruel thou hast been.

Iseult

Blame me not, poor sufferer! that I tarried;
    Bound I was, I could not break the band.
Chide not with the past, but feel the present!
    I am here—we meet—I hold thy hand.

Tristram

Thou art come, indeed—thou hast rejoin'd me;
    Thou hast dared it—but too late to save.
Fear not now that men should tax thine honour!
    I am dying: build—(thou may'st)—my grave!

Iseult

Tristram, ah, for love of Heaven, speak kindly!
    What, I hear these bitter words from thee?
Sick with grief I am, and faint with travel—
    Take my hand—dear Tristram, look on me!

Tristram

I forget, thou comest from thy voyage—
    Yes, the spray is on thy cloak and hair.
But thy dark eyes are not dimm'd, proud Iseult!
    And thy beauty never was more fair.

Iseult

Ah, harsh flatterer! let alone my beauty!
    I, like thee, have left my youth afar.
Take my hand, and touch these wasted fingers—
    See my cheek and lips, how white they are!

Tristram

Thou art paler—but thy sweet charm, Iseult!
  Would not fade with the dull years away.
Ah, how fair thou standest in the moonlight!
  I forgive thee, Iseult!—thou wilt stay?

Iseult

Fear me not, I will be always with thee;
  I will watch thee, tend thee, soothe thy pain;
Sing thee tales of true, long-parted lovers,
  Join'd at evening of their days again.

Tristram

No, thou shalt not speak! I should be finding
  Something alter'd in thy courtly tone.
Sit—sit by me! I will think, we've lived so
  In the green wood, all our lives, alone.

Iseult

Alter'd, Tristram? Not in courts, believe me,
  Love like mine is alter'd in the breast;
Courtly life is light and cannot reach it—
  Ah! it lives, because so deep-suppress'd!

What, thou think'st men speak in courtly chambers
  Words by which the wretched are consoled?
What, thou think'st this aching brow was cooler,
  Circled, Tristram, by a band of gold?

Royal state with Marc, my deep-wrong'd husband—
  That was bliss to make my sorrows flee!
Silken courtiers whispering honied nothings—
  Those were friends to make me false to thee!

Ah, on which, if both our lots were balanced,
  Was indeed the heaviest burden thrown—
Thee, a pining exile in thy forest,
  Me, a smiling queen upon my throne?

Vain and strange debate, where both have suffer'd,
    Both have pass'd a youth consumed and sad,
Both have brought their anxious day to evening,
    And have now short space for being glad!

Join'd we are henceforth; nor will thy people,
    Nor thy younger Iseult take it ill,
That a former rival shares her office,
    When she sees her humbled, pale, and still.

I, a faded watcher by thy pillow,
    I, a statue on thy chapel-floor,
Pour'd in prayer before the Virgin-Mother,
    Rouse no anger, make no rivals more.

She will cry: "Is this the foe I dreaded?
    This his idol? this that royal bride?
Ah, an hour of health would purge his eyesight!
    Stay, pale queen! for ever by my side."

Hush, no words! that smile, I see, forgives me.
    I am now thy nurse, I bid thee sleep.
Close thine eyes—this flooding moonlight blinds them!—
    Nay, all's well again! thou must not weep.

Tristram

I am happy! yet I feel, there's something
    Swells my heart, and takes my breath away.
Through a mist I see thee; near—come nearer!
    Bend—bend down!—I yet have much to say.

Iseult

Heaven! his head sinks back upon the pillow—
    Tristram! Tristram! let thy heart not fail!
Call on god and on the holy angels!
    What, love, courage!—Christ! he is so pale.

Tristram

Hush, 'tis vain, I feel my end approaching!
    This is what my mother said should be,

When the fierce pains took her in the forest,
  The deep draughts of death, in bearing me.

"Son," she said, "thy name shall be of sorrow;
  Tristram art thou call'd for my death's sake."
So she said, and died in the drear forest.
  Grief since then his home with me doth make.

I am dying.—Start not, nor look wildly!
  Me, thy living friend, thou canst not save.
But, since living we were ununited,
  Go not far, O Iseult! from my grave.

Close mine eyes, then seek the princess Iseult;
  Speak her fair, she is of royal blood!
Say, I will'd so, that thou stay beside me—
  She will grant it; she is kind and good.

Now to sail the seas of death I leave thee—
  One last kiss upon the living shore!

                    Iseult

Tristram!—Tristram!—stay—receive me with thee!
  Iseult leaves thee, Tristram! never more.

            *   *   *   *

You see them clear—the moon shines bright.
Slow, slow and softly, where she stood,
She sinks upon the ground;—her hood
Had fallen back; her arms outspread
Still hold her lover's hand; her head
Is bow'd, half-buried, on the bed.
O'er the blanch'd sheet her raven hair
Lies in disorder'd streams; and there,
Strung like white stars, the pearls still are,
And the golden bracelets, heavy and rare,
Flash on her white arms still.
The very same which yesternight
Flash'd in the silver sconces' light,

When the feast was gay and the laughter loud
In Tyntagel's palace proud.
But then they deck'd a restless ghost
With hot-flush'd cheeks and brilliant eyes,
And quivering lips on which the tide
Of courtly speech abruptly died,
And a glance which over the crowded floor,
The dancers, and the festive host,
Flew ever to the door.
That the knights eyed her in surprise,
And the dames whispered scoffingly:
"Her moods, good lack, they pass like showers!
But yesternight and she would be
As pale and still as wither'd flowers,
And now to-night she laughs and speaks
And has a colour in her cheeks;
Christ keep us from such fantasy!"—

Yes, now the longing is o'erpast,
Which, dogg'd by fear and fought by shame
Shook her weak bosom day and night,
Consumed her beauty like a flame,
And dimm'd it like the desert-blast.
And though the bed-clothes hide her face,
Yet were it lifted to the light,
The sweet expression of her brow
Would charm the gazer, till his thought
Erased the ravages of time,
Fill'd up the hollow cheek, and brought
A freshness back as of her prime—
So healing is her quiet now.
So perfectly the lines express
A tranquil, settled loveliness,
Her younger rival's purest grace.

The air of the December-night
Steals coldly around the chamber bright,
Where those lifeless lovers be;
Swinging with it, in the light
Flaps the ghostlike tapestry.
And on the arras wrought you see

A stately Huntsman, clad in green,
And round him a fresh forest-scene.
On that clear forest-knoll he stays,
With his pack round him, and delays.
He stares and stares, with troubled face,
At this huge, gleam-lit fireplace,
At that bright, iron-figured door,
And those blown rushes on the floor.
He gazes down into the room
With heated cheeks and flurried air,
And to himself he seems to say:
"What place is this, and who are they?
Who is that kneeling Lady fair?
And on his pillows that pale Knight
Who seems of marble on a tomb?
How comes it here, this chamber bright,
Through whose mullion'd windows clear
The castle-court all wet with rain,
The drawbridge and the moat appear,
And then the beach, and, mark'd with spray,
The sunken reefs, and far away
The unquiet bright Atlantic plain?
—What, has some glamour made me sleep,
And sent me with my dogs to sweep,
By night, with boisterous bugle-peal,
Through some old, sea-side, knightly hall,
Not in the free green wood at all?
That Knight's asleep and at her prayer
That Lady by the bed doth kneel—
Then hush, thou boisterous bugle-peal!"
—The wild boar rustles in his lair;
The fierce hounds snuff the tainted air;
But lord and hounds keep rooted there.

Cheer, cheer thy dogs into the brake,
O Hunter! and without a fear
Thy golden-tassell'd bugle blow,
And through the glades thy pastime take—
For thou wilt rouse no sleepers here!
For these thou seest are unmoved;
Cold, cold as those who lived and loved
A thousand years ago.

III

ISEULT OF BRITTANY

A year had flown, and o'er the sea away,
In Cornwall, Tristram and Queen Iseult lay;
In King Marc's chapel, in Tyntagel old—
There in a ship they bore those lovers cold.

The young surviving Iseult, one bright day,
Had wander'd forth. Her children were at play
In a green circular hollow in the heath
Which borders the sea-shore—a country path
Creeps over it from the till'd fields behind.
The hollow's grassy banks are soft-inclined,
And to one standing on them, far and near
The lone unbroken view spreads bright and clear
Over the waste. This cirque of open ground
Is light and green; the heather, which all round
Creeps thickly, grows not here; but the pale grass
Is strewn with rocks, and many a shiver'd mass
Of vein'd white-gleaming quartz, and here and there
Dotted with holly-trees and juniper.
In the smooth centre of the opening stood
Three hollies side by side, and made a screen,
Warm with the winter-sun, of burnish'd green
With scarlet berries gemm'd, the fell-fare's food.
Under the glittering hollies Iseult stands,
Watching her children play; their little hands
Are busy gathering spars of quartz, and streams
Of stagshorn for their hats; anon, with screams
Of mad delight they drop their spoils, and bound
Among the holly-clumps and broken ground,
Racing full speed, and startling in their rush
The fell-fares and the speckled missel-thrush
Out of their glossy coverts;—but when now
Their cheeks were flush'd, and over each hot brow,
Under the feather'd hats of the sweet pair,
In blinding masses shower'd the golden hair—
Then Iseult call'd them to her, and the three
Cluster'd under the holly-screen, and she
Told them an old-world Breton history.

Warm in their mantles wrapt the three stood there,
Under the hollies, in the clear still air—
Mantles with those rich furs deep glistering
Which Venice ships do from swart Egypt bring.
Long they stay'd still—then, pacing at their ease,
Moved up and down under the glossy trees.
But still, as they pursued their warm dry road,
From Iseult's lips the unbroken story flow'd,
And still the children listen'd, their blue eyes
Fix'd on their mother's face in wide surprise;
Nor did their looks stray once to the sea-side,
Nor to the brown heaths round them, bright and wide,
Nor to the snow, which, though 't was all away
From the open heath, still by the hedgerows lay,
Nor to the shining sea-fowl, that with screams
Bore up from where the bright Atlantic gleams,
Swooping to landward; nor to where, quite clear,
The fell-fares settled on the thickets near.
And they would still have listen'd, till dark night
Came keen and chill down on the heather bright;
But, when the red glow on the sea grew cold,
And the grey turrets of the castle old
Look'd sternly through the frosty evening-air,
Then Iseult took by the hand those children fair,
And brought her tale to an end, and found the path,
And led them home over the darkening heath.

And is she happy? Does she see unmoved
The days in which she might have lived and loved
Slip without bringing bliss slowly away,
One after one, to-morrow like to-day?
Joy has not found her yet, nor ever will—
Is it this thought which makes her mien so still,
Her features so fatigued, her eyes, though sweet,
So sunk, so rarely lifted save to meet
Her children's? She moves slow; her voice alone
Hath yet an infantine and silver tone.
But even that comes languidly; in truth,
She seems one dying in a mask of youth.
And now she will go home, and softly lay
Her laughing children in their beds, and play
Awhile with them before they sleep; and then

She'll light her silver lamp, which fishermen
Dragging their nets through the rough waves, afar,
Along this iron coast, know like a star,
And take her broidery-frame, and there she'll sit
Hour after hour, her gold curls sweeping it;
Lifting her soft-bent head only to mind
Her children, or to listen to the wind.
And when the clock peals midnight, she will move
Her work away, and let her fingers rove
Across the shaggy brows of Tristram's hound
Who lies, guarding her feet, along the ground;
Or else she will fall musing, her blue eyes
Fixt, her slight hands clasp'd on her lap; then rise,
And at her prie-dieu kneel, until she have told
Her rosary-beads of ebony tipp'd with gold,
Then to her soft sleep—and to-morrow'll be
To-day's exact repeated effigy.

Yes, it is lonely for her in her hall.
The children, and the grey-hair'd seneschal,
Her women, and Sir Tristram's aged hound,
Are there the sole companions to be found.
But these she loves; and noisier life than this
She would find ill to bear, weak as she is.
She has her children, too, and night and day
Is with them; and the wide heaths where they play,
The hollies, and the cliff, and the sea-shore,
The sand, the sea-birds, and the distant sails,
These are to her dear as to them; the tales
With which this day the children she beguiled
She gleaned from Breton grandames, when a child,
In every hut along this sea-coast wild.
She herself loves them still, and, when they are told,
Can forget all to hear them, as of old.

Dear saints, it is not sorrow, as I hear,
Not suffering, which shuts up eye and ear
To all that has delighted them before,
And lets us be what we were once no more.
No, we may suffer deeply, yet retain
Power to be moved and soothed, for all our pain,
By what of old pleased us, and will again.

No, 'tis the gradual furnace of the world,
In whose hot air our spirits are upcurl'd
Until they crumble, or else grow like steel—
Which kills in us the bloom, the youth, the spring—
Which leaves the fierce necessity to feel,
But takes away the power—this can avail,
By drying up our joy in everything,
To make our former pleasures all seem stale.
This, or some tyrannous single thought, some fit
Of passion, which subdues our souls to it,
Till for its sake alone we live and move—
Call it ambition, or remorse, or love—
This too can change us wholly, and make seem
All which we did before, shadow and dream.

And yet, I swear, it angers me to see
How this fool passion gulls men potently;
Being, in truth, but a diseased unrest,
And an unnatural overheat at best.
How they are full of languor and distress
Not having it; which when they do possess,
They straightway are burnt up with fume and care,
And spend their lives in posting here and there
Where this plague drives them; and have little ease,
Are furious with themselves, and hard to please.
Like that bald Caesar, the famed Roman wight,
Who wept at reading of a Grecian knight
Who made a name at younger years than he;
Or that renown'd mirror of chivalry,
Prince Alexander, Philip's peerless son,
Who carried the great war from Macedon
Into the Soudan's realm, and thundered on
To die at thirty-five in Babylon.

What tale did Iseult to the children say,
Under the hollies, that bright winter's day?

She told them of the fairy-haunted land
Away the other side of Brittany,
Beyond the heaths, edged by the lonely sea;
Of the deep forest-glades of Broce-liande,
Through whose green boughs the golden sunshine creeps,

Where Merlin by the enchanted thorn-tree sleeps.
For here he came with the fay Vivian,
One April, when the warm days first began.
He was on foot, and that false fay, his friend,
On her white palfrey; here he met his end,
In these lone sylvan glades, that April-day.
This tale of Merlin and the lovely fay
Was the one Iseult chose, and she brought clear
Before the children's fancy him and her.

Blowing between the stems, the forest-air
Had loosen'd the brown locks of Vivian's hair,
Which play'd on her flush'd cheek, and her blue eyes
Sparkled with mocking glee and exercise.
Her palfrey's flanks were mired and bathed in sweat,
For they had travell'd far and not stopp'd yet.
A brier in that tangled wilderness
Had scored her white right hand, which she allows
To rest ungloved on her green riding-dress;
The other warded off the drooping boughs.
But still she chatted on, with her blue eyes
Fix'd full on Merlin's face, her stately prize.
Her 'haviour had the morning's fresh clear grace,
The spirit of the woods was in her face.
She look'd so witching fair, that learned wight
Forgot his craft, and his best wits took flight;
And he grew fond, and eager to obey
His mistress, use her empire as she may.

They came to where the brushwood ceased, and day
Peer'd 'twixt the stems; and the ground broke away,
In a sloped sward down to a brawling brook;
And up as high as where they stood to look
On the brook's farther side was clear, but then
The underwood and trees began again.
This open glen was studded thick with thorns
Then white with blossom; and you saw the horns,
Through last year's fern, of the shy fallow-deer
Who come at noon down to the water here.
You saw the bright-eyed squirrels dart along
Under the thorns on the green sward; and strong
The blackbird whistled from the dingles near,

113

And the weird chipping of the woodpecker
Rang lonelily and sharp; the sky was fair,
And a fresh breath of spring stirr'd everywhere.
Merlin and Vivian stopp'd on the slope's brow,
To gaze on the light sea of leaf and bough
Which glistering plays all round them, lone and mild,
As if to itself the quiet forest smiled.
Upon the brow-top grew a thorn, and here
The grass was dry and moss'd, and you saw clear
Across the hollow; white anemonies
Starr'd the cool turf, and clumps of primroses
Ran out from the dark underwood behind.
No fairer resting-place a man could find.
"Here let us halt," said Merlin then; and she
Nodded, and tied her palfrey to a tree.

They sate them down together, and a sleep
Fell upon Merlin, more like death, so deep.
Her finger on her lips, then Vivian rose,
And from her brown-lock'd head the wimple throws,
And takes it in her hand, and waves it over
The blossom'd thorn-tree and her sleeping lover.
Nine times she waved the fluttering wimple round,
And made a little plot of magic ground.
And in that daisied circle, as men say,
Is Merlin prisoner till the judgment-day;
But she herself whither she will can rove—
For she was passing weary of his love.

King Ban

A Fragment

ALGERNON CHARLES SWINBURNE

These three held flight upon the leaning lands
At undern, past the skirt of misty camps
Sewn thick from Benwick to the outer march—
King Ban, and, riding wrist by wrist, Ellayne,
And caught up with his coloured swathing-bands
Across her arm, a hindrance in the reins,
A bauble slipt between the bridle-ties,
The three months' trouble that was Launcelot.
For Claudas leant upon the land, and smote
This way and that way, as a pestilence
Moves with vague patience in the unclean heat
This way and that way; so the Gaulish war
Smote, moving in the marches. Then King Ban
Shut in one girdled waist of narrow stones
His gold and all his men, and set on them
A name, the name of perfect men at need,
And over them a seneschal, the man
Most inward and entailed upon his soul,
That next his will and in his pulses moved
As the close blood and purpose of his heart,
And laid the place between his hands, and rode
North to the wild rims of distempered sea

115

That, crossed to Logres, his face might look red [sic]
The face of Arthur, and therein light blood
Even to the eyes and to the circled hair
For shame of failure in so near a need,
Failure in service of so near a man.
Because that time King Arthur would not ride,
But lay and let his hands weaken to white
Among the stray gold of a lady's head.
His hands unwedded: neither could bring help
To Ban that helped to rend his land for him
From the steel wrist of spoilers, but the time
A sleep like yellow mould had overgrown,
A pleasure sweet and sick as marsh-flowers.
Therefore about his marches rode King Ban
With eyes that fell between his hands to count
The golden inches of the saddle-rim,
Strange with rare stones; and in his face there rose
A doubt that burnt it with red pain and fear
All over it, and plucked upon his heart,
The old weak heart that loss had eaten through,
Remembering how the seneschal went back
At coming out from Claudas in his tent;
And how they bound together, chin by chin,
Whispered and wagged, and made lean room for words,
And a sharp mutter fed the ears of them.
And he went in and set no thought thereon
To waste; fear had not heart to fear indeed,
The king being old, since any fear in such
Is as a wound upon the fleshly sense
That drains a parcel of his time thereout,
Therefore he would not fear that as it fell
This thing should fall. For Claudas the keen thief
For some thin rounds and wretched stamps of gold
Had bought the tower and men and seneschal,
Body and breath and blood, yea, soul and shame.
They knew not this, at halt upon a hill.
Only surmise was dull upon the sense
And thin conjecture sickened in the speech;
So they fell silent, riding in the hills.
There on a little terrace the good king
Reined, and looked out. Far back the white lands lay;
The wind went in them like a broken man,

Lamely; the mist had set a bitter lip
To the rimmed river, and the moon burnt blank.
But outward from the castle of King Ban
There blew a sound of trouble, and there clomb
A fire that thrust an arm across the air,
Shook a rent skirt of dragging flame, and blanched
The grey flats to such cruel white as shone
Iron against the shadow of the sky
Blurred out with its blind stars; for as the sea
Gathers to lengthen a bleached edge of foam
Whole weights of windy water, and the green
Brine flares and hisses as the heap makes up,
Till the gaunt wave writhes, trying to breathe,
Then turns, and all the whited rims of steel
Lean over, and the hollowed round roars in
And smites the pebble forward in the mud,
And grinds the shingle in cool whirls of white,
Clashed through and crossed with blank assault of foam,
Filled with hard thunder and drenched dregs of sand—
So leant and leapt the many-mouthèd fire,
So curled upon the walls, dipt, crawled, smote, clung,
Caught like a beast that catches on the flesh,
Waxed hoar with sick default, shivered across,
Choked out, a snake unfed.
                              Thereat King Ban
Trembled for pain in all his blood, and death
Under the heart caught him and made his breath
Wince, as a worm does, wounded in the head;
And fear began upon his flesh, and shook
The chaste and inly sufferance of it
Almost to ruin; a small fire and keen
Eating in muscle and nerve and hinge of joint
Perilous way; so bitter was the blow
Made on his sense by treason and sharp loss.
Then he fell weeping tears, with blood in them,
Like that red sweat that stained Gethsemane
With witness, when the deadly kiss had put
Shame on the mouth of Judas; and he cried,
Crying on God, and made out words and said:
Fair lord, sweet lord, most pleasant to all men,
To me so pleasant in clean days of mine
That now are rained upon with heavy rain,

Soiled with grey grime and with the dusty years,
Because in all those tourneys and hot things
I had to do with, in all riding times
And noise of work, and on smooth holidays
Sitting to see the smiting of hard spears,
And spur-smiting of steeds and wrath of men,
And gracious measure of the rounded game,
I held you in true honour and kept white
The hands of my allegiance as a maid's,
Being whole of faith and perfect in the will.
Therefore I pray you, O God marvellous,
See me how I am stricken among men,
And how the lip I fed with plenteousness
And cooled with wine of liberal courtesy
Turns a snake's life to poison me and clings—

The Last Ballad

JOHN DAVIDSON

By coasts where scalding deserts reek,
    The apanages of despair;
In outland wilds, by firth and creek,
    O'er icy bournes of silver air;

In storm or calm delaying not,
    To every noble task addressed,
Year after year, Sir Lancelot
    Fulfilled King Arthur's high behest.

He helped the helpless ones; withstood
    Tyrants and sanctioners of vice;
He rooted out the dragon brood,
    And overthrew false deities.

Alone with his own soul, alone
    With life and death, with day and night,
His thought and strength grew great and shone
    A tongue of flame, a sword of light.

And yet not all alone. On high,
    When midnight set the spaces free,
And brimming stars hung from the sky
    Low down, and spilt their jewellery,

ir Launcelot greets Queen Guinevere:

From *The Story of the Champions of the Round Table,*
written and illustrated by Howard Pyle.
New York: Scribner's, 1905.

Behind the nightly squandered fire,
　　Through a dark lattice only seen
By love, a look of rapt desire
　　Fell from a vision of the Queen.

From heaven she bent when twilight knit
　　The dusky air and earth in one;
He saw her like a goddess sit
　　Enthroned upon the noonday sun.

In passages of gulfs and sounds,
　　When wild winds dug the sailor's grave,
When clouds and billows merged their bounds,
　　And the keel climbed the slippery wave,

A sweet sigh laced the tempest; nay,
　　Low at his ear he heard her speak;
Among the hurtling sheaves of spray
　　Her loosened tresses swept his cheek.

And in the revelry of death,
　　If human greed of slaughter cast
Remorse aside, a violet breath,
　　The incense of her being passed

Across his soul, and deeply swayed
　　The fount of pity; o'er the strife
He curbed the lightning of his blade,
　　And gave the foe his forfeit life.

Low on the heath, or on the deck,
　　In bloody mail or wet with brine,
Asleep he saw about her neck
　　The wreath of gold and rubies shine;

He saw her brows, her lovelit face,
　　And on her cheek one passionate tear;
He felt in dreams the rich embrace,
　　The beating heart of Guinevere.

"Visions that haunt my couch, my path,
　　Although the waste, unfathomed sea

Should rise against me white with wrath
    I must behold her verily,

"Once ere I die," he said, and turned
    Westward his faded silken sails
From isles where cloudy mountains burned,
    And north to Severn-watered Wales.

Beside the Usk King Arthur kept
    His Easter court, a glittering rout.
But Lancelot, because there swept
    A passion of despair throughout

His being, when he saw once more
    The sky that canopied, the tide
That girdled Guinevere, forebore
    His soul's desire, and wandered wide

In unknown seas companionless,
    Eating his heart, until by chance
He drifted into Lyonesse,
    The wave-worn kingdom of romance.

He leapt ashore and watched his barque
    Unmastered stagger to its doom;
Then doffed his arms and fled baresark
    Into the forest's beckoning gloom.

The exceeding anguish of his mind
    Had broken him. "King Arthur's trust,"
He cried; "ignoble, fateful, blind!
    Her love and my love, noxious lust!

"Dupes of our senses! Let us eat
    In caverns fathoms underground,
Alone, ashamed! To sit at meat
    In jocund throngs?—the most profound

"Device of life the mountebank,
    Vendor of gilded ashes! Steal
From every sight to use the rank
    And loathsome needs that men conceal;

"And crush and drain in curtained beds
　　The clusters called of love; but feed
With garlanded uplifted heads;
　　Invite the powers that sanction greed

"To countenance the revel; boast
　　Of hunger, thirst; be drunken; claim
Indulgence to the uttermost,
　　Replenishing the founts of shame!"

He gathered berries, efts, and snails,
　　Sorrel, and new-burst hawthorn leaves;
Uprooted with his savage nails
　　Earth-nuts; and under rocky eaves

Shamefast devoured them, out of sight
　　In darkness, lest the eye of beast,
Or bird, or star, or thing of night
　　Uncouth, unknown, should watch him feast.

At noon in twilight depths of pine
　　He heard the word Amaimon spoke;
He saw the pallid, evil sign
　　The wred-eld lit upon the oak.

The viper loitered in his way;
　　The minx looked up with bloodshot leer;
Ill-meaning fauns and lamiae
　　With icy laughter flitted near.

But if he came upon a ring
　　Of sinless elves, and crept unseen
Beneath the brake to hear them sing,
　　And watch them dancing on the green,

They touched earth with their finger-tips;
　　They ceased their roundelay; they laid
A seal upon their elfin lips
　　And vanished in the purple shade.

At times he rent the dappled flank
　　Of some fair creature of the chase,

Mumbled its flesh, or growling drank
    From the still-beating heart, his face

And jowl ruddled, and in his hair
    And beard, blood-painted straws and burs,
While eagles barked screening the air,
    And wolves that were his pensioners.

Sometimes at night his mournful cry
    Troubled all waking things; the mole
Dived to his deepest gallery;
    The vixen from the moonlit knoll

Passed like a shadow underground,
    And the mad satyr in his lair
Whined bodeful at the world-old sound
    Of inarticulate despair.

Sir Lancelot, beloved of men!
    The ancient earth gat hold of him;
A year was blotted from his ken
    In the enchanted forest dim.

At Easter when the thorn beset
    The bronzing wood with silver sprays,
And hyacinth and violet
    Empurpled all the russet ways;

When buttercup and daffodil
    A stainless treasure-trove unrolled,
And cowslips had begun to fill
    Their chalices with sweeter gold,

He heard a sound of summer rush
    By swarthy grove and kindled lawn;
He heard, he sighed to hear the thrush
    Singing alone before the dawn.

Forward he stalked with eyes on fire
    Like one who keeps in sound and sight
An angel with celestial lyre
    Descanting rapturous delight.

He left behind the spell-bound wood;
    He saw the branchless air unfurled;
He climbed a hill and trembling stood
    Above the prospect of the world.

With lustre in its bosom pent
    From many a shining summer day
And harvest moon, the wan sea leant
    Against a heaven of iron-grey.

Inland on the horizon beat
    And flickered, drooping heavily,
A fervid haze, a vaporous heat,
    The dusky eyelid of the sky.

White ways, white gables, russet thatch
    Fretted the green and purple plain;
The herd undid his woven latch;
    The bleating flock went forth again;

The skylarks uttered lauds and prime;
    The sheep-bells rang from hill to hill;
The cuckoo pealed his mellow chime;
    The orient bore a burden shrill.

His memory struggled half awake;
    Dimly he groped within to see
What star, what sun, what light should break
    And set his darkened spirit free.

But from without deliverance came:
    Afar he saw a horseman speed,
A knight, a spirit clad in flame
    Riding upon a milkwhite steed.

For now the sun had quenched outright
    The clouds and all their working charms,
Marshalled his legionary light,
    And fired the rider's golden arms.

Softly the silver billows flowed;
    Beneath the hill the emerald vale

Dipped seaward; on the burnished road
  The milkwhite steed, the dazzling mail

Advanced and flamed against the wind;
  And Lancelot, his body rent
With the fierce trial of his mind
  To know, reeled down the steep descent.

Remembrances of battle plied
  His soul with ruddy beams of day.
"A horse! a lance! to arms!" he cried,
  And stood there weeping in the way.

"Speak!" said the knight. "What man are you?"
  "I know not yet. Surely of old
I rode in arms, and fought and slew
  In jousts and battles manifold."

Oh, wistfully he drew anear,
  Fingered the reins, the jewelled sheath;
With rigid hand he grasped the spear,
  And shuddering whispered, "Life and death,

"Love, lofty deeds, renown—did these
  Attend me once in days unknown?"
With courtesy, with comely ease,
  And brows that like his armour shone,

The golden knight dismounting took
  Sir Lancelot by the hand and said,
"Your voice of woe, your lonely look
  As of a dead man whom the dead

"Themselves cast out—whence are they, friend?"
  Sir Lancelot a moment hung
In doubt, then knelt and made an end
  Of all his madness, tensely strung

In one last effort to be free
  Of evil things that wait for men
In secret, strangle memory,
  And shut the soul up in their den.

"Spirit," he said, "I know your eyes:
          They bridge with light the heavy drift
Of years. . . . A woman said, 'Arise;
          And if you love the Queen, be swift!'

"The token was an emerald chased
          In gold, once mine. Wherefore I rode
At dead of night in proudest haste
          To Payarne where the Queen abode.

"A crafty witch gave me to drink:
          Almost till undern of the morn
Silent, in darkness. . . . When I think
          It was not Guinevere, self-scorn

"Cuts to the marrow of my bones,
          A blade of fire. Can wisdom yield
No mood, no counsel, that atones
          For wasted love! . . . Heaven had revealed

"That she should bear a child to me
          My bed-mate said. . . . Yet am I mad?
The offspring of that treachery!
          The maiden knight! You—Galahad,

"My son, who make my trespass dear!"
          His look released his father's thought—
The darkling orbs of Guinevere;
          For so had Lancelot's passion wrought.

With tenderer tears than women shed
          Sir Galahad held his father fast.
"Now I shall be your squire," he said.
          But Lancelot fought him long. At last

The maiden gently overpowered
          The man. Upon his milkwhite steed
He brought him where a castle towered
          Midmost a green enamelled mead;

And clothed his body, clothed his heart
          In human garniture once more.

127

"My father, bid me now depart.
    I hear beside the clanging shore,

"Above the storm, or in the wind,
    Outland, or on the old Roman street,
A chord of music intertwined
    From wandering tones deep-hued and sweet.

"Afar or near, at noon, at night,
    The braided sound attends and fills
My soul with peace, as heaven with light
    O'erflows when morning crowns the hills.

"And with the music, seen or hid,
    A blood-rose on the palace lawn,
A fount of crimson, dark amid
    The stains and glories of the dawn;

"Above the city's earthly hell
    A token ominous of doom,
A cup on fire and terrible
    With thunders in its ruddy womb;

"But o'er the hamlet's fragrant smoke,
    The dance and song at eventide,
A beating heart, the gentle yoke
    Of life the bridegroom gives the bride;

"A ruby shadow on the snow;
    A flower, a lamp—through every veil
And mutable device I know,
    And follow still the Holy Grail

"Until God gives me my new name
    Empyreal, and the quest be done."
Then like a spirit clad in flame,
    He kissed his father and was gone.

Long gazed Sir Lancelot on the ground
    Tormented till benign repose
Enveloped him in depths profound
    Of sweet oblivion. When he rose

The bitterest was past. "And I
    Shall follow now the Holy Grail,
Seen, or unseen, until I die:
    My very purpose shall avail

"My soul," he said. By day, by night,
    He rode abroad, his vizor up;
With sun and moon his vehement sight
    Fought for a vision of the cup—

In vain. For evermore on high
    When darkness set the spaces free,
And brimming stars hung from the sky
    Low down, and spilt their jewellery,

Behind the nightly squandered fire,
    Through a dim lattice only seen
By love, a look of rapt desire
    Fell from a vision of the Queen.

From heaven she bent when twilight knit
    The dusky air and earth in one;
He saw her like a goddess sit
    Enthroned upon the noonday sun.

Wherefore he girt himself again:
    In lawless towns and savage lands,
He overthrew unrighteous men,
    Accomplishing the King's commands.

In passages of gulfs and sounds
    When wild winds dug the sailor's grave,
When clouds and billows merged their bounds,
    And the keel climbed the slippery wave,

A sweet sigh laced the tempest; nay,
    Low at his ear he heard her speak;
Among the hurtling sheaves of spray
    Her loosened tresses swept his cheek.

And in the revelry of death,
    If human greed of slaughter cast

Remorse aside, a violet breath,
    The incense of her being passed

Across his soul, and deeply swayed
    The fount of pity; o'er the strife
He curbed the lightning of his blade,
    And gave the foe his forfeit life.

His love, in utter woe annealed,
    Escaped the furnace, sweet and clear—
His love that on the world had sealed
    The look, the soul of Guinevere.

MERLIN

JOHN VEITCH

The Merlin of this poem is Merlin Caledonius, known also as Merlin Wylt and Silvestris. He ought not to be identified with Myrdin Emrys, or Merlin Ambrosius, who was the *vates* of Vortigern, and also apparently of Aurelius Ambrosianus,—the man of Roman descent who superseded Vortigern in the Cymric supremacy, and lost it again about 465. This Myrdin Emrys was probably also the Merlin of Uther Pendragon and of Arthur. While the name of the latter is associated with Dinas Emrys, or Fort of Emrys, in the Vale of the Waters—Nant Gwynant, which circles round the rugged grandeur of the southern slopes of Snowdon—that of the former, Merlin Caledonius, is inseparably joined to the wavy, far-spreading, and heather-streaked hills between which the Powsail Burn makes its way to the Tweed in the haugh of Drummelzier. Out of the two Merlins—the earlier and the later—the romancers of the eleventh and following centuries formed a third or legendary Merlin. Now the personage appears as a vulgar wizard and soothsayer, master of the art of glamoury, to be finally overcome by a woman's wiles, and kept for ever in hopeless captivity.

The Caledonian Merlin is a sufficiently distinct historical personage. He was the son of Morvryn, who was descended from Coel Godebawc, the head of one of the main royal lines of the Cymri. He had a twin-sister Gwendydd. He was the friend of the Prince Gwenddoleu, a lord or king of the North, and he was present at the decisive battle of Ardderyd in 573, when the contest lay between the

Pagan and Christian forces of the time. Merlin was on the Pagan or losing side. After the defeat and the death of his leader Gwenddoleu, he fled to the wilds of Drummelzier, in the wood of Caledon. There he spent some years, reputed insane, probably only heart-broken, and despairing of the Cymric cause and his own fortunes,—perhaps doubting the trustworthiness of his original faith or Nature-worship. Finally, he is said to have died at the hands—rather stones and clubs—of the herdsmen of a princeling of the district, then incorporated in the kingdom afterwards known as Strathclyde, and ruled over by Rydderch Hael, originally lord of Llanerch, or Lanark. Merlin's grave is pointed out by tradition near the village of Drummelzier, by the side of the Powsail Burn as it joins the Tweed. There can be little doubt, looking to external and internal evidence, that this Merlin was the author of certain poems now preserved in the "Four Ancient Books of Wales," and that to him also are to be assigned portions of the Merlinian poems, in which there occur interpolations of a later date. The poems show a peculiarly delicate feeling for nature and natural objects—tree, hill, and fountain—and they are pervaded by a cry of wailing and despair for the fortunes of the Cymric race. Many of the lines show the deepest pathos; some of them are incorporated in the following poem.

Merlin's relation to the Christianity of the time is indicated in the poem. Originally a Nature-worshipper—probably with priestly functions—one who reverenced the powers and objects of Nature, and the sun above all, as the lord and symbol of creative and sustaining power, he was more or less affected by the Christianity of the time, but he never fully embraced it. If it ever had a hold on him, he appears to have relapsed from it in his later years; although conceptions from the faith which was making progress around him mingled with his original beliefs and pretensions to supernatural power and prophetic insight. This is the Merlin as depicted in the poem. It opens immediately after the battle of Arddderyd, when, in doubt and despair, the hopes of his life broken, he had fled to the retreat and shelter afforded by the hills and glens of Upper Tweeddale, where, more than a thousand years afterwards, men whose faith was of quite another type found refuge. Here, in the centre of the wood of Caledon, frequenting a fountain on the hills, he is said to have lived for some years ere he met his violent fate. Merlin was to a certain extent contemporary with Kentigern, who is said to have met him on the wilds which he haunted, and sought to convert him to the Christianity of the time, with, however, but partial and temporary effect. The details of the interview, as given hundreds of years afterwards in the "Scotichronicon," are of course a priestly invention, and wholly untrustworthy. The character of the Merlin of the poem is, I venture to think, in accordance with all the earliest and genuine information we have regarding him. His sister Gwendydd, The Dawn,—her affection and companionship in his life and troubles—and his early love, Hwimleian, The Gleam,—have their warrant in the original poems, and in the later ones, still of a very early time, in which reference is made to the Bard and Seer of this semi-historic, semi-mythic epoch of the ancient Cymri.

J.V.

PERSONS

MERLIN—Bard, Seer, Wizard.
GWENDYDD (The Dawn)—His twin-sister.
HWIMLEIAN (The Gleam)—His early love.

MERLIN (*in the Glen, and on Drummelzier Law*).

All night I've wandered in the glen, 'mid hum
Of hidden waters moving in the gloom,
And eerie sounds, strange voices from th' unseen,
And things have shaped themselves upon the air,
Some mocking me, and some soliciting
My evil will;—dim, weird sprites, that pass
'Twixt sky and earth in dark hours ere the morn,—
Form after form in crowding mystery,
Where none can mark the mien of living thing,
Or pause upon a face for love or light;
But all that seems to be doth also pass
In mockery of show to mortal eye.

The hill-top now is gained, and lo! afar
The eastern summits redden with the dawn;
The moor around me wakes to growing sound
And stir of life, all tremulous before
The high on-coming of the lord of day.

This morn I bow before thee, lord of light
And life!—my hope, my fear, my reverence!
Of thee unworthy, and my early vows.
Far-gleaming arrows, piercing feeble mists,

Herald thine uprise; low down in the vales,
That pour their loving tribute to the Tweed,
The waters shimmer 'mid the morning's joy;
Around me burn-heads croon, and moorland birds
Awake, a-wing, pipe brief glad notes to thee,
The brightening lord of happy melody.
Now part in twain the curtains of the dawn,
Each hill-top is aflame, and thou hast set
Thyself, full-orbed, in empire o'er the day:—
Aglow as in that dawn when first enthroned,
The wasting ages taking nought from thee,
Nor tainted by the evil of this earth,
Thou layest now, as new birth of the morn,
Thy strength of glory on the circling hills.
I worship thee, O sovereign of the sky,
The symbol of the God who is unseen.

Inspirer, thou, of life and hope and joy,
My pulses beat with thine. Again I feel
The blood that leaps to high ambition's quest,
And wakes, as sudden flash, my vanished dream,
To hold in leash the powers of all this world,
Be lord of nature and of human lives,—
Phantasm of youth that beckoned and beguiled
To empire and emprise, wild, subtle, vain—
As if this feeble hand could pluck from thee,
O king of day, thy lofty radiance,
And usurp thy throne.

To know the soul of things has been my quest,
To feel the beating of the inmost heart
That pulses through the world,—to know and be
As God,—a king o'er kings, with subtler power
Than that of lords who rule by force of arm,
Or wavering tie of human sympathy,—
This, this, the dream that dazzled all my youth;
And I have dared and done, in this my quest,
What no man knows, seen what no eye hath seen—
Weird sights not utterable in mortal words,
Strange forms o' morn, shapes in the weather-gleam,
That silent move and pass along the rim,
Clear-set, of the dim world that engirds the hills.

Ay, at grey dawn, I've struggled with the bird
Of wrath, until the sun came to mine aid,
And smote the hovering shadow, beak and wing.—
And now the dream is riven, shatterëd,
As when the great west wind in strength has struck
The summer heaven; and lo! we see but shreds
Of all its gilded towers, and broken shapes
Athwart the storm-cleft sky.

To stand supreme in mystery of might;
To lead the battle on to victory;
Mine was the pledge, assurance, and the hope,
The inspiration, and the faith of men.
Their trusting look to me as on the morn
They passed, fiend-blessed, to that green plain that lay
Between the Liddel's tide and Carwinelow;
This lives for aye deep scarred upon my heart.
I see the shock, and hear the frusch of spears,
Edge grinding edge, all through the fatal hours;
Twice seven armies locked in deadly grip,
Until at length that Cross, upraised against
The evening sky, shot o'er the struggling hosts
One blinding ray, as of the wrath of heaven;
And in that hour supreme of fate my power
Was stricken, and each sprite grew palsied-pale,
And passed away before my 'wildered eye,
Dissolved as phantom of the feeble air;
And then—was nought but faces of the dead,
Upturned, upbraiding, in the gloamin' grey;
And all was laid 'neath cover of the shade,
And all was hushed save the unheeding stream.

My prince, my Gwenddoleu, whose golden torques
I wore, and thou, well-lovëd Gwendydd's son,
Thou fearless bearer of the white-rimmed shield,
Where may I seek you now? Where are my dead,
The dead of Ardderyd? To me ye come
No more; no more again your hands I touch,—
To me your eyes glance never light of life!
"Hath not the burden been consigned to earth?
And every one must give up what he loves."
The budding thorn is green, the birch is blest,

135

And sweet the melody and chirp of birds;
But ye are still, my Moryen and Mordav!
Are ye now spirits of the nerveless clouds
That speck the shadowed hills and sweep the moor;
That dwell in air, and come, and passing wail,
Behold the misery of race and kin,
But have no power to stretch a hand in aid
Of their fell lot? Oft I hear a voice
A-crying in the night, see glimpsing forms
In outbreak of the moon through riven sky.
Oh! unavailing wail and stricken arm!
Is this your heaven?

Or are these seemings of the strainëd sense—
The fond heart's quickening of the hopeless dead?
And is it so that all are surely gone,
As is the creed of that far Orient,
Whence my race has sprung—to Nirvana's shade,
The formless state where nought is marked or known,
No sense, no thought, pain, pleasure, or desire;
Where keen emotion hath no quickening,
And resolute will, unstrung, can dare no deed
Of good or ill, and hath no fate to bear:
Where comes not e'en a passing dream to stir
The unconscious brain, or glint of memory
Across the darkened past; but all is one—
An absolute repose, alike for those
Once harassed by the pains of earthly life,
And souls that lived spell-bound in human bliss,
Heroes in battle slain, the weak who passed
From cottage couch, the proud from palace-hall,
The maiden in her bloom, the mother, child;
In the absorbing All are life and death alike,—
Close folded in unconscious unity?

What, then, this life of ours but pain and wreck!—
Mirage that hovers fair o'er youthful sky;
Inwoven dream that parts as mist before
The sun of noon; mid-life a battle 'gainst
Fierce striving powers for issues no one knows
Are in their final outcome good or ill,—
None seeing whither tends the deed we do
In the mysterious process of the world!

GWENDYDD (*The Dawn—his twin-sister—sings; she addresses him as Lallo-gen, twin-brother*).

Lallogen! princely Morvryn's son,
    Of olden heroes born,
Spirit divine, incarnate god,
    To thee I bow this morn!

Thou, lord of airy powers, that dwell
    In speed of the towering cloud,
In far out-flash of the levin fell,
    In the croak of the raven brood;

In the hurrying mist of the moor,
    Thy vassal spirits troop,
In the striving blast that tears the pine,
    In eagle forms that swoop

From their course in the rack of the sky—
    Playmates of the stormy gleam—
Winging to earth the stroke of fate,
    As well to thee may beseem!

At thy bidding the wrath of the storm
    Suddenly smites earth's rest,
And swiftly the burns arise and roar
    In awe of thy dread behest.

The gentle milkwort bows its head,
    Cowering beneath the hour,
When thy spirit feels not a bound
    To its lust of evil power.

All unlovely, O brother, is might,
    When slave of the wayward will;
And passion that knows but to smite
    Is self-accursed with its ill.

Once blameless wert thou in thy strength,
    As on that eve of old,
When Saxons fierce from the Frisian Sea
    Crept in the mist's grey fold,

And sudden swooped on the Meldon green,
    From old Penjacob glen,—
Thou and I in the lonely Caer,—
    No hope or help from men!

At calm upraising of thy hand,
    And far gleam of thine eye,
The rainbow rose round that airy Caer
    In sacred majesty.

And we two forms within its rim
    Shone god-like on the gaze,
And every sieging eye was held
    In wild and weird amaze!

So arched in splendour Meldon's top,
    Our blinded foes dismayed,
Paled, fled before the Power of Heaven
    In its awesome robe arrayed.

Now turn thee from the tempter's thrall,
    Dream of one bygone day,—
The flickering shade o'er the woodland glade
    When thou and I were at play,—

And thou touched thy harp to a gentle tune
    Of happy melody;
The deer stood charmed; the golden leaves
    Dropped from the quivering tree.

Oh, brother! take that harp once more,
    All-thrilling to the gleams
That pass now o'er the mountain's brow,
    'Mid the music of the streams:

As from the heaven's height they come,
    Bright messengers to earth:
Ethereal love doth shine in them,
    They speak a god-like birth.

And high they bear our human heart
    O'er grief, and fear, and pain:

Ah, brother! shall thy harp resound
   No more in holy strain!

MERLIN.

My heart is dust,
And callous is the soul that once was thrilled
By every pure and gentle thing of earth;
No more for me is blessing or to bless,—
Mine,—the power that smites, but cannot save;
Mine,—dreaded memory that wakes to hate;
Mine,—vision more than man's that can foresee
The future of my race, and what befalls
Of fateful contest and of storied deed.
Ghosts of the mountain mutter in mine ear;
Sea-birds, sky-borne, aye clang it on my brain,—
The Bard dishonoured, worthless Priest extolled,
The kingless Cymri trampled on the plain,
Blood-spilling from the sea to shoreless land,
Their Caers all desolate on the windy hills,
Haunted by wailing spirits of the dead,—
This powerless I behold in my despair.
Once I could bend each sprite to subtle art,
And I could sport with all their fiendish power,
And sway it to mine end, but now,—so ripe
In me the habit of the evil will,—
Each mocks my fainting purpose after good,
And I, proud master once, am now the slave!

GWENDYDD (*takes Merlin's harp and sings*).

Fresh as of old the breeze of the morn,
   Plaintive the notes that float
O'er the moor with the sunny thyme,
   And the blue forget-me-not.

The rock-rose lifts its face to the sun,
   It droops when its lord is set;
The tormentil peers, the heather-bell glows;
   Sweet-eyed is the violet.

The lowly gale looks forth from the grass,
   Silver-starring the brae;

139

Th' Idaean vine holds its cup for the dew,
    High where the burn-heads play,

As they flash in ripples of light,
    Ere down they break to the glen
By green bank, red scaur, and grey rock,
    Where the rowan shades the linn:

And the sun o'er all is moving in joy,
    The strong lord of the sky;
He stoops to bless the earth with his love,
    Benign in his majesty.

And nought but raises its face to him,
    Both herb and flower of earth;
He, lord of all, that rules in heaven,
    Hath care for the lowliest birth.

And thou art far from the face of God—
    Whate'er thy craft or power—
Who knowest not first to bless with thy might,
    As the sun in the morning hour.

MERLIN.

Ah! gentle sister, thou hast touched my heart;
I live, again, in the green fields of memory,
A swift-winged hour of bright enchanting hope.
Would I were clothed again in innocence
Of youth, when every breeze was life and love,
Each ripple of the stream a soothing sound,
Each sparkle leapt to joy before mine eye;
Each mountain flower the darling of my heart;
When, with my shield on shoulder, sword on thigh,
I roamed by day the wood of Caledon,
And in the silence of the summer night
Lay folded in a dreamless sleep,—the hours
Unvisited by ghostly forms of air.
E'en now the vision rises,—that fair form,
The sportive maid, the Gleam amid the trees,
Whereon the spring had spread the apple-bloom,

Low by the river's side,—my Hwimleian,
Earth's paragon of movement and of grace,
The jewel of this heart, a faithless guardian!
Stale heart of mine! now no dew of heaven
Can freshen thee, no dawn bring quickening.
Ah me! the blossoms were untimely frayed,
Ne'er golden autumn theirs; and yet 'twas well,
Hwimleian, thou didst not wed with devil's son!

HWIMLEIAN (*The Gleam—Merlin's early love—appearing as a glint on the
hill, sings*).

The daughter of the Sun, I come,
    His joy, his free first-born;
As birthright fair the gleam I wear
    Of the golden hair of morn.

Above the earth's dark orb I soar,
    Nought there eludes my ken;
The wide o'erarching heaven is mine—
    The Queen of hill and glen.

I smite the darkness from the cloud,
    And pierce its dusky fold;
I lay my hand on the dark-browed storm,
    And charm it into gold.

The grey moor mists transfigured pass,
    And every evil sprite
And power of air, that threatened earth,
    Flees stricken in my sight.

Over the mottled hills I fly,
    My brother shade with me;
With light wing drape the peace that broods
    O'er the moorland spaces free.

O' night my paler robe is cast
    O'er the trembling waters clear;
I peer into depths of the silent glen,
    The lonely herdsman's cheer.

141

The brow of pain I touch with joy;
  My face—my power unfurled,
Dark spirits cowering pass away—
  Mine homage of the world!

MERLIN.

Ah me! this voice once more—this voice to me—
The faithless to the truest love on earth!
She has conquered death, and calls from th' unseen
To me, dim groper after truth and power,
Yet missing bliss! man mocked and satisfied
With outward show and sensual pageantry.
The outer seeming, not the truth itself,
Has been my portion; husk, not fruit, was mine,—
The trick of art which awes, destroys, but builds
Not for the world: when it hath passed, remain
The waste of ashes, cowering dread, despair,
The glare of power that briefly flames in space,
Its whole reward—the dazzling snare whereby
The spirit of the world leads captive souls
Whose trust is in their strength, divorced from love,
And silent working, patient thought and faith,
That move the springs of progress and of hope—
Not waited on by fame or noisy talk
Of buzzing tongues, or clamour of the crowd—
Yet in the course of ages moulding men
To noble likeness, life of higher grade.
The stream of order from th' Eternal Fount
Flows free and full, unmeasured in its might,
Unthwarted, suffering not disharmony,
But thrusting all our rebel strokes aside,
And mocking all our puny might to grasp,
And turn aside from its unerring aim.
One Will there is in heaven and on earth—
'Tis mirrored in the open-visioned soul.
Who waits the revelation only knows,
Who bows before the Power hath true control.

GWENDYDD.

The dew is on the grave that holds my son;
The grass upon the mound is green where lies

Our Gwenddoleu. They have no ear to list
The twittering birds at opening of the dawn.
But, O Lallogen, lord of lucid verse,
Thou wise diviner, fearless in the fight,
"The fosterer of song among the streams,"
Thy locks are hoar as when the winter lays
Its snowy fingers on Trahenna's brow;
And thou art nearing mortal's dreaded doom,
And saddest to my sight will be the cairn
Of thine entrenchment,—there my heart will yearn
For thee in separation long and cold.
I pray thee, loved one, pass not from the world
In mood of wrath, vengeful, unreconciled;
The Priest shall bear to thee the sacred rite
That heals and saves.

MERLIN.

Sister! no rite shall be for me at hand
Of cloak-draped monk, the ally of our foes.
He gives, forgives, as he were Lord—purblind:
"May my communion be with God alone!"

(*After an interval.*)

Gwendydd! to my fountain lead me once again,
Then leave me,—I would see once more alone
The well-eye 'mong the hills that has for fringe
The solitary fern of tender mien,
That bends, leaf-charmëd, o'er the gleam it loves,
Where birk and hazel fleck with shifting shades
The waters, as they move in gentle rise
And fall, and pour soft music ceaselessly;
Where mosses, green and brown, cling to the stones,
And eyes of fair forget-me-not are bright
With blessings for the spray that leaps to kiss
It by the way. There may I commune free
With creatures of the wild that come at eve,
Whose language is the depth of loving eyes,
Who err not from the order of the world.

O Spirit of my fountain—pure, benign,
Whose dwelling is in depths of Nether Erd,

Far down, beyond the turmoil of the world,
Serene and sanctified, untouched by storm,
Or aught that can defile,—who wearest aye
Unstainèd face in trouble or in calm
Of earth or air,—I pray this evil heart
In me may pass. Now would I be at peace
With thee, O Spirit, and all gentle things.
I know mine hour is come.

RUSTICS (*herdsmen find him at the fountain*).

Lo! Wizard Merlin, lo! the devil's son!
Destroyer of our crops, bringer fell of storms,
Nor sparing herdsman in the moorland drift,
Nor tender lamb in bitter wind of March,—
Grip, bind him with the green withes from the tree
Blessed by the priest. Then swiftly to the stream.
                    [*They carry him to the Tweed.*
Son of air and earth! let water hide thee,
Gurgling o'er, when thou, sunk deep, art dead
In wheeling Debbit,—devil's pool, where dwells
The iron-toed, the fiend who waits thee there:
On earth or in the air not thine to die.

Strong Spirit of the flood! we give to thee
The lord of all the elements of air,—
Who from the hills sent torrent through the haugh,
That strove and roared, and bore its tawny mane,
Outsweeping, merciless, in joy of wrath,—
To be for ever thine, ne'er more to touch
Our earth with wizard spell.

MERLIN (*raising his head once from the current ere he sinks*).

One gleam upon the stream! My Hwimleian!
My love! fair daughter of the sun,—thou, thou
Alone art faithful unto passing death
Of this poor feeble framework of the soul
That fears the dread unknown and yearns for love,
E'en in that future baffling all our ken.
I am for ever consecrate to thee!
What boots it aye to be, if not to be

With love!—the loved and lost, the soul that waits
In ever-living love! With thee I grasp
Anew the golden thread of life,—to be
No more 'mong living men where life is not.

Hwimleian (*in the air over the stream*).

Now hold I thee, the spirit, free from taint
Of mortal flesh, and from the tempter's thrall.
Now we are one—one in our strength and love—
Ne'er one before in all that checkered world
Which men call earth, where passions rage and rule,
And love but seems, and gilded guilt has sway;
And the brute hand that understandeth not
Can strike the brave, the noble, and the wise—
God-sped, whose kingdom is where earth is not:
There to the best doth e'er befall the worst.
Base earth no longer dominates the soul!
We know it now, one orb among the stars,
A speck upon infinity; and far
Beneath our wingèd flight, through ether borne,
In pure and simple vision we shall see
Free beauty undefaced, the truth undimmed,
And purity unsullied—face to face
In that unbroken light which faintly here
Gleams through the veil, and seeks with pitying heart
To win the unheeding darkness of the world!

And seeing, we shall be what we behold,
Through the unwavering purpose of the soul,
Transfixed by glory of th' Eternal Throne,
Boundless as craving of the heart for bliss.
Here effort wanders not in devious ways,
And strength wails not its wasted energy,
Nor love is pain, but will and heart are one
In high endeavour after nobler good,
As life on life evolves, infinite life,
Th' unwearied process of th' eternal years.

When I Set Out for Lyonnesse

THOMAS HARDY

When I set out for Lyonnesse,
  A hundred miles away,
  The rime was on the spray,
And starlight lit my lonesomeness
When I set out for Lyonnesse
  A hundred miles away.

What would bechance at Lyonnesse
  While I should sojourn there
  No prophet durst declare,
Nor did the wisest wizard guess
What would bechance at Lyonnesse
  While I should sojourn there.

When I came back from Lyonnesse
  With magic in my eyes,
  All marked with mute surmise
My radiance rare and fathomless,
When I came back from Lyonnesse
  With magic in my eyes!

Knights of King Arthur's Court

JESSIE WESTON

The scent of the may is in the air,
    And its stars on each bough are hung,
With largesse of blossom and perfume rare
    To the wandering breezes flung,
And the fairies tread a measure fair
    To the chime by the blue-bells rung.

And the wood-birds carol unafraid,
    For no man hath done them wrong,
While King Arthur's knights pass adown the glade,
    And each, as he rides along,
Wending his way by sun and shade,
    Beguileth the hour with song.

SIR GAWAYNE

"A song, a song for the springtide,
    A song for the golden days,
For the lovelit eyes of the maidens,
    And the knight whom their lips shall praise
And who but I should sing it,
    Who was ever the Maidens' Knight?
Such honour hath been my guerdon
    For many a fair-fought fight.

"Oh, my heart is fain for the clamour
  And cry of the battle-field,
For the crash of the splintered spear-shaft,
  And the clang of the smitten shield.
But 'tis sweeter when toil is over
  To lay me a while to rest
In the arms that so soft enfold me,
  And for pillow a snow-white breast.

"And what if such joys be fleeting?
  Ah, little I reck the while
I ride adown thro' the sunlight,
  With ever a song and a smile!
For when my last fight is foughten
  I know that a white-robed band
Of maidens shall bid me greeting
  On the shores of a sunlit land!"

SIR TRISTAN

"Tho' the springtide sun be fair,
Brighter far beyond compare
Shineth Iseult's golden hair!

"Springtide hours pass all too fleet,
Haste, my steed, on flying feet,
Ah, but Iseult's lips are sweet!

"Iseult, lily, Iseult, rose,
At my heart the love-drink glows,
Thro' my veins like fire it flows!

"Iseult, Iseult, when the light
Fadeth, clasp me, hold me tight,
Kiss me, dearest, into night!"

SIR LANCELOT

"Art thou waiting for me, my Lady,
Alone in thy royal bower?
Dost thou send a word thro' the silence
To hasten the passing hour,

148

'Hath he ever a thought for me, my knight?
Will he come to my arms with the fading light?'

"I am coming, love, I am coming—
Breathe soft, O wind of Spring,
Sail fast, O fleecy cloudlet,
Speed, bird, on glancing wing,
Whisper a word in my Lady's ear,
Tell her the sound of my feet ye hear!

"Ah, never had knight a lady
Fair as my queen is fair;
On a golden throne she sitteth,
In the blaze of her red-gold hair—
And little he dreams, my lord the king,
Of the secret that maketh her heart to sing.

"Are we false? are we true? I know not,
The twain are so wrought in one;
But whether for joy or for sorrow,
The sands of our fate must run—
And what matter if men condemn us quite,
Since all the world shall be ours to-night?"

SIR PERCEVAL

"I ride adown the forest aisles
    From morn till evening shade,
Beneath the stars of heaven my head,
    At fall of night, is laid.
No comrade wendeth at my side,
    No voice bids me God-speed,
Alone by hill and vale I ride,
    Alone by wood and mead.

"For somewhere, near, or far away,
    One waiteth long mine aid,
I may not rest, by night or day,
    Until his grief be stayed.
For many a year, with prayer and tear,
    I've sought to find the way,
But rough or smooth, the path I choose
    Still leadeth me astray.

149

"I may not rest from off my quest,
   I may not stay my hand,
Tho' Life and Love be waiting me,
   Far in a distant land.
I may not see my wife's fair face,
   I may not faint nor fail,
Till I have won Anfortas grace,
   And found the Holy Grail."

         . . . .

Sir Gawayne hath sought the isles of light
   Beyond the shores of day,
Where morn never waneth to shades of night,
   And the silver fountains play;
There he holdeth high court as the Maidens' Knight,
   In the Maidens' Isle, for aye.

And Tristan sleeps by his lady's side,
   To the dirge of the sounding sea;
And the foaming wave and the flowing tide
   Hide the twain, that no man may see
Where they take their rest, and their fate abide,
   Till the dawn of Eternity.

But Lancelot wrought a penance hard
   To win from his sin release,
And his face was by fast and vigil marred
   Or ever his pain might cease.
Now his body lieth in Joyous Gard,
   And his soul hath gotten peace.

And Perceval, doth he wake or sleep?
   Ah, no man shall tell that tale—
Perchance he lieth in slumber deep
   With the Eastern sands for veil;
Or perchance, in a distant land, doth keep
   Watch and ward o'er the Holy Grail.

But when the archangel trump shall call,
   And the Heavenly Feast be spread,
Say, which of those heroes, among them all,

150

Shall lift up a fearless head,
And walk the pavement of Heaven's high Hall
With unashamèd tread?

Sir Gawayne, methinks, shall hide his face,
    Abashed and overawed,
And the lovers twain, by Jesu's grace,
    Sit low at the Heavenly board;
But the King of Heaven shall rise from His place
    When He seeth Monsalväsch' lord—

"Welcome, O Brother, who bare thy part
    In the travail of My soul,
Who knew no rest of hand or heart
    Till thy brother might be made whole;
Come thou, and sit at My side, apart,
    While the stars 'neath our footstool roll."

The Castle of Carbonek

ERNEST RHYS

1

The wind and the dark,
   The wind and we,
We parleyed together
   And put to sea,—
      To sea!

2

The waves they followed
   Like hounds let go;
The salt froth spotted
   The deck like snow.

3

The fireball sate
   On our tall mast-head,
And lit the pit
   Of the long-drown'd dead.

From *The Story of the Champions of the Round Table,*
written and illustrated by Howard Pyle,
New York: Scribner's, 1905.

4

We stood like sheep
    On the after-deck,
When we sighted the Castle
    Of Carbonek,—
        Carbonek.

5

Not once, but thrice
    We gave the hail!
For the Fisher King
    And the Holy Grail.

6

But the wind went round
    On the winter sea
And blew us back
    Over Collibë.

7

And twice it shifted,
   And twice about
The steersman steer'd us
   Within a shout.

*   *   *

8

'Tis ten years gone
   Since we stood on deck
And sighted the Castle
   Of Carbonek,—
      Carbonek.

The Quest of the Grail: On the Eve

ERNEST RHYS

"And then the king and all estates went home unto Camelot, and so went to evensong to the great minster. And so after upon that to supper."

I

"Before you take this Quest," (he said), "in order set,—
Each knight around the Table,—come, sup with me yet;
Come, keep the feast, that after us men never shall forget!"

II

Now, round the Table seated, each tall knight in his place,—
Hears noises like to thunder, and sees a light whose rays
Make shine his fellows by him, with brows more bright than day's.

III

Not one could speak, for wonder. Then lo, within the hall
Wrapt round with snow-white samite, the blessèd Sancgreal
And sweetest savours filled the board; and meat and drink for all.

IV

The mystic Vessel like a gleam went by: it could not stay:
And the knights all fell to feasting, and the vision passed away,
That all shall quest, but few shall find, until the earth's last day.

V

And then they fell to babbling, their hands upon their knees,
And babbled of the morrow, and all the joy there is
For them that quest, and ride the lands, and cross the winter seas.

VI

But the tears fell down King Arthur's cheeks, as he sate with his men:
"Ye have set me in great sorrow," said Arthur to them then:
"For oh, I doubt, my fellowship, shall meet no more again!"

Sir Launcelot and the Sancgreal

ERNEST RHYS

"Car il [le Gréail] n'or à nul pech'eour
Ne compaignie ne amour."

He found a chamber where the door was shut,
    And thereto set his hand to open it;
And mightily he tried, and still might not:
    And then he heard a voice which sang so sweet,
It seemed none earthly thing that he heard sing,
        "Honour and joy be given
        To the High King of Heaven!"

It seemed none earthly thing that sung therein,
    So sweet the voice, it near had made him greet,—
For well he knew his body, stained with sin,
    Was for that mystic chamber all unmeet,
Wherein those voices rang, yes, choired and sang;
        "Honour and joy be given
        To the High King of Heaven!"

For well he knew that there the Sancgreal
    Upon the board was set for sinless souls,
While the three rays shone sidelong down the wall;
    While he without did kneel with many a stain,

And there to that hid noise he joined his voice,
    "Pity and grace be given,
    To me, lost child of Heaven!"

With that he saw the chamber door unclose,
    And out there shone a clearness and a light
As all the torches in the world that house
    Had lighted and been borne there burning bright
About the Sancgreal, while sang they all,
    "Honour and joy be given,
    To the sweet lord of Heaven!"

Oh, much he marvelled, and would enter in,
    And cried, "Fair Father Jesu" in his need,
Remembering then men's woe and mortal sin
    For which the Christ upon the Cross did bleed,—
Yes, crying still that prayer, he entered there,—
    "Pity and grace be given
    To me, poor knight of Heaven!"

Right so he entered, where the Sancgreal
    Did shine to greet him; but a gust of fire,
And a grim smoke, there smote and made him fall;
    It took his body's might, and all desire;
He had no voice nor will, though they sang still,
    "Honour and joy be given
    To the High King of Heaven!"

Then many hands did raise and bear him out,
    And there all night he lay, till morning time;
And many a day like dead lay Launcelot,
    He heard no bell at matin or at prime:
Nathless he deem'd did sing, none earthly thing,
    "Honour and joy be given
    To the High King of Heaven!"

Then came a dayspring and a fair white dawn,
    And he rose up, yet did not rise the same:
For all the bitterness and pain were gone:
    For he who sinn'd the sin had borne the shame,
And seen the Sancgreal, and heard them call,
    "Honour and joy be given
    To the High King of Heaven!"

*   *   *   *   *

Oh now, frail sons of earth, who fell in sin;
    Learn from the piteous deed of this dread knight,
Beat at the door, and cry, and enter in,
    And you shall win the Grail, and see the Light,
Yes, like none earthly thing, shall hear them sing,
        "Honour and joy be given
        To the High King of Heaven!"

The Song of the Four Knights

ERNEST RHYS

From "Gwenevere" a Lyric Play.

Merlin. But tell me now, how went this fight
Of Camlan field?" . . .

I

The First Knight.

One star was bright,—the cold dawn-star!
I saw a thousand lift the spear
In Modred's camp, to end the night,
As grey, we rode in the morning light.

II

The Second Knight.

The King rode with us,—and his head
Was grown grey too, we saw and said:
When he cried Halt! on Camlan Hill
The dawn-star pale above him still.

III

The Third Knight.

His face too, grey beneath his helm:
Then: "For the Table and the Realm
Ride now!" he cried, and on we flowed
Each spear athirst for Modred's blood.

IV

The Fourth Knight.

But Modred met us, spear for spear.
Was he afraid? He showed no fear:
When Arthur riding, shining, thrust
The death-spear through him, to the dust.

V

"Kneel now, Haut King!" he cried, "and save
My soul the travail it shall have,
Were this not told of my remorse!"
And Arthur lighted off his horse.

VI

The First Knight.

Ah Snake! he crept upon the shaft
Could not be drawn: and dying, laught,
And with his sword struck at the head
Bent there to hear what thing he said.

VII

The Third Knight.

So Modred died,—a traitor still,
Up to the end, by Camlan Hill!
And as we bore the King away,—
On Modred's lips the death-laugh lay.

VIII

The Four Knights.

Now, of the Flower of Camelot,—
Knights, Arthur loved, and Launcelot,
What is there left but stricken men
That bear the Haut King home again.

The Unfinished Book of Bleise

ERNEST RHYS

All the battles that were won
    Merlin bade his master, Bleise,
Put on parchment. Caerleon,—
    Blazoned round with crimson rays
Was that page of night and sun:
    And the siege of Ile Maleise,—
Black and purple, marching on.
    But when he wrote the fierce assays
The Haut King had in Caledon,
    The letters fought: the rampant A's,
The S's all awry—each one
    Recall'd the burning tower of Pase,
Wherein the knights in agony spun.
    For so the letters twirl'd, till Bleise
Left Merlin's book of wars undone.
    Yet fame hath still her splendent ways:
Camlan,—Cardoile,—Caerleon—
    Still shall keep the Haut King's praise
    Sounding to the end of days.

From *Idylls of the King,*
by Alfred Tennyson, illustrated by George and Louis Rhead.
New York: R. H. Russell, 1898.

King Arthur's Sleep
A Ballad of Bala Fair.

ERNEST RHYS

I

On the morn of sweet St. Martin
    Davie drew a hazel wand,
And he singing came to Bala,
    With the hazel in his hand.

What he sang, the cock-thrush echoed,
    some wild rhyme of Merlin's doom,
Or the sad refrain of Rhuddlan,
    Or the love of Hob and Twm.

From the hill, he heard the harpers,
    And the hagglers, in the town,
And his heart leapt up to hear them,
    As he sang, and hastened down.

II

What cobbled ancientry is this comes coughing thro' the fair,
     Davie dear?
Like one from out the grave arisen, the grave-mould in his hair?

The shepherd boys cry "Druan!" the Bala maids "Beware!
     Davie dear!"
Yea sure, at sight of Davie's wand, he waits a while to stare.

"If thou'll take me where thy hazel grew,—ah, this cough has made
          me old!"
     Davie's told,—
"I'll twine thy wand with silver, and bind thy belt with gold!"

Can you bear to leave untasted all the fun of Bala Fair,
     Davie dear?
"Davie dear!" the maids keep calling. His wand leads otherwhere.

III

Far from Bala fair, the Lonnen
     Leans against the mountain side;
Far above the Lonnen haystacks,
     Drops the brook the hazels hide.

Davie leads, the grey-man follows,
     As grey-eve, St. Martin's morn;
While across the Lonnen haystacks,
     Now the pale frost-fog is borne.

Davie leads, the grey-man follows;
     And he coughs; but Davie sighs
As they climb, and mark the night-fall;
     With no lantern but their eyes.

By the torrent, mid the hazels,
     Hardly may the grey-man see,
Groping, kneeling, there, a gravestone,
     Cast with Druid charactry.

165

Ach, he coughs; his lean long fingers
    Strain upon it, till it stirs,
But a cry from out the torrent,
    And the hazels Davie hears!

IV

Deep as Merlin's grave, the stairway
    That descended, gloom on gloom,
Into darkness that no window
    Ever yet let sun illume.

Davie fears, but he must follow:
    Till the darkness soars and falls,—
Arched and groined, and looped and lifted,
    Like St. David's twilit walls.

And within, a trembling twilight
    Surely shewed a thousand men,
All asleep, in shining helmets.
    Ah, to see them wake again.

"They are mighty Arthur's warriors!"
    Said the grey-man; "Till the day
When the bell shall ring to wake them,
    They must sleep. Then wake for aye!

"With his Knights at the Round Table,—
    Owain, Kai, and Percival,—
See,—the little star that crowns him,
    There sleeps Arthur, King of all.

"But as Merlin said, not waking
    In our time, save yonder bell
Ring,—and see the gold around them
    That is ours. Oh, Sirs, sleep well!"

Davie's lips part, wide with wonder,
    At the warriors in their sleep,
With such spears, and splendid helmets;
    "Ah," he cries, "to see them leap

"Forth to life, and march to music,
    Flashing all their thousand spears;
Ring, you bell, until King Arthur
    Rises, royal, when he hears!"

Still the old man gropes and grumbles
    O'er his gold, as Davie's gone;
Hark, ye mystic hall of warriors,
    Hark, the bell rings, night is done!

At its stroke, the mountain trembled,
    And the thousand spears replied,
Grounding on the mouldy pavement,
    As the men rose, side by side.

Oh, the soldiers rise in radiance,
    All in motion, helm and spear!
And King Arthur's crown, above them,
    Like a star shines steadfast there!

But a voice cried,—"Sleep, King Arthur!
    Greed of gold, a boy at play,
Wake thy destined sleep; far distant
    Still is the awakening day!"

And King Arthur cried,—"Sleep, soldiers!
    Sleep, my spears!" They sank again
Into silence. Round the table
    Arthur slept with all his men!

But the old man hastened, stumbling,
    From his gold, and grumbling crept,
And drew Davie up the stairway,
    Looking back at those who slept.

Far below, the Lonnen windows,
  Sent one gleam forth lonelily,
As alone stood Davie, asking,—
  "Old man, gold man, where is he?"

VI

Many a morn, up from the Lonnen,
  Davie led his sheep to seek
For the door, but never found it,—
  Many a morn, week after week!

Many an eve, too, Davie waited,
  Year by year, till he was grown
Stalwart, and the Lonnen pastures,
  And the sheep there were his own.

And when he was grey, he told it,
  In his sounding mountain tongue
To his grandsons; and they told it
  To the harp when songs were sung.

So my grandsire told the story
  O'er to me: and long I sought
For King Arthur's Hall,—and seeking,
  Yet must wander, finding nought.

Yet we wait the day of waking!
  But the grave its counsel keeps:
Still within his Hall of Waiting,
  With his warriors Arthur sleeps.

The Riddles of Merlin

ALFRED NOYES

I

As I was walking
    Alone by the sea,
"What is that whisper?"
    Said Merlin to me.
"Only," I answered,
    "The sigh of the wave."
"Oh no," replied Merlin,
    "'Tis the grass on your grave."

As I lay dreaming
    In churchyard ground,
"Listen," said Merlin,
    "What is that sound?"
"The green grass is growing,"
    I answered; but he
Chuckled, *"Oh no!*
    'Tis the sound of the sea."

As I went homeward
    At dusk by the shore,
"What is that crimson?"
    Said Merlin once more.

"Only the sun," I said,
    Sinking to rest."
"*Sunset for East,*" he said,
    "*Sunrise for West.*"

II

Tell me, Merlin—it is I
    Who call thee, after a thousand Springs,—
Tell me by what wizardry
    The white foam wakes in whiter wings
Where surf and sea-gulls toss and cry
Like sister-flakes, as they mount and fly,
Flakes that the great sea flings on high,
    To kiss each other and die?

Tell me, Merlin, tell me why
    These delicate things that feast on flowers,
Red admiral, brown fritillary,
Sister the flowers, yet sail the sky,
Frail ships that cut their cables, yet still fly
    The colours we know them by?

Tell me, Merlin, tell me why,
The sea's chaotic colour grows
Into these rainbow fish whose Tyrian dye
In scales of gold and green reply
To blue-striped mackerel waves, to kelp-brown caves,
And deep-sea blooms of gold and green and rose?
Why colours that the sea at random throws
Were ordered into this living harmony,
This little world, no bigger than the hand,
Gliding over the raw tints whence it came,
This opal-bellied patch of sand,
That floats above the sand, or darts a flame
Through woods of crimson lake, and flowers without a name?
See all their tints around its body strewn
In planetary order. Sun, moon, star,
Are not more constant to their tune
Than those light scales of colour are;
Where each repeats the glory of its neighbour,
In the same pattern, with the same delight,

As if, without the artist's labour,
The palette of rich Chaos and old Night
Should spawn a myriad pictures, every line
True to the lost Designer's lost design.

Tell me, Merlin, for what eye
Gathers and grows this cosmic harmony?
Can sea-gulls feed, or fishes brood
On music fit for angels' food?
Did Nescience this delight create
To lure the conger to his mate?

If this be all that Science tells
The narrowest church may peal its bells,
And Merlin work new miracles;
While every dreamer, even as I,
May wonder on, until he die.

The Ballad of Sir Bors

JOHN MASEFIELD

Would I could win some quiet and rest, and a little ease,
In the cool grey hush of the dusk, in the dim green place of the trees,
Where the birds are singing, singing, singing, crying aloud
The song of the red, red rose that blossoms beyond the seas.

Would I could see it, the rose, when the light begins to fail,
And a lone white star in the West is glimmering on the mail;
The red, red passionate rose of the sacred blood of the Christ,
In the shining chalice of God, the cup of the Holy Grail.

The dusk comes gathering grey, and the darkness dims the West,
The oxen low to the byre, and all bells ring to rest;
But I ride over the moors, for the dusk still bides and waits,
That brims my soul with the glow of the rose that ends the Quest.

My horse is spavined and ribbed, and his bones come through his
                    hide,
My sword is rotten with rust, but I shake the reins and ride,
For the bright white birds of God that nest in the rose have called,
And never a township now is a town where I can bide.

It will happen at last, at dusk, as my horse limps down the fell,
A star will glow like a note God strikes on a silver bell,
And the bright white birds of God will carry my soul to Christ,
And the sight of the Rose, the Rose, will pay for the years of hell.

The Sailing of Hell Race

JOHN MASEFIELD

When Arthur came from warring, having won
A name in Britain and a peace secure,
He felt the red horizon cast her lure
To set him hunting of the setting sun,
To take a ship and sail
West, through the grassless pastures of the whale,
West, to the wilderness of nothing sure
But tests for manhood in the deeds undone.

So, in his ship, the *Britain*, with her crew,
He sailed at all adventure for the west:
The Severn glittered at the *Britain's* breast
As first her set sail wrinkled and then drew;
She dropped down with the tide,
Then, ere the changing, leaned upon her side
And smote the spindrift from the billow-crest
And strode from raddled waters into blue.

Westward she sailed, beyond familiar seas,
Beyond the landmarks and the ships of home,
To seas where never ship had broken foam,
Past all encounter with man's argosies.
The skies shone blue; the sun
Burned hotter at each marking of the run;

Out of the sea the summer islands clomb;
For many happy days they passt by these.

And there, between the surf-break and the snow
Bright on the pinnacles of crags, the land
Grew fruits of blessing ready to man's hand,
In deathless green an ever-golden glow:
And brown-skinned Indians came
Bringing them wreaths of flowers red as flame,
And plaques of gold-leaf beaten from the sand,
And begged them stay and wept to see them go.

But on they stood, until the sea-most peak
Was sunken as Polaris; till the day
No longer burned with summer but was gray
With iron snow-clouds over waters bleak.
A granite coast appeared,
Beaten by breakers; thither Arthur steered
Into the desolation of a bay
Where the sacred seahawks made the echoes shriek.

All still it was, save for the seabird's cry
And for the thunder when the glacier broke
Her seaward iceberg in a spray like smoke.
All iron-gray the land was, like the sky;
But on the beach were heapt
The harvest wreckage which the sea had reapt,
Mastings of pine, fir plankings, ribs of oak;
The bones of ships, suckt bloodless, flung up dry.

There lay the helm, the yard, the figurehead;
Nay, even a ship that had been painted green;
Nay, all the wreckings that had ever been
Seemed to have stored that dockyard of the dead.
And there a cairn of stones
Rose as a tomb above the broken bones,
And on the cairn a wooden box was seen
Which held a script in heart's blood. Thus it read:

"Beyond this harbour are the granite rocks
Which are the gates of Hell, where courage dies.
Brother, I call upon you to be wise;

174

Return, before the Key turns in the locks.
Return, and do not dare
Death beyond death, the Cities of Despair.
Return, to where the lark sings in the skies
And on the Down the shepherd keeps his flocks."

Then Arthur said: "We have adventured far,
And tread upon the bones of what has failed;
The door of hell is dark until assailed,
But every night of blackness hides a star.
Come: even if we end,
Courage will bring immortals to befriend,
By whom the precipices shall be scaled
And bolted doors forever flung ajar."

Then: "On," they cried, "good captain, let us go."
Onward they sailed, till sunset, when they neared
Two forms (or were they goddesses?) upreared
On crags with wrack above and foam below,
And from their granite lips
A laughter cackled like the death of ships.
Into the race between them Arthur steered,
Dreading lest they should murder him. But no . . .

Under those awful figures and between
He passed into a race of toppling seas
That broke and back-lasht at the granite knees
And scurft with salt the figures of each queen.
Those Furies' shadows fell
Dark on that channel of the way to Hell;
But Arthur's ship was built of sacred trees,
She stood, although the billows swept her clean.

On, through the turmoil of Hell Race, she swept,
The darkness, with her rooky wings of fear,
Covered the starless sunset's crimson smear;
Into the midnight of the sky there crept
Ahead, a glare, as though
The world were all afire smouldering slow.
Black towers on the glaring stood up sheer,
Lit windows in them sleepless vigil kept.

"Friends," Arthur called, "we have adventured well:
Ahead is all the glittering and pride
Of power of the devils satisfied,
The triple City where destructions dwell.
We will adventure on
And face their death together." Then anon
Furling their sail, they made the *Britain* glide
Safe to a pier below the citadel.

Hell Race, the channel of the ocean, thrust
Tongue-like throughout the City: her two banks
Glittered and glowed with lamplight, ranks on ranks,
Higher than March's madness flings the dust;
Within some topmost towers
Flames out of cressets tosst like scarlet flowers
Where some exultant devil uttered thanks
For will indulged in executed lust.

Where Arthur lay, the City's dreadful joy
Came to him from the streets, for devils dirled
Pan upon iron pan, for glee; or hurled
Crockery crash, to shatter and destroy;
With shrieking horns they sped;
Explosions burst; the fire rusht up red;
Devils of discord, dancing, shriekt and skirled,
Beating at doors their brothers to annoy.

The naked women devils lured their prey
To dens or corners where, alert, in wait,
Murder stood tiptoe by the side of Hate;
Vice stole in flusht, and, glutted, slunk out gray.
And all life went at speed,
Each for himself and let the other heed.
Life was a fury roaring like a spate,
To fall, and to keep falling, or to slay.

And, drunk with vanity, their poets barkt
The glory of great Hell, the joy, the pride,
Of being devil-born in Hell to bide,
As devil-spawn by other devils sharkt.
The shrieks of women sped:
"Bring us your brother's blood if you would wed;

Blood, that our day-old mantles may be dyed,
That Mammon may be snared and we be markt."

Within his vast and dirty temple sat
Mammon, the god and monarch of that Hell,
With sharp suspicion blinking through his fell,
Toad-throated, hooft, yet pinioned like a bat.
Athwart the temple's span,
Across the walls, a fire-writing ran,
Blazing the prices of the souls to sell
For all to read, the devils yelled thereat.

Multitudes trampled in the temple nave,
Fighting like wolves in quarrel for a bone;
The brazen forehead with the heart of stone,
Rat with hyena, murderer with knave;
Then from a gallery's height
The tiger devils cast into the fight
Spirits of men like dirty papers blown
That raved in dropping down as madmen rave.

And at the dropping down, the mob beneath
Leapt, like starved dogs at feeding time, to snatch
Each one a dropping from the tempter's catch;
With filthy claws they clutcht, or filthy teeth;
They tattered into rags
Those faded floatings that had once been flags;
Roaring they fought for them with kick and scratch:
They trod the quivering anguish underneath.

Yet more than Mammon, Lady Self was lord
Within that city of the lust for gold,
The jewelled thing, bespiced, bepainted, cold,
Whom Mammon purchased for his bed and board.
A varnisht shell was she,
Exquisite emptiness of vanity,
Unbodied and unminded and unsouled,
The mirror Self, whom all who saw adored.

She, and her mighty husband, and the game,
The roar, the glitter, and the zest of sin,
The prices offered by the Mammon Kin,

The gold all chinking when the moment came,
All these temptations drew
Some of the seamen of King Arthur's crew;
They stole ashore to Mammon, there to win
The worm's eternity in lasting flame.

So ere they all should leave him, and because
The Mammon people, hating foreign breeds,
Denounced him as perverter of their creeds,
One fit for burning by their holy laws,
King Arthur cut his ropes
And thrust to seaward, leaving to their hopes
His nine deserters, there to reap their seeds.
He sailed, with bubbling water at his hawse.

Soon in Hell Race a City loomed ahead,
Unlit, unlovely, under a dark star,
Girded by forts, each scaled with many a scar,
And topped by cloud where fire glittered red.
A roaring filled the air
With thunder and destruction and despair,
As engines flung the fireballs afar
And fireballs Hell's dissolution shed.

And here the Searcher-Devils, grim with steel,
Boarded them out at sea and led them in
Within defences jaw-tootht like a gin
That kept without the port the foeman's keel.
"We are at war," they said,
"The justest war that devils ever made,
Waged as a vengeance on our neighbour's sin,
To blast them into carrion till they kneel.

Why are we fighting? That's forgotten now;
No matter why; we are, let that suffice . . .
Yes, and those cannibals shall pay the price
Before we end, nor shall we scruple how.
And you . . . remember here . . .
We end all question-askers with the spear.
Wisdom is treason not committed twice;
We make it Death with branding on the brow."

Then did those devils prison ship and crew
Under grim guard, where, natheless, they could tell
The progress of that war of Nether Hell:
No peace nor any joy that City knew.
The trumpet called the hours,
Trampling of troops had trodden out the flowers,
The trees were rampikes blasted by the shell;
Babes starved and women maddened, and men slew.

Bright-eyed with sharp starvation and with hate,
Twitching their bitter mouths from nerves gone mad,
With homes long since destroyed, in rags half clad,
(No craft save war being practist in the state)
They lusted, like the stoat,
To meet their teeth within a foeman's throat,
Or, like the wolf, to see the corpses shrad
With even thirsty Earth blood-satiate.

All day, all night, the shrieking and the crash
Of battle shook the town, as hate grew worse.
The elements were peopled with the fierce;
Insanity was captain of the rash.
Then cries arose: "Kill, kill! . . .
Those foreigners are workers of our ill,
Spies to a man and bringers of the curse;
Brothers, come slay and burn them to an ash."

Then some of Arthur's crew were killed; and all
Would have been killed, had not the stunt and wizen
Starved doers of the slaughtering arisen
Against their Emperor and General,
And forkt to hideous ends
Those profiters by battle and their friends.
They hurried Arthur and his crew from prison,
Then made their town a pyre of funeral.

As Arthur sailed, he saw a lightning run
Along that City's ramparts with the thirst
Of fire licking up those bricks accurst;
Then thunder blasted from it and did stun;
Then its immense strength shot
Skywards in sooty fire withering hot,

179

Where trembling planks and figures were immerst
In glare that slowly darkened into dun.

Then as that fiery cloud came scattering down,
Blackness oppresst that City from the sight;
The foeman's fireballs came flaming bright
Into the crater that had been a town;
The devil's laughter cackled,
As fever laughs, like fetters being shackled.
King Arthur's ship drove on into the night;
A darkness toppt the battle like a crown.

Throughout the night they sailed, till morning showed
Mudbanks and salted marshes with sparse hair
Or stubble-stalks, of herbage blasted bare.
Then, the wind failing, up the creek they rowed:
Grey wisps of vapour curled
Above that marish of the underworld;
A droning and a whining filled the air
As though small devils in the mist abode.

Then, as the sullen sun rose, they beheld
Smoke rising up from pyres of the dead;
A granite statue sat there without head;
Beyond, arose a City gray with eld,
Nay, green with dropping mould;
That which had ruined her had made her old;
Cricketless were her ovens without bread;
A wind-stirred jangle from her ruins knelled.

There the pale fevers issued from the fen
To yellow human cheeks and cloud the mind;
There tetters dwelt, that writhel skin to rind,
Or rash the forehead with a savage pen;
Palsies, that twitch the lips
Or hamstring men with anguish in the hips;
These, too, were there, and sloughings that make blind,
And all the madnesses that unmake men.

They forct those Britons to that City's Queen,
A winged and browless fireceness on the throne,
Vert-adamantine in her hall of bone,

Fang'd, sting'd and mail'd in metal gleaming green:
No thought was in her eyes;
In where her victims' blood ran she was wise;
Her death-horns filled the palace with their drone,
Her dart of death out-quivered and was keen.

"Arthur," she said, "you stand in Nether Hell
Upon the sediments of greed and pride,
The rotted dust of nations that have died,
Amidst the foulness where destructions dwell.
Here the strong hand grows faint;
Here poison saps the manhood of the saint;
Here beauty sickens, joy goes hollow-eyed;
What else of glory is, my minions quell.

I slay the nations, one by one, that stood
Fierce-eyed in rapine and the fire of sacks,
Bright-eyed in ringing breaches in attacks,
Glad-eyed in glory from the beauty good.
I am the final Death,
Unseen and unsuspected as the breath,
Yet fatal as the crashing of the axe.
I am the ender of all hardihood.

You, too, with your adventurers, are sealed
As mine already: see, your cheeks are pale,
Your scarlet currents in their courses fail;
However lusty, they will swiftly yield,
And you will dwindle down
To beg among the ruins of the town."
Then Arthur felt a weariness assail,
Nor could he struggle, nor oppose a shield.

And there with yellowing skins his seamen drooped,
Their arms too sick to pull upon the oar,
Forgetting how the sail rose to the roar
Of singing, as the gleaming clipper swooped.
"We've done enough," they cried,
"Leave us alone." There seven of them died:
Their burials were the vulture and the boar,
Whose scavengings the shallow graveyards scooped.

There Arthur saw the chickweed green the deck,
The halliard rot, the anchor-cable rust;
Gone was all order, gone were hope and lust,
The sick mind stared contented with the wreck.
Then in a midnight drear,
As Arthur tossed, a brightness hurried near,
A sudden glory on his senses thrust,
A terror prickt the hair upon his neck.

There, in her blue robe, the immortal queen
His Helper, stood, the calm one, the benign,
Crowned with forget-me-not and columbine,
And speedwells blue and never-withering green;
No darkness nor disgrace
Could bide the beauty of that steadfast face.
"Arthur," she said, "from birth devoted mine,
Now flung as straw for devils' hands to glean,

Take power from my touch; arise, arise,
Cast loose these prison-tacklings and begone
Forth from these dens where sunlight never shone,
Nor flower throve, nor spirit saw the skies.
My power gives you strength."
Then spirit kindled Arthur, and at length
It stirred his seamen from the malison
Of that third monarchy of the unwise.

So, with that Helper at the helm, they stood
Clear from that City's mudbanks, and away,
To seas where flying fishes skimmed the spray
And every blowing air gave hardihood.
Homeward the *Britain* cleft,
Of all her company but seven left.
Soon the blue water dimmed into the gray
And bright Polaris rose as they pursued.

Till, as they sailed, they saw the seaweed float
And felt a changing tide. When darkness came
They watched for sight of land or beacon-flame,
Or any friendly sail or fisher's boat.
The steering lantern purred;
Then through the haze before the dawn they heard

Triumphantly a red cock call his dame,
Making a stallion challenge with full throat.

Then as the haze blew seaward, they beheld
The hills of home, the country green with corn,
Blossom upon the blackness of the thorn,
The hedgerows with the pretty primrose stelled;
They heard the blackbird sing,
They heard the chiff-chaff and the birds of spring,
The early cuckoo wandering forlorn
In woods whose millioned green was still unshelled.

Till noon they coasted, reach by lovely reach,
Beyond King Dyved's, past King Ryence' lands,
Past mountains casting shadows on the sands
And river water shining over beach.
Then lo, a brazen-poled
Bright chariot driving, all aflame with gold,
A chariot driven by princesses' hands:—
A princess drove to welcome them with speech.

Two stallions dragged that chariot like a spate,
White stallions lovely as the leaping pard,
Pickt stallions of King Ocvran's bodyguard,
Urged by a green-clad woman, who, elate,
With streaming red-gold hair
And eyes like stars illumined and aware,
Croucht watchful, to the grippt reins straining hard,
As one who lifts a winner up the Straight.

There did the giant Ocvran leave the car
And welcome Arthur to the shining shore;
There Arthur furled the sail and tosst the oar
And dragged the ship where billows could not mar.
The red-gold lady dear
Was Ocvran's daughter, princess Gwenivere,
Whom Arthur worshippt then and evermore,
As in the night the traveller the star.

The Fight at Camlan

JOHN MASEFIELD

Soon the two armies were in touch, and soon
Camped, face to face, upon the windy, high,
Thyme-scented barren where the wild bees croon.
Southward and westward was the wrinkled sea
Where Kolgrim's ships lay black.
Now must they treat or battle, since to fly
No longer was a solace that might be.
The season neared midsummer and full moon;
His impulse urged King Arthur to attack.

Then thought, and pity of his son, and hate
Of shedding subjects' blood, made him resolve
To make an offer ere he shut the gate
On every end save battle to the death.
He sent Sir Bedwyr forth
To Modred, to discover what might solve
Their quarrel without quell of living breath.
Modred replied, "Let Arthur abdicate
This southern half the realm, and keep the north.

If he contemn this, say I shall not treat
Or commune, save as King with equal King.
Here is my army, yonder is my fleet;
Cornwall is mine, I can maintain it mine;
I am prepared to fight.

But if my modest terms can end the thing,
And all this southern realm be paid as fine,
We'll choose ambassadors and let them meet
There on that barrow, in the armies' sight."

So, to be brief, both men empowered peers
To make discussion of the terms of peace.
The barrow, of the King of ancient years,
Topped by a thorn tree, was the meeting-place.
There six from either side
Went, while the heralds bade all warfare cease,
No sword to leave its sheath, no bow its case,
The horsemen to dismount and pile their spears
And all keep camp till all were ratified.

The twelve Knights went unarmed up to the howe
Between the armies, to debate together;
They hung a white flag on the hawthorn bough
And started talking, while the troops in camp
Disarmed, and cleaned their gear,
Or stretcht to sleep upon the matted heather;
Or with their comrades sat upon the ramp,
Sure that the quarrel would be settled now;
Each hailed the other side with mock or cheer.

To eastwards of the campments was a mound
Or rise of earth from some old fallen fence
Of ancient village, camp, or cattle-pound;
Three rebels flung themselves upon its top
With Kolgrim, Modred's friend,
Who mocked and said: "There talkers have no sense."
Then, hours later, "Let this folly stop . . .
There goes King Arthur; let us shoot the hound,
Crown Modred King and bring it to an end."

Prone in the heath the four uncased their bows,
They strung them, on each other's bodies stayed;
Then from their quivers each an arrow chose.
Arthur was sitting with Sir Kai in talk,
Making an easy mark.
Back to the ears the arrow-feathers laid,
Then, as the hornet leaves his hollow balk

Humming with evil, so the arrows rose,
Shot from the string to strike the victim stark.

Sweeping the space those shafted barbings sped,
Like golden birds athwart the light they thrilled:
One pierced Kai's bitter heart and struck him dead,
Another cut King Arthur's purple cloak;
Another, by his hand
Stuck quivering in the table till it stilled;
The last struck sideways on a shield and broke
Below the barbs, its venomed fang unfed.
"Quick, mates, again," said Kolgrim to his band.

But as they drew, King Arthur's herald cried:
"Treason! The men are shooting! Quick. Beware."
Then, leaping up, he thrust the King aside
And shouted "Treason! Fall in, Arthur's men."
And as he snatcht a shield
The second flighting shafted through the air
That struck him through and put him out of ken
Of wife and home by pleasant Severnside.
Then trumpets blew and tumult filled the field.

The counsellors upon the barrow fled,
Each to his camp, not knowing what betid;
King Arthur's men into their cohorts sped,
Swearing, "We'll pay those breakers of the truce,
Oath-breaking, treacherous swine."
The black-backt adder to her cavern glid;
Now Modred's archers let their arrows loose,
And many a grey goose-feather was made red,
Ere either army formed a battle-line.

Now the two armies stood as walls of spears
Beneath the ever-passing shriek and strike
Of arrows wavering in their careers.
Modred came swooping as a falcon swoops,
On horseback down his ranks,
Crying: "Behold your sparrows: play the shrike."
The trumpets blared among the rebel troops,
King Arthur galloped to his front with cheers;
He cried: "If fronts are stubborn, try the flanks."

Then as in thunderstorms the wind-vanes shift
On towers, against blackness, with a gleam,
So did his riders' spearheads glitter swift
Above the blowing pennons as they drooped
As one, down to the charge.
Then did the stallions bare their gums and scream,
The bright bits tightened as the riders stooped;
Then like a lightning from a thunder rift
The squadrons clashed together, lance on targe.

For hours they fought: then Arthur, beaten back
From camp and downland to the planted fields,
Steadied his line against the spent attack;
The armies stopped the battle to re-form.
Thirst-broken soldiers quencht
Their thirsts, and dropped their lances and their shields.
There fell the central quiet of the storm,
And spearmen strayed, to rob the haversack
Of friend or rebel prone with muscles clencht.

And while the battle stayed, Sir Modred found
No plenishment of spears and arrows spent
Save what the fight had scattered on the ground;
But Arthur formed upon his waggon-train
That brought him up new gear.
Archers and lancers took fresh armament
And faced to front, resolved to fight again.
Then Arthur heard a distant trumpet sound,
And, looking, saw strange horsemen in his rear.

And as he moved some lancers as a guard,
Thinking that Modred threatened his retreat,
He saw the banner of the golden pard;
Sir Lancelot was riding in to aid
With squadrons of picked horse.
Lancelot said, "Though banisht, let us meet
To put an ending to this renegade:
See, his line wavers: let us push him hard;
He'll break as sure as prickles grow on gorse."

It was now drawing to the summer dusk,
The sun, low fallen, reddened on the sea,
Dog-rose and honeysuckle shed their musk,

Lancelot's troops moved up upon the left,
King Arthur took the right.
It was the hour of the homing bee.
Then up the bright blades glittered on the heft,
The dragon of red battle bared her tusk,
King Arthur's tattering trumpets sounded Fight.

At a slow trot they started, keeping touch,
Elbow to elbow, upon rested horses
That strove to get the bits within their clutch;
Troop after troop the hoof-beat thunder grew;
Slowly the trot increast
As Lammas torrents grow in watercourses;
Then, utterly triumphant trumpets blew
And as a mounting wave, already much,
Mounts mighty ere it smashes into yeast,

So mounted there that billow ere it broke;
Then, at its breaking, Modred, branch and root,
Horseman and footman, scattered like blown smoke
From burning leaves on an October blast.
Then mile on moorland mile,
King Arthur's army had them in pursuit;
Arthur with six Knights followed Modred fast,
Till on a beach he turned to strike a stroke.
Ten, against Arthur's seven, seemed worth while.

Launcelot

C. S. LEWIS

When the year dies in preparation for the birth
Of other seasons, not the same, on the same earth,
Then saving and calamity together make
The Advent gospel, telling how the heart will break
With dread, and stars, unleaving from the rivelled sky,
Scatter on the wind of man's Redemption drawing nigh,
Man's doom and his Redeeming and the wreck of man.
     Therefore it was in Advent that the Quest began;
In wail of wind the flower of the Britons all
Went out, and desolation was in Arthur's hall,
And stillness in the City of Legions. Then the Queen
Expected their returning when the woods were green;
But leaves grew large, and heaviness of August lay
Upon the woods. Then Guinever began to say,
"Autumn will bring them home again." But autumn passed
With all its brown solemnities, and weathers fast
Came driving down the valley of the Usk with hail
At Advent, and the hearts of men began to fail,
And Lucan said, "If summer brings the heathen men
From over-seas, or trouble of Picts beyond the wall,
Britain will break. The Sangrail has betrayed us all,
According to the prophecy Pelles the king
Once made, that at the moving of this holy thing

Our strength would fail." But Arthur, who was daily less
Of speech, through all these winter days, gave answer, "Yes.
I know it, and I knew it when they rode away."

The year turned round and bettered, and the coloured May
Crept up the valley of the Usk, and softening green
Rounded the form of forests. But this year the Queen
Said nothing of the knight's return; and it became
A custom in that empty court never to name
The fear all felt, and not to listen any more
For rumours, nor to watch the roads, nor pace the shore;
Patience, most like conspiracy, had hushed them all,
Women, old men, and boys.
                                        That year was heavy fall
Of snows. And when amid its silence Gawain, first
Defeat from the long Quest, came riding home, their thirst
For news he could not or he would not satisfy.
He was unlike the Gawain they had known, with eye
Unfrank, and voice ambiguous, and his answers short.
Gulfs of unknowing lay between him and the court,
Unbreakable misunderstandings. To the King,
He answered, No; he had not seen the holy thing.
And, No; he had heard no news of Launcelot and the rest,
But, for his own part, he was finished with the Quest
And now asked leave to journey North and see his own
Estates. And this was granted, and he went, alone,
Leaving a hollow-heartedness in every man
And, in the Queen, new fear. Then, with the spring, began
The home-coming of heroes from the Quest, by two's
And three's, unlike their expectations, without news,
A dim disquiet of defeated men, and all
Like Gawain, changed irrelevant in Arthur's hall,
Strange to their wives, unwelcome to the stripling boys.
Ladies of Britain mourned the losing of their joys:
"What have they eaten, or in what forgetful land
Were their adventures? Now they do not understand
Our speech. They talk to one another in a tongue
We do not know. Strange sorrows and new jests, among
Themselves, they have. The Sangrail has betrayed us all."
So leaf by leaf the old fellowship of Arthur's hall
Felt Autumn's advent. New divisions came, and new
Allyings: till, of all the Table Round, those few
Alone who had not ridden on the dangerous Quest

Now bore the name of courteous and were loved the best
Mordred, or Kai, or Calburn, or Agravaine.
    And the Queen understood it all. And the drab pain,
Now for two years familiar in her wearied side,
Stirred like a babe within her. Every nerve woke wide
To torture, with low-moaning pity of self, with tears
At dawn, with midnight jealousies; and dancing fears
Touched with their stabs and quavers and low lingerings
Her soul, as a musician plays the trembling strings;
And loud winds from the cruel countries of despair
Came roaring through her, breaking down, and laying bare,
Till naked to the changing of the world she stood
At Advent. And no tidings now could do her good
Forever; the heart failing in her breast for fear
—Of Launcelot dead—of Launcelot daily drawing near
And bringing her the sentence that she knew not of,
The doom, or the redeeming, or the change of love.
    Yet, like a thief surprising her, the moment came
At last, of his returning. The tormented flame
Leaned from the candle guttering in the noisy gloom
Of wind and rain, where Guinever amid her room
Stood with scared eyes at midnight on the windy floor,
Thinking, forever thinking. From beyond her door
Came foot of sentry and change of countersign; and then
A murmur of their rough-mouthed talk between the men
She heard, that on one moment like an arrow flew
Into the deepest crimson of her heart and slew
Hopes and half-doubts and self-deceits; and told the Queen
That Launcelot already had returned—had been
Three days now in the city and sent to her no word.
    The rain was gone, the sky was pale, when next she stirred,
Having no memory of the passing of that night,
And in her cold, small fingers took her pen to write,
And wrote five words, and sent it by her aged nurse.
    Then the cold hours began their march again, not worse,
Not better, never-ending. And that night he came,
Out of the doorway's curtained darkness to the flame
Of candlelight and firelight. And the curtains fell
Behind him, and they stood alone, with all to tell,
Not like that Launcelot tangled in the boughs of May
Long since, nor like the Guinever he kissed that day,
But he was pale, with pity in his face writ wide,

191

And she a haggard woman, holding to her side
A pale hand pressed, asking "What is it?" Slowly then
He came to her and took her by the hand, as men
Take tenderly a daughter's or a mother's hand
To whom they bring bad news she will not understand.
So Launcelot led the Queen and made her sit: and all
This time he saw her shoulders move and her tears fall,
And he himself wept not, but sighed. Then, like a man
Who ponders, in the fire he gazed; and so began
Presently, looking always in the fire, the tale
Of his adventures seeking for the Holy Grail.

. . . How Launcelot and his shining horse had gone together
So far that at the last they came to springy weather;
The sharpened buds like lances were on every tree,
The little hills went past him like the waves of the sea,
The white, new castles, blazing on the distant fields
Were clearer than the painting upon new-made shields.
Under the high forests many days he rode, and all
The birds made shrill with marriage songs their shadowy hall
Far overhead. But afterwards the sun withdrew,
And into barren countries, having all gone through
The fair woods and the fortunate, he came at last.
He sees about him noble beeches overcast.
And aged oaks revealing to the rainless sky
Shagg'd nakedness of roots uptorn. He passes by
Forsaken wells and sees the buckets red with rust
Upon the chains. Dry watercourses filled with dust
He crosses over; and villages on every side
Ruined he sees, and jaws of houses gaping wide,
And abbeys showing ruinously the peeling gold
In roofless choirs and, underneath, the churchyard mould
Cracking and far subsiding into dusty caves
That let the pale light in upon the ancient graves.
All day he journeys in a land of ruin and bones
And rags; and takes his rest at night among the stones
And broken things; till, after many leagues he found
A little stone-built hermitage in barren ground.
And at his door the hermit stands, so pined and thin
The bone-face is scarce hidden by the face of skin.
"Now fair, sweet friend," says Launcelot, "Tell me, I pray
How all this countryside has fallen into decay?"

The good man does not look on Launcelot at all,
But presently his loud, high voice comes like the call
Of a sad horn that blows to prayer in Pagan lands:
"This is the daughter of Babylon who gnaws her hands
For thirst and hunger. Nine broad realms in this distress
Are lying for the sake of one man's heedlessness
Who came to the King Fisherman, who saw the Spear
That burns with blood, who saw the Sangrail drawing near,
Yet would not ask for whom it served. Until there come
The Good Knight who will kneel and see, yet not be dumb,
But ask, the Wasted Country shall be still accursed
And the spell upon the Fisher King be unreversed,
Who now lies sick and languishing and near to death."
So far the hermit's voice pealed on: and then his breath
Rattled within the dry pass of his throat: his head
Dropped sideways, and the slender trunk stands upright, dead,
And tall against the lintel of the narrow door.
And Launcelot alighted there, and in the floor
Of that low house scraped in the dust a shallow grave
And laid the good man in it, praying God to save
His soul; and for himself such grace as may prevail
To come to the King Fisherman and find the Grail.
      Then up he climbed and rode again, and from his breath
The dust was cleared, and from his mind the thought of death,
And in the country of ruin and rags he came so far
That over the grey moorland, like a shining star,
He sees a valley, emerald with grass, and gleam
Of water, under branches, from a winding stream,
A respite in the wilderness, a pleasant place,
Struck with the sun. His charger sniffs and mends his pace,
And down they go, by labyrinthine paths, until
They reach the warm green country, sheltered by the hill.
Jargon of birds angelical warbles above,
And Launcelot throws his mail'd hood back, and liquid love
Wells in his heart. He looks all round the quartered sky
And wonders in what region Camelot may lie
Singing "The breezes here have passed my lady's mouth
And stol'n a paradisal fragrance of the South."
Singing "All gentle hearts should worship her and sing
The praises of her pity and Fair-Welcoming."
So carolling he trotted under lights and shadows
Of trembling woods, by waterfalls and sunny meadows,

And still he wandered, following where the water flows
To where, at the blue water's edge, a shrine arose
On marble pillars slender, with no wall between;
Through every arch the blueness of the sky was seen.
And underneath the fragile dome three narrow beds
Of lilies raised in windless air their silver heads.
Beside them sat a damosel, all clothed in bright,
Pale, airy clothes, and all her countenance filled with light,
And parted lips as though she had just ceased to sing.
Launcelot thinks he never has seen a fairer thing,
And checks his horse, saluting her. "God send you bliss.
Beautiful one! I pray you tell, what place is this?"
The damsel said, "The corseints in the praise of whom
This tomb is built are yet far distant from the tomb.
Here, when the Wasted Country is no longer dry,
The three best knights of Christendom shall come to lie."
Launcelot remembers often to have heard them named
And guesses who is one of them: so half ashamed,
He asks her, with his eyes cast down, "What knights are these?"
And waits; and then lifts up his eyes again, and sees
No lady there: an empty shrine, and on the grass
No print of foot, where in grey dew the blackbirds pass.
Then came on high a disembodied voice and gave
Solitude tongue. "A grave for Bors," it cried, "A grave
For Percivale, a grave for Galahad: but not
For the Knight recreant of the Lake, for Launcelot!"
Then came clear laughter jingling in the air like bells
On horses' manes, thin merriment of that which dwells
In light and height, unaging and beyond the sense
Of guilt and grieving, merciless with innocence.
    And presently he catches up his horse's head
And rides again, still following where the water led.
The sun rose high: the shadow of the horse and man
Came from behind to underneath them and began
To lengthen out in front of them. The river flowed
Wider and always slower and the valley road
Was soft with mud, and winding, like a worm, between
Wide swamps and warm entanglement of puddles green;
And multitude of buzzing and of stinging flies
Came round his sweated forehead and his horse's eyes;
The black turf squeaked and trembled at the iron hoofs.

Then Launcelot looks and sees a huddle of flat roofs
Upon a little island in the steaming land,
A low, red, Roman manor-house; and close at hand
A lady, riding softly on a mule, who came
Towards him, and saluted him, and told her name,
The Queen of Castle Mortal; but to Launcelot
Somewhat like Morgan the enchantress, and somewhat
Like Guinever, her countenance and talking seemed;
And golden, like a dragon's back, her clothing gleamed
And courteously she prayed him, "Since the night is near
Turn now and take your lodging in my manor here."
"Lady, may God repay you," says the Knight, and so
Over the bridge, together, to the gate they go
And enter in. Young servitors enough he found
That kneeled before the lady, and came pressing round;
One took his helm, another took his spear, a third
Led off his horse; and chamberlains and grooms were stirred
To kindle fires and set him at the chimney side,
And clothe him in a long-sleeved mantle, soft and wide.
They go to dine. And presently her people all
Were gone away, he saw not where; and in the hall
He and the Lady sat alone. And it was night;
More than a hundred candles burned both still and bright.
His hostess makes great joy for him, and many a cup
Of strong wine, red as blood, she drinks; then rises up
And prays him bear her company and look on all
The marvels of her manor house. So out of hall,
Laughing, she leads him to the chapel-door: and when
That door was opened, fragrance such as dying men
Imagine in immortal countries, blown about
Heaven's meadows from the tree of life, came floating out.
No man was in the chapel, but he sees a light
There too of many hundred candles burning bright.
She led him in, and up into the choir, and there
He saw three coffins all of new cut stone, and fair
With flowers and knots, and full of spices to the brim
And from them came the odour that by now makes dim
His sense with deathly sweetness. But the heads of all
Those coffins passed beneath three arches in the wall.
On these he gazes; then on her. The sweet smell curls
About their brains. Her body is shaking like a girl's

Who loves too young; she has a wide and swimming eye;
She whispers him, "The three best knights of earth shall lie
Here in my house"; and yet again, "Lo, I have said,
The three best knights." But Launcelot holds down his head,
And will not speak. "What knights are these?" she said. And "Nay."
He answered, "If you name them not, I dare not say."
She laughed aloud—"A coffin for Sir Lamorake,
For Tristram; in the third lies Launcelot du Lake."
He crossed himself and questioned her when these should die.
She answered, "They shall all be living when they lie
Within these beds; and then—behold what will be done
To all, or even to two of them, or even to one,
Had I such grace." She lifts her hand and turns a pin
Set on the wall. A bright steel blade drops down within
The arches, on the coffin-necks, so razor-keen
That scarce a movement of the spicey dust was seen
Where the edge sank. "Ai! God forbid that you should be
The murderer of good knights," said Launcelot. And she
Said, "But for the endless love of them I mean to make
Their sweetness mine beyond recovery and to take
That joy away from Morgan and from Guinever
And Nimue and Isoud and Elaine, and here
Keep those bright heads and comb their hair and make them lie
Between my breasts and worship them until I die."

The Crowning of Arthur

CHARLES WILLIAMS

The king stood crowned; around in the gate,
midnight striking, torches and fires
massing the colour, casting the metal,
furnace of jubilee, through time and town,
Logres heraldically flaunted the king's state.

The lords sheathed their swords; they camped
by Camelot's wall; thick-tossed torches,
tall candles flared, opened, deployed;
between them rose the beasts of the banners;
flaring over all the king's dragon ramped.

Wars were at end; the king's friend stood
at the king's side; Lancelot's lion
had roared in the pattern the king's mind cherished,
in charges completing the strategy of Arthur;
the king's brain working in Lancelot's blood.

Presaging intelligence of time climbed,
Merlin climbed, through the dome of Stephen,
over chimneys and churches; from the point of Camelot
he looked through the depth to the dome of Sophia;
the kingdom and the power and the glory chimed.

He turned where the fires, amid burning mail,
poured, tributaried by torches and candles,
to a point in a massive of colour, one
aureole flame; the first shield's deep azure,
sidereally pointed, the lord Percivale.

Driving back that azure a sea rose black;
on a fess of argent rode a red moon.
The Queen Morgause leaned from a casement;
her forehead's moon swallowed the fires,
it was crimson on the bright-banded sable of Lamorack.

The tincture changed; ranged the craft
of the king's new champion in a crimson field;
mockery in mockery, a dolphin naiant;
a silver fish under bloody waters,
conquered or conquering, Dinadan laughed.

A pelican in golden piety struck well
the triple bloody drops from its wound;
in strong nurture of instinct, it smote
for its young its breast; the shield of Bors
bore its rich fervours, to itself most fell.

Shouldering shapes through the skies rise and run,
through town and time; Merlin beheld
the beasts of Broceliande, the fish of Nimue,
hierarchic, republican, the glory of Logres,
patterns of the Logos in the depth of the sun.

Taliessin in the crowd beheld the compelled brutes,
wildness formalized, images of mathematics,
star and moon, dolphin and pelican,
lion and leopard, changing their measure.
Over the mob's noise rose gushing the sound of the flutes.

Gawaine's thistle, Bedivere's rose, drew near:
flutes infiltrating the light of candles.
Through the magical sound of the fire-strewn air,
spirit, burning to sweetness of body,
exposed in the midst of its bloom the young queen Guinevere.

Lancelot moved to descend; the king's friend kneeled,
the king's organic motion, the king's mind's blood,
the lion in the blood roaring through the mouth of creation
as the lions roar that stand in the Byzantine glory.
Guinevere's chalice flew red on an argent field.

So, in Lancelot's hand, she came through the glow,
into the king's mind, who stood to look on his city:
the king made for the kingdom, or the kingdom made for the king?
Thwart drove his current against the current of Merlin:
in beleaguered Sophia they sang of the dolorous blow.

Doom in shocks sprinkled the burning gloom,
molten metals and kindling colours pouring
into the pyre; at the zenith lion and dragon
rose, clawed, twisted, screamed;
Taliessin beheld a god lie in his tomb.

At the door of the gloom sparks die and revive;
the spark of Logres fades, glows, fades.
It is the first watch; the Pope says Matins in Lateran;
the hollow call is beaten on the board in Sophia;
the ledge of souls shudders, whether they die or live.

The Departure of Merlin

CHARLES WILLIAMS

The Pope stands at Lateran's stone; man's
heart throbs from his vicarious hands.
The themes are pointed with a new device of brightness,
Trebizond with sun, Archangel with ice.

The blessing of Byzantium befriends the world's ends;
the great heretical doctors, Moslem and Manichaean,
fly; in time-spanned Camelot the Table changes;
the method of phenomena is indrawn to Broceliande.

Merlin bore Lancelot's child to a moon of white nuns,
a knot of nurture in a convent of spirits and suns;
thence in the perilous throne is the Child's moon risen,
pillars of palace and prison changed to the web of a wood.

The joyous moon waxes in the chair;
the blessed young sorcerer, a boy and less than a boy,
rose and ran, turning on the roads; he span
into the heart's simultaneity of repose.

Joseph of Nazareth, Joseph of Arimathea,
came dancing through the coeval-rooted world's idea.
They saw Merlin descending: they met him in the wood,
foster-fathers of beatitude to the foster-father of Galahad;

twin suns of womb and tomb; there no strife
is except growth from the roots, nor reaction but repose;
vigours of joy drive up; rich-ringed moments
thick in their trunks thrive, young-leaved their voices.

Moons and suns that rose in rites and runes
are come away from sequence, from rules of magic;
here all is cause and all effect; the laws
of Merlin's boyhood are unknown in Nimue's wood.

I saw from the deck of a galley becalmed in the seas
Merlin among the trees; the headless form faded;
throngs of trunks covered the volcanic waters;
only the flat djongs float into alien P'o-Lu.

The sailors stared at the thick wood; one,
ghastly and gaping, despaired of joy; he yelled
for horror and leapt from the deck to the phosphorescence,
to the wreck of wisdom, the drowned last of love.

The purple sail moved in the wind of Broceliande;
the sailors sprang to the oars; the sea-call sang
bidding tack—near and far infinite and equal—
on the visionary ocean track to the port of Byzantium.

More than the fable of Dryads is troth to the Table
in the growth of hazel and elm, oak and bamboo;
voice of all moments covers who hears as he goes
rich-ringed, young-leaved, monstrous trunks rejoice.

Time's president and precedent, grace ungrieved,
floating through gold-leaved lime or banked behind beech
to opaque green, through each membraned and tissued experience
smites in simultaneity to times variously veined.

She who is Nimue, lady of lakes and seas,
articulation of limbs, accumulation of distance,
brings all natural becoming to her shape of immortal being,
as to a flash of seeing the women in the world's base.

Well has Merlin spoken the last spell,
worked the last image, gone to his own:
the moon waxes and wanes in the perilous chair,
where time's foster-child sits, Lancelot's son.

Merlin

EDWIN MUIR

O Merlin in your crystal cave
Deep in the diamond of the day,
Will there ever be a singer
Whose music will smooth away
The furrow drawn by Adam's finger
Across the meadow and the wave?
Or a runner who'll outrun
Man's long shadow driving on,
Break through the gate of memory
And hang the apple on the tree?
Will your magic ever show
The sleeping bride shut in her bower,
The day wreathed in its mound of snow
And Time locked in his tower?

Merlin in the Cave:
He Speculates Without a Book

THOM GUNN

This was the end and yet, another start:
Held by the arms of lust from lust I pace
About the dim fulfilment of my art,
Impatient in the flesh I eye a space
Where, warlock, once I might have left this place,
A form of life my tool, creeping across
The shelving rock as rank convolvulus.

The Rock. The space, too narrow for a hand.
Pressing my head between two slopes of stone
I peer at what I do not understand,
The movement: clouds, and separate rooks blown
Back on their flight. Where do they fly, alone?
I lost their instinct. It was late. To me
The bird is only meat for augury.

And here the mauve convolvulus falls in,
Its narrow stalk as fat and rich in sap
As I was rich in lusting to begin
A life I could have had and finished up
Years, years before. With aphrodisiac
I brought back vigour; oiled and curled my hair;
Reduced my huge obesity, to wear

MERLIN AND VIVIEN

From *The Book of Romance,*
by Andrew Lang, illustrated by Henry Ford.
London: Longmans, Green and Co., 1902.

The green as tightly girdled at my waist
As any boy who leapt about the court;
And with an unguent I made my chest
Fit for the iron plate. I still held short
Of wrestling as the boys did: from their sport
They slid back panting on the tiles to look
At one distinguished now by scent, not book.

Love was a test: I was all-powerful,
So failed, because I let no fault intrude.
A philosophic appetite. By rule
I calculated each fond attitude
But those that self-distrust makes more than mood,
The quick illogical motions, negative
But evidence that lovers move and live.

I watch the flux I never guessed: the grass;
The watchful animal that gnaws a root,
Knowing possession means the risk of loss;
Ripeness that rests an hour in the fruit.
Yet locked here with the very absolute
I challenged, I must try to break the hold:
This cave is empty, and is very cold.

I must grow back through knowledge, passing it
Like casual landmarks in a well-known land,
Great mausoleums over ancient wit,
Doors that would swing at my complacent hand;
And come at last, being glad to understand
The touched, the seen, and only those, to where
I find the earth is suddenly black and near.

And having reached the point where there remain
No knacks or habits, and these empty cells
Are matched by a great emptiness in my brain:
Unhampered by remembered syllables,
The youth I wasted at precocious spells
Will grow upon me, and my wants agree
In the sweet promiscuity of the bee.

And yet, the danger. All within my mind
Hovers complete, and if it never grows

It never rots; for what I leave behind
Contains no fight within itself: the rose
Is full and drops no petal, emblems doze
Perfect and quiet as if engraved in books,
Not like the fighting boys and wind-torn rooks.

The bee's world and the rook's world are the same:
Where clouds do, or do not, let through the light;
Too mixed, unsimple, for a simple blame;
Belligerent: but no one starts the fight,
And nothing ends it but a storm or night.
Alchemists, only, boil away the pain,
And pick out value as one small dry grain.

And turned upon the flooding relative,
What could I do but start the quest once more
Towards the terrible cave in which I live,
The absolute prison where chance thrust me before
I built it round me on my study floor;
What could I do but seek the synthesis
As each man does, of what his nature is?

Knowing the end to movement, I will shrink
From movement not for its own wilful sake.
—How can a man live, and not act or think
Without an end? But I must act, and make
The meaning in each movement that I take.
Rook, bee, you are the whole and not a part.
This is an end, and yet another start.

The Vision of Sir Launfal

JAMES RUSSELL LOWELL

Author's Note: According to the mythology of the Romancers, the San Greal, or Holy Grail, was the cup out of which Jesus partook of the last supper with his disciples. It was brought into England by Joseph of Arimathea, and remained there, an object of pilgrimage and adoration, for many years in the keeping of his lineal descendants. It was incumbent upon those who had charge of it to be chaste in thought, word, and deed; but one of the keepers having broken this condition, the Holy Grail disappeared. From that time it was a favorite enterprise of the knights of Arthur's court to go in search of it. Sir Galahad was at last successful in finding it, as may be read in the seventeenth book of the Romance of King Arthur. Tennyson has made Sir Galahad the subject of one of the most exquisite of his poems.

The plot (if I may give that name to any thing so slight) of the following poem is my own, and, to serve its purposes, I have enlarged the circle of competition in search of the miraculous cup in such a mannner as to include, not only other persons than the heroes of the Round Table, but also a period of time subsequent to the date of King Arthur's reign.

Prelude to Part First

Over his keys the musing organist,
    Beginning doubtfully and far away,

From *The Vision of Sir Launfal,*
by James Russell Lowell, illustrated by Sol Eytinge, Jr.
Boston: Ticknor & Fields, 1867.

First lets his fingers wander as they list,
    And builds a bridge from Dreamland for his lay:
Then, as the touch of his loved instrument
    Gives hopes and fervor, nearer draws his theme,
First guessed by faint auroral flushes sent
    Along the wavering vista of his dream.

    Not only around our infancy
      Doth heaven with all its splendors lie;
    Daily, with souls that cringe and plot,
      We Sinais climb and know it not;
Over our manhood bend the skies;
    Against our fallen and traitor lives
The great winds utter prophecies;
    With our faint hearts the mountain strives;
Its arms outstretched, the druid wood
    Waits with its benedicite;
And to our age's drowsy blood
    Still shouts the inspiring sea.

Earth gets its price for what Earth gives us;
    The beggar is taxed for a corner to die in,
The priest hath his fee who comes and shrives us,
    We bargain for the graves we lie in;
At the Devil's booth are all things sold
Each ounce of dross costs its ounce of gold;
    For a cap and bells our lives we pay,
Bubbles we earn with a whole soul's tasking:
    'T is heaven alone that is given away,
'T is only God may be had for the asking;
There is no price set on the lavish summer,
And June may be had by the poorest comer.

And what is so rare as a day in June?
    Then, if ever, come perfect days;
Then Heaven tries the earth if it be in tune,
    And over it softly her warm ear lays:
Whether we look, or whether we listen,
We hear life murmur, or see it glisten;
Every clod feels a stir of might,
    An instinct within it that reaches and towers,
And, grasping blindly above it for light,
    Climbs to a soul in grass and flowers;

The flush of life may well be seen
  Thrilling back over hills and valleys;
The cowslip startles in meadows green,
  The buttercup catches the sun in its chalice,
And there's never a leaf or a blade too mean
  To be some happy creature's palace;
The little bird sits at his door in the sun,
  Atilt like a blossom among the leaves,
And lets his illumined being o'errun
  With the deluge of summer it receives;
His mate feels the eggs beneath her wings,
And the heart in her dumb breast flutters and sings;
He sings to the wide world, and she to her nest,—
In the nice ear of Nature which song is the best?

Now is the high-tide of the year,
  And whatever of life hath ebbed away
Comes flooding back, with a ripply cheer,
  Into every bare inlet and creek and bay;
Now the heart is so full that a drop overfills it,
We are happy now because God so wills it;
No matter how barren the past may have been,
'T is enough for us now that the leaves are green;
We sit in the warm shade and feel right well
How the sap creeps up and the blossoms swell;
We may shut our eyes, but we cannot help knowing
That skies are clear and grass is growing;
The breeze comes whispering in our ear,
That dandelions are blossoming near,
  That maize has sprouted, that streams are flowing,
That the river is bluer than the sky,
That the robin is plastering his house hard by;
And if the breeze kept the good news back,
For other couriers we should not lack;
  We could guess it all by yon heifer's lowing,—
And hark! how clear bold chanticleer,
Warmed with the new wine of the year,
  Tells all in his lusty crowing!

Joy comes, grief goes, we know not how;
Every thing is happy now,
  Every thing is upward striving;

'T is as easy now for the heart to be true
As for grass to be green or skies to be blue,—
　　　'T is the natural way of living:
Who knows whither the clouds have fled?
　　　In the unscarred heaven they leave no wake;
And the eyes forget the tears they have shed,
　　　The heart forgets its sorrow and ache;
The soul partakes the season's youth,
　　　And the sulphurous rifts of passion and woe
Lie deep 'neath a silence pure and smooth,
　　　Like burnt-out craters healed with snow.
What wonder if Sir Launfal now
Remembered the keeping of his vow?

Part First

I

"My golden spurs now bring to me,
　　　And bring to me my richest mail,
For to-morrow I go over land and sea
　　　In search of the Holy Grail;
Shall never a bed for me be spread,
Nor shall a pillow be under my head,
Till I begin my vow to keep;
Here on the rushes will I sleep,
And perchance there may come a vision true
Ere day create the world anew."
　　　Slowly Sir Launfal's eyes grew dim,
　　　Slumber fell like a cloud on him,
And into his soul the vision flew.

II

The crows flapped over by twos and threes,
In the pool drowsed the cattle up to their knees,
　　　The little birds sang as if it were
　　　The one day of summer in all the year,
And the very leaves seemed to sing on the trees:
The castle alone in the landscape lay
Like an outpost of winter, dull and gray;
'T was the proudest hall in the North Countree,
And never its gates might opened be,

Save to lord or lady of high degree;
Summer besieged it on every side,
But the churlish stone her assaults defied;
She could not scale the chilly wall,
Though round it for leagues her pavilions tall
Stretched left and right,
Over the hills and out of sight;
    Green and broad was every tent,
    And out of each a murmur went
Till the breeze fell off at night.

III

The drawbridge dropped with a surly clang,
And through the dark arch a charger sprang,
Bearing Sir Launfal, the maiden knight,
In his gilded mail, that flamed so bright
It seemed the dark castle had gathered all
Those shafts the fierce sun had shot over its wall
    In his siege of three hundred summers long,
And, binding them all in one blazing sheaf,
    Had cast them forth: so, young and strong,
And lightsome as a locust-leaf,
Sir Launfal flashed forth in his unscarred mail,
To seek in all climes for the Holy Grail.

IV

It was morning on hill and stream and tree,
    And morning in the young knight's heart;
Only the castle moodily
Rebuffed the gifts of the sunshine free,
    And gloomed by itself apart;
The season brimmed all other things up
Full as the rain fills the pitcher-plant's cup.

V

As Sir Launfal made morn through the darksome gate,
    He was ware of a leper, crouched by the same,
Who begged with his hand and moaned as he sate;
    And a loathing over Sir Launfal came,

The sunshine went out of his soul with a thrill,
    The flesh 'neath his armor did shrink and crawl,
And midway its leap his heart stood still
    Like a frozen waterfall;
For this man, so foul and bent of stature,
Rasped harshly against his dainty nature,
And seemed the one blot on the summer morn,—
So he tossed him a piece of gold in scorn.

VI

The leper raised not the gold from the dust:
"Better to me the poor man's crust,
Better the blessing of the poor,
Though I turn me empty from his door;
That is no true alms which the hand can hold;
He gives nothing but worthless gold
    Who gives from a sense of duty;
But he who gives a slender mite,
And gives to that which is out of sight,
    That thread of the all-sustaining Beauty
Which runs through all and doth all unite,—
The hand cannot clasp the whole of his alms,
The heart outstretches its eager palms,
For a god goes with it and makes it store
To the soul that was starving in darkness before."

Prelude to Part Second

Down swept the chill wind from the mountain peak,
    From the snow five thousand summers old;
On open wold and hill-top bleak
    It had gathered all the cold,
And whirled it like sleet on the wanderer's cheek;
It carried a shiver everywhere
From the unleafed boughs and pastures bare;
The little brook heard it and built a roof
'Neath which he could house him, winter-proof;
All night by the white stars' frosty gleams
He groined his arches and matched his beams;
Slender and clear were his crystal spars
As the lashes of light that trim the stars;

He sculptured every summer delight
In his halls and chambers out of sight;
Sometimes his tinkling waters slipt
Down through a frost-leaved forest-crypt,
Long, sparkling aisles of steel-stemmed trees
Bending to counterfeit a breeze;
Sometimes the roof no fretwork knew
But silvery mosses that downward grew;
Sometimes it was carved in sharp relief
With quaint arabesques of ice-fern leaf;
Sometimes it was simply smooth and clear
For the gladness of heaven to shine through, and here
He had caught the nodding bulrush-tops
And hung them thickly with diamond drops,
Which crystalled the beams of moon and sun,
And made a star of every one:
No mortal builder's most rare device
Could match this winter-palace of ice;
'T was as if every image that mirrored lay
In his depths serene through the summer day,
Each flitting shadow of earth and sky,
    Lest the happy model should be lost,
Had been mimicked in fairy masonry
    By the elfin builders of the frost.

Within the hall are song and laughter,
    The cheeks of Christmas glow red and jolly,
And sprouting is every corbel and rafter
    With the lightsome green of ivy and holly;
Through the deep gulf of the chimney wide
Wallows the Yule-log's roaring tide;
The broad flame-pennons droop and flap
    And belly and tug as a flag in the wind;
Like a locust shrills the imprisoned sap,
    Hunted to death in its galleries blind;
And swift little troops of silent sparks,
    Now pausing, now scattering away as in fear,
Go threading the soot-forest's tangled darks
    Like herds of startled deer.

But the wind without was eager and sharp,
Of Sir Launfal's gray hair it makes a harp,
　　And rattles and wrings
　　The icy strings,
Singing, in dreary monotone,
A Christmas carol of its own,
Whose burden still, as he might guess,
Was—"Shelterless, shelterless, shelterless!"

The voice of the seneschal flared like a torch
As he shouted the wanderer away from the porch,
And he sat in the gateway and saw all night
　　The great hall-fire, so cheery and bold,
　　Through the window-slits of the castle old,
Build out its piers of ruddy light
　　Against the drift of the cold.

Part Second

I

There was never a leaf on bush or tree,
The bare boughs rattled shudderingly;
The river was dumb and could not speak,
　　For the frost's swift shuttles its shroud had spun;
A single crow on the tree-top bleak
　　From his shining feathers shed off the cold sun;
Again it was morning, but shrunk and cold,
As if her veins were sapless and old,
And she rose up decrepitly
For a last dim look at earth and sea.

II

Sir Launfal turned from his own hard gate,
For another heir in his earldom sate;
An old, bent man, worn out and frail,
He came back from seeking the Holy Grail;
Little he recked of his earldom's loss,
No more on his surcoat was blazoned the cross,
But deep in his soul the sign he wore,
The badge of the suffering and the poor.

Sir Launfal's raiment thin and spare
Was idle mail 'gainst the barbed air,
For it was just at the Christmas time;
So he mused, as he sat, of a sunnier clime,
And sought for a shelter from cold and snow
In the light and warmth of long ago;
He sees the snake-like caravan crawl
O'er the edge of the desert, black and small,
Then nearer and nearer, till, one by one,
He can count the camels in the sun,
As over the red-hot sands they pass
To where, in its slender necklace of grass,
The little spring laughed and leapt in the shade,
And with its own self like an infant played,
And waved its signal of palms.

IV

"For Christ's sweet sake, I beg an alms";
The happy camels may reach the spring,
But Sir Launfal sees naught save the grewsome thing,
The leper, lank as the rain-blanched bone,
That cowered beside him, a thing as lone
And white as the ice-isles of Northern seas
In the desolate horror of his disease.

V

And Sir Launfal said,—"I behold in thee
An image of Him who died on the tree;
Thou also hast had thy crown of thorns,—
Thou also hast had the world's buffets and scorns,—
And to thy life were not denied
The wounds in the hands and feet and side:
Mild Mary's Son, acknowledge me;
Behold, through him, I give to thee!"

VI

Then the soul of the leper stood up in his eyes
    And looked at Sir Launfal, and straightway he

Remembered in what a haughtier guise
    He had flung an alms to leprosie,
When he caged his young life up in gilded mail
And set forth in search of the Holy Grail.
The heart within him was ashes and dust;
He parted in twain his single crust,
He broke the ice on the streamlet's brink,
And gave the leper to eat and drink;
'T was a mouldy crust of coarse brown bread,
    'T was water out of a wooden bowl,—
Yet with fine wheaten bread was the leper fed,
    And 't was red wine he drank with his thirsty soul.

VII

As Sir Launfal mused with a downcast face,
A light shone round about the place;
The leper no longer crouched at his side,
But stood before him glorified,
Shining and tall and fair and straight
As the pillar that stood by the Beautiful Gate,—
Himself the Gate whereby men can
Enter the temple of God in Man.

VIII

His words were shed softer than leaves from the pine,
And they fell on Sir Launfal as snows on the brine,
Which mingle their softness and quiet in one
With the shaggy unrest they float down upon;
And the voice that was calmer than silence said,
"Lo, it is I, be not afraid!
In many climes, without avail,
Thou had spent thy life for the Holy Grail;
Behold, it is here,—this cup which thou
Didst fill at the streamlet for me but now;
This crust is my body broken for thee,
This water His blood that died on the tree;
The Holy Supper is kept, indeed,
In whatso we share with another's need,—
Not that which we give, but what we share,—
For the gift without the giver is bare;

Who bestows himself with his alms feeds three,—
Himself, his hungering neighbor, and me."

IX

Sir Launfal awoke, as from a swound:—
"The Grail in my castle here is found!
Hang my idle armor up on the wall,
Let it be the spider's banquet-hall;
He must be fenced with stronger mail
Who would seek and find the Holy Grail."

X

The castle-gate stands open now,
      And the wanderer is welcome to the hall
As the hangbird is to the elm-tree bough;
      No longer scowl the turrets tall,
The Summer's long siege at last is o'er;
When the first poor outcast went in at the door,
She entered with him in disguise,
And mastered the fortres by surprise;
There is no spot she loves so well on ground,
She lingers and smiles there the whole year round;
The meanest serf on Sir Launfal's land
Has hall and bower at his command;
And there 's no poor man in the North Countree
But is lord of the earldom as much as he.

Merlin I

RALPH WALDO EMERSON

Thy trivial harp will never please
Or fill my craving ear;
Its chords should ring as blows the breeze,
Free, peremptory, clear.
No jingling serenader's art,
Nor tinkle of piano strings,
Can make the wild blood start
In its mystic springs.
The kingly bard
Must smite the chords rudely and hard,
As with hammer or with mace;
That they may render back
Artful thunder, which conveys
Secrets of the solar track,
Sparks of the supersolar blaze.

Merlin's blows are strokes of fate,
Chiming with the forest tone,
When boughs buffet boughs in the wood;
Chiming with the gasp and moan
Of the ice-imprisoned flood;
With the pulse of manly hearts;
With the voice of orators;

With the din of city arts;
With the cannonade of wars;
With the marches of the brave;
And prayers of might from martyrs' cave.

Great is the art,
Great be the manners, of the bard.
He shall not his brain encumber
With the coil of rhythm and number;
But, leaving rule and pale forethought,
He shall aye climb
For his rhyme.
"Pass in, pass in," the angels say,
"In to the upper doors,
Nor count compartments of the floors,
But mount to paradise
By the stairway of surprise."

Blameless master of the games,
King of sport that never shames,
He shall daily joy dispense
Hid in song's sweet influence.
Forms more cheerly live and go,
What time the subtle mind
Sings aloud the tune whereto
Their pulses beat,
And march their feet,
And their members are combined.

By Sybarites beguiled,
He shall no task decline;
Merlin's mighty line
Extremes of nature reconciled,—
Bereaved a tyrant of his will,
And made the lion mild.
Songs can the tempest still,
Scattered on the stormy air,
Mold the year to fair increase,
And bring in poetic peace.
He shall not seek to weave,
In weak, unhappy times,
Efficacious rhymes;

Wait his returning strength.
Bird that from the nadir's floor
To the zenith's top can soar,—
The soaring orbit of the muse exceeds that journey's length.
Nor profane affect to hit
Or compass that, by meddling wit,
Which only the propitious mind
Publishes when 'tis inclined.
There are open hours
When the God's will sallies free,
And the dull idiot might see
The flowing fortunes of a thousand years;—
Sudden, at unawares,
Self-moved, fly-to the doors,
Nor sword of angels could reveal
What they conceal.

Merlin II

RALPH WALDO EMERSON

The rhyme of the poet
Modulates the king's affairs;
Balance-loving Nature
Made all things in pairs.
To every foot its antipode;
Each color with its counter glowed;
To every tone beat answering tones,
Higher or graver;
Flavor gladly blends with flavor;
Leaf answers leaf upon the bough;
And match the paired cotyledons.
Hands to hands, and feet to feet,
In one body grooms and brides;
Eldest rite, two married sides
In every mortal meet.
Light's far furnace shines,
Smelting balls and bars,
Forging double stars,
Glittering twins and trines.
The animals are sick with love,
Lovesick with rhyme;
Each with all propitious Time
Into chorus wove.

Like the dancers' ordered band,
Thoughts come also hand in hand;
In equal couples mated,
Or else alternated;
Adding by their mutual gage,
One to other, health and age.
Solitary fancies go
Short-lived wandering to and fro,
Most like to bachelors,
Or an ungiven maid,
Not ancestors,
With no posterity to make the lie afraid,
Or keep truth undecayed.
Perfect-paired as eagle's wings,
Justice is the rhyme of things;
Trade and counting use
The self-same tuneful muse;
And Nemesis,
Who with even matches odd,
Who athwart space redresses
The partial wrong,
Fills the just period,
And finishes the song.

Subtle rhymes, with ruin rife,
Murmur in the house of life,
Sung by the Sisters as they spin;
In perfect time and measure they
Build and unbuild our echoing clay,
As the two twilights of the day
Fold us music-drunken in.

Merlin's Song

RALPH WALDO EMERSON

Of Merlin wise I learned a song,—
Sing it low, or sing it loud,
It is mightier than the strong,
And punishes the proud.
I sing it to the surging crowd,—
Good men it will calm and cheer,
Bad men it will chain and cage.
In the heart of the music peals a strain
Which only angels hear;
Whether it waken joy or rage,
Hushed myriads hark in vain,
Yet they who hear it shed their age,
And take their youth again.

Cerdic and Arthur

JOHN LESLIE HALL

Hengist went off to All-Father's keeping,
Wihtgils's son, to the Wielder's protection,
Earl of the Anglians. From the east came, then,
Cerdic the Saxon a seven-year thereafter;
The excellent atheling, offspring of Woden
Came into Albion. His own dear land
Lay off to the eastward out o'er the sea-ways,
Far o'er the flood-deeps. His fair-haired, eagle-eyed
Liegeman and son sailed westwardly,
O'er the flint-gray floods, with his father and liegelord,
O'er the dashing, lashing, dark-flowing currents
That roll and roar, rumble, grumble
Eastward of Albion. Not e'er hath been told me
Of sea-goers twain trustier, doughtier
Than Cerdic and Cynric, who sailed o'er the waters
Valiant, invincible vikings and sea-dogs
Seeking adventure. Swift westwardly,
O'er the fallow floods, fared they to Albion,
Would look for the land that liegemen-kinsmen
Of Hengist and Horsa and high-mooded Aella
And Cissa had come to. Cerdic was mighty,
Earl of the Saxons. His excellent barks,
His five good floats, fanned by the breezes,

Gliding the waters were wafted to Albion,
Ocean-encircled isle of the sea-waves,
Delightsomest of lands. Lay then at anchor
The five good keels close to the sea-shore;
The swans of the sea sat on the water
Close by the cliff-edge. The clever folk-leader
Was boastful and blithesome, brave-mooded Saxon,
Said to his earlmen: "Excellent thanes
True-hearted, trusty table-companions,
See the good land the loving, generous
Gods have given you: go, seize on it.
I and my son have sailed westwardly,
To gain with our swords such goodly possessions
As Hengist and Aella did erstwhile win
On the island of Albion. On to the battle,
The foe confronteth us." Folk of the island,
Earlmen of Albion, angry-mooded, then,
Stood stoutly there, striving to hurl them
Off in the ocean east to the mainland,
Back o'er the billows. Bravely Albion's
Fearless defenders fought with the stranger
Then and thereafter: early did Cerdic
See and declare that slowly, bloodily,
And foot by foot, must the folk of the Saxons
Tear from the Welsh their well-lovèd, blithesome,
Beautiful fatherland. Brave were the men that
So long could repel the puissant, fearless
Sons of the Saxons that had sailed o'er the oceans
To do or to die, doughty, invincible
Earls of the east. The excellent kinsmen,
Father and son, scions of Woden,
Burned in their spirit to build in the south the
Greatest of kingdoms: 't was granted to Cerdic
To be first of the famous folk-lords of Wessex,
Land-chiefs belovèd; to lead, herald the
World-famous roll of the wise, eminent
Athelings of Wessex, where Egbert and Ethelwulf,
Alfred and Edward, ever resplendently,
Spaciously shine, shepherds of peoples,
Excellent athelings, and Athelstan, Godwin
And Harold the hero, helms of the Saxons,
Have their names written in record of glory

In legend and story, leaving their fame as an
Honor forever to England, peerless
Mother of heroes.—The men of the east
Slowly, bloodily builded a kingdom
Where Aesc and Aella not e'er had been able
To bear their banners, though both these athelings
Were in might marvellous, mood-brave, heroic
Leaders of liegemen.—Beloved of the Welsh
Was the atheling Arthur, excellent, valiant
Lord of the Silurians, land-prince, warrior
Famed 'mid the races. He rued bitterly
That father and son, Saxon invaders,
To the left and right were wresting, tearing
From races no few their fond-lovèd, blood-bought
Homesteads and manors, were hacking and sacking
Folk of the southland, and far westwardly
Had bitterly banished the best of the heroes
And earlmen of Albion. Arthur was mighty,
Uther Pendragon's offspring belovèd,
His fame far-reaching. Afar and anear then,
All men of Albion honored and loved him;
Sent over Severn beseeching the mighty
Silurian leader no longer to tarry
In crushing the foemen, but quickly to drive them
Back to their bottomless bogs in the eastward
O'er the rime-cold sea; said wailingly:
"The fierce, pitiless folk of the eastward,
Mighty, remorseless men of the waters,
Treacherous, terrible, will take speedily
Our name and nation, and naught will be left us
But to dare and to die." The doughty, invincible
Atheling Arthur, earl of Siluria,
Offspring of Uther, early was ready;
Feared not, failed not, fared on his journey
Seeking for Cerdic. Severn's waters
Saw him and laughed, little expecting
That Arthur the king and the excellent knights
Of the Table Round, with troopers a-many,
Would suffer the foemen to seize and possess the
Lands of Siluria, would let the remorseless,
Implacable, pitiless pagan and heathen
Sail over Severn; not soon did it happen

While Arthur the atheling his earth-joys tasted
Here under heaven. That hero was brave,
Great, all-glorious: God fought for him:
Nor Cerdic nor Cynric could soon injure that
Hero of Heaven; his horrible destiny
Wyrd the weaver wove in her eerie,
Mysterious meshes, mighty, taciturn
Goddess of gods: she gives whom she will to
Speed in the battle. Brave-mooded Arthur,
Offspring of Uther, was eager for glory,
Peerless of prowess: proudly, dauntlessly
Fought he for Albion. Not e'er heard I
Of better battle-knight, more bold, fearless,
That sun ever shone on: the sheen of his glory
With lustre illumined the land where his mother
Gave birth to the bairn; and broad, mighty,
Spacious his fame was; his splendid achievements
Were known to all nations. None could e'er dare to
Cope with that hero, till the conquering, dauntless
Earl of the Anglians, ever-belovèd
Founder of freedom and father of kings,
O'er the seas sailing, slowly, bloodily
Builded the best and broadest of kingdoms
Heroes e'er heard of. The heart of king Arthur
Was sad as he saw the Saxon invader
How, foot by foot, forward, onward,
He ever proceeded, eastward, westward,
Far to the north, founding and building
A kingdom and country to crush and destroy the
Land that he long had lived for, thought for,
Fiercely had fought for. Famed was Arthur,
Wide his renown; but Wyrd the spinster
Taketh no heed of hero or craven;
Her warp and her woof she weaveth and spinneth
Unmindful of men. The mighty war-hero,
Atheling Arthur, set out on his journey,
Laid down his life-joys; the belovèd folk-lord's
Feasting was finished. Unflinching, fearless,
Doomed unto death, dead on the battle-field
Fell the brave folk-prince. Foul was the traitor,
Hated of heroes. The hope of his countrymen
Sank into darkness; for dead was Arthur,

The last and the best and bravest of Albion's
Athelings of eld. Not ever thereafter
Could the Welshman withstand the sturdy, mighty
Tread of the Saxon as tramping, advancing,
Onward he went, eastward, westward,
Far to the northward: none withstood him,
Now Arthur was lifeless; he alone was able
To stay for a moment that sturdy, mighty,
Invincible march.—The valiant, doughty
Kinsmen of Cerdic, conquering earlmen,
Forward then bare bravely, unfalt'ringly,
Daringly, dauntlessly, the dragon of Wessex
Fuming and flaming; fearlessly bare it
Northward, eastward, on to the westward,
O'er Severn and Thames and Trent and Humber
And east oceanward, till all the great races
Of Albion's isle owned as their liegelords
The children of Cerdic, sire of kings and
Founder of freedom. Few among athelings
Were greater than he, gift-lord eminent,
Wielder of Wessex; the wise-mooded, far-seeing,
Brave-hearted folk-prince builded his kingdom
As a bulwark of freedom. His brave, high-hearted
Table-companions, trusty, faithful
Liegemen and thanes, leaped to his service
In peace and in war: well did they love him,
Bowed to his bidding; blithely followed him
Where the fight was fiercest; would fall in the battle
Gladly, eagerly, excellent heroes,
Ere they'd leave their dear lord alone on the battle-field,
Bearing unaided the onset of foes and
The brunt of the battle. The brave ones were mindful
Of the duties of liegemen; dastardly thought it
To flee from the field while their fond, loving
Leader and liegelord lingered thereon
Dead or alive; deemed him a nidering
Who stood not stoutly, sturdily, manfully
Close to his lord as he led in the battle,
Facing the foemen. The free-hearted earlmen
Minded the days when their dear-honored liegelord
Feasted the throngs of thanemen-kinsmen
In the handsomest of halls heroes e'er sat in

229

'Neath dome of the welkin. Well they remembered
How their lord lovingly lavished his treasures
On all earlmen older and younger,
Greater and lesser: 't were loathsomest treason
To leave such a lord alone in the battle,
With a foe facing him. The folk-ruler mighty
King-like requited them with costliest gems,
Most bountiful banqueting. The brave-hearted man
Builded his kingdom, broadly founded it
Northward, eastward, on to the westward,
South to the seaward. He said tenderly,
Cerdic discoursed, king of the Saxons,
Father of England: "Old, hoary is
Cerdic your king, kinsmen-thanemen,
Warriors of Wessex. Well have ye served me,
Ye and your fathers. I yet remember
How, ere age came on me, I ever was foremost
In deeds of daring, in doughty achievements,
In feats of prowess. I fought valiantly
Alone, unaided, with only my faithful,
Well-lovèd sword, and swept away hundreds
Of earlmen of Albion: now age, ruthless,
Horrible foe of heroes and warriors,
Hath marred my might, though my mood is as daring,
My spirit as stout and sturdy as ever
In years of my youth. I yearn in my soul, now,
To cross over Severn and cut into slivers
The wolf-hearted Welshmen. Well-nigh a forty
Years in their circuits have seen me a-conquering
Here under heaven: from hence, early
I go on my way. Woden will bid me
To the halls of Valhalla, where heroes will meet me,
Gladly will seat me 'mid the glory-encircled
Heroes of heaven. In my heart it pains me
To feel my war-strength fading and waning
And ebbing away. Would I might leap now
Like a king to the battle, not cow-like breathe out my
Soul in the straw. The son of my bosom,
Cynric my bairn, bravely will lead you
When I am no more: he ever hath proved him
A bold battle-earl. My blade I will give him,
Sigbrand my sword: he hath served me faithfully

230

Sixty of winters: well do I love him,
Bold-hearted battle-brand." The brave earlmen, then,
Shouted lustily, loudly commending
The words of good Cerdic. Cynric they loved, too,
Son of the hero; themselves had beheld him
How valiant, adventurous, invincible, king-like
He ever had borne him, since erst he landed
To fight, with his father, the fierce, implacable,
Wolf-hearted Welshmen: well did they love him,
And oft on the ale-benches earlmen asserted
That, when good king Cerdic, gracious, belovèd
Ward of the kingdom, went on his journey,
Laid down his life-joys, his liegefolk would never
Find them a folk-lord fonder, truer,
More honored of all men, than atheling Cynric
Surely would prove him. Shouted they lustily,
"Wes hael, wes hael! hero of Wessex,
Cerdic the conqueror," clanging their lances
And beating their bucklers, bellowed like oxen,
Blew in their shields, shouting, yelling
Glad-hearted, gleefully. The good one discoursed, then,
Cerdic the king said to his liegemen
(Henchmen all hearkened): "Hear ye, good troopers,
Of Sigbrand my sword. I said he was trusty,
And bitter in biting. I brought him to Albion
Far from the eastward. I fared, long ago,
East over Elbe and Oder and Weser
And thence to the northward, never wearying,
Greedy for glory; 'mid the Goths found it,
Old, iron-made, excellent sword-blade,
Weland his work. Well I remember
How I heard high-hearted heroes and athelings,
My true-hearted troopers, tell how a dragon,
His cave guarding, kept there a treasure
Age after age; how earls of the eastward
Said that Sigbrand, the sword-blade of Hermann,
Was kept in that cave covered with magic,
Encircled with sorcery, secretly guarded,
Bound with enchantments. I boldly adventured
A grim grapple with that grisly, terrible
Fire-spewing dragon, to fetch to the westward
The well-lovèd, warlike, wide-famous brand

231

Of Hermann the hero. I hied o'er the rivers
And off to the eastward: earls of those lands there
Laughed when they learned that a lad from the westward
Would dare the great dragon that had daunted their fathers
Five hundred winters. I fared eastward then,
Met with the monster, mightily smote him,
To earth felled him; flamings of battle
Horribly hurled he, hotly he snorted,
Would seethe me in poison. Wtih the point of my blade
I proudly did prick him. Prone he fell forward,
Dead lay the dragon. His den was no more
A horror to heroes; hastened I in, then,
To joy in the sight of jewels and treasures
And song-famous swords that had slept on the wall there
From earliest eras, edge-keen, famous,
Magic-encircled swords of the ancients,
Old-work of giants. With joy, saw I
World-famous Sigbrand, sword-blade of Hermann,
Men-leader mighty, matchless battle-knight,
Hero of Germany. I hastily seized it
All rusting to ruin; the rime-carved, ancient
Sword of the hero was soon hanging then
Safe at my side: it hath served me faithfully
Sixty of winters, well-tried, trusty
Friend-in-the-battle. When I fare, troopers,
Hence to Valhalla, high-hearted Cynric,
My fond-lovèd son, folk-lord of Wessex,
Will take up the brand borne by his father
And carve out a kingdom clean to the northward and
Wide to the westward; the Welshman will cower
And shudder and shake, as the shout of the Saxon
Frightens afresh forest and river
And meadow and plain. I shall pass on my journey
Early anon: old and hoary,
Death will subdue me. Dear young heroes,
Do as I bid ye. Bear ye onward
The banner of Wessex. Wyrd will help you
If doughty your valor. I dare to allege it,
That the gods have given this goodly, bountiful
Land of Albion to the liegemen and children
Of Cerdic the Saxon; seize, hold to it
Forever and ever. Ye early will see me

Lorn of my life-joys, lying unwarlike,
Dead in my armor. I urge you, good heroes,
To build me a barrow broad-stretching, lofty,
High on the cliff-edge, that comers from far
May see it and say that so did Angle-folk
Honor the atheling that erstwhile led their
Fathers of old in founding a kingdom."

The Last Love of Gawaine

RICHARD HOVEY

You will betray me—oh, deny it not!
What right have I, alas, to say you nay?
I, traitor of ten loves, what shall I say
To plead with you that I be not forgot?
My love has not been squandered jot by jot
In little loves that perish with the day.
My treason has been ever to the sway
Of queens; my faith has known no petty blot.
You will betray me, as I have betrayed,
And I shall kiss the hand that does me wrong.
And oh, not pardon—I need pardon more—
But in proud torment, grim and unafraid,
Burn in my hell nor cease the bitter song
Your beauty triumphs in forevermore.

The Vision of the Holy Grail

EUGENE FIELD

Deere Chryste, let not the cheere of earth,
To fill our hearts with heedless mirth
This holy Christmasse time;
But give us of thy heavenly cheere
That we may hold thy love most deere
And know thy peace sublime.

———

Full merry waxed King Pelles court
With Yuletide cheere and Yuletide sport,
    And, when the board was spread,
Now wit ye well 'twas good to see
So fair and brave a companie
    With Pelles at the head.

"Come hence, Elaine," King Pelles cried,
"Come hence and sit ye by my side,
    For never yet, I trow,
Have gentle virtues like to thine
Been proved by sword nor pledged in wine,
    Nor shall be nevermo!"

"Sweete sir, my father," quoth Elaine,
"Me it repents to give thee pain—
    Yet, tarry I may not;
For I shall soond and I shall die
If I behold this companie
    And see not Launcelot!

"My heart shall have no love but this—
My lips shall know no other kiss,
    Save only, father, thine;
So graunt me leave to seek my bower,
The lonely chamber in the toure,
    Where sleeps his child and mine."

Then frowned the King in sore despite;
"A murrain seize that traitrous knight,
    For that he lies!" he cried—
"A base, unchristian paynim he,
Else, by my beard, he would not be
    A recreant to his bride!

"Oh, I had liefer yield my life
Than see thee the deserted wife
    Of dastard Launcelot!
Yet, an' thou has no mind to stay,
Go with thy damosels away—
    Lo, I'll detain ye not."

Her damosels in goodly train
Back to her chamber led Elaine,
    And when her eyes were cast
Upon her babe, her tears did flow
And she did wail and weep as though
    Her heart had like to brast.

The while she grieved the Yuletide sport
Waxed lustier in King Pelles' court,
    And louder, houre by houre,
The echoes of the rout were borne
To where the lady, all forlorn,
    Made moning in the toure,

"Swete Chryste," she cried, "ne let me hear
Their ribald sounds of Yuletide cheere
    That mock at mine and me;
Graunt that my sore affliction cease
And give me of the heavenly peace
    That comes with thoughts of thee!"

Lo, as she spake, a wondrous light
Made all that lonely chamber bright,
    And o'er the infant's bed
A spirit hand, as samite pail,
Held sodaine foorth the Holy Grail
    Above the infant's head.

And from the sacred golden cup
A subtle incense floated up
    And filled the conscious air,
Which, when she breathed, the fair Elaine
Forgot her grief, forgot her pain.
    Forgot her sore despair.

And as the Grail's mysterious balm
Wrought in her heart a wondrous calm,
    Great mervail 'twas to see
The sleeping child stretch one hand up
As if in dreams he held the cup
    Which none mought win but he.

Through all the night King Pelles' court
Made mighty cheer and goodly sport.
    Nor never recked the joy
That was vouchsafed that Christmass tide
To Launcelot's deserted bride
    And to her sleeping boy.

Swete Chryste, let not the cheere of earth
To fill our hearts with heedless mirth
    This present Christmasse night;
But send among us to and fro
Thy Holy Grail, that men may know
    The joy withe wisdom dight.

The Lady Guinevere

From *The Story of King Arthur and His Knights,*
writen and illustrated by Howard Pyle.
New York: Scribner's, 1903.

Guenevere

SARA TEASDALE

I was a queen, and I have lost my crown;
A wife, and I have broken all my vows;
A lover, and I ruined him I loved:—
There is no other havoc left to do.
A little month ago I was a queen,
And mothers held their babies up to see
When I came riding out of Camelot.
The women smiled, and all the world smiled too.
And now, what woman's eyes would smile on me?
I am still beautiful, and yet what child
Would think of me as some high, heaven-sent thing,
An angel, clad in gold and miniver?
The world would run from me, and yet I am
No different from the queen they used to love.
If water, flowing silver over stones,
Is forded, and beneath the horses' feet
Grows turbid suddenly, it clears again,
And men will drink it with no thought of harm.
Yet I am branded for a single fault.

I was the flower amid a toiling world,
Where people smiled to see one happy thing,
And they were proud and glad to raise me high;

They only asked that I should be right fair,
A little kind, and gownèd wondrously,
And surely it were little praise to me
If I had pleased them well throughout my life.

I was a queen, the daughter of a king.
The crown was never heavy on my head,
It was my right, and was a part of me.
The women thought me proud, the men were kind,
And bowed down gallantly to kiss my hand,
And watched me as I passed them calmly by,
Along the halls I shall not tread again.
What if, to-night, I should revisit them?
The warders at the gates, the kitchen-maids,
The very beggars would stand off from me,
And I, their queen, would climb the stairs alone,
Pass through the banquet-hall, a hated thing,
And seek my chambers for a hiding-place,
And I should find them but a sepulchre,
The very rushes rotted on the floors,
The fire in ashes on the freezing hearth.

I was a queen, and he who loved me best
Made me a woman for a night and day,
And now I go unqueened forevermore.

A queen should never dream on summer nights,
When hovering spells are heavy in the dusk:—
I think no night was ever quite so still,
So smoothly lit with red along the west,
So deeply hushed with quiet through and through.
And strangely clear, and sharply dyed with light,
The trees stood straight against a paling sky,
With Venus burning lamp-like in the west.
I walked alone among a thousand flowers,
That drooped their heads and drowsed beneath the dew,
And all my thoughts were quieted to sleep.
Behind me, on the walk, I heard a step—
I did not know my heart could tell his tread,
I did not know I loved him till that hour.
The garden reeled a little, I was weak,
And in my breast I felt a wild, sick pain.

Quickly he came behind me, caught my arms,
That ached beneath his touch; and then I swayed,
My head fell backward and I saw his face.

All this grows bitter that was once so sweet,
And many mouths must drain the dregs of it,
But none will pity me, nor pity him
Whom Love so lashed, and with such cruel thongs.

Elaine

EDNA ST. VINCENT MILLAY

Oh, come again to Astolat!
    I will not ask you to be kind.
And you may go when you will go,
    And I will stay behind.

I will not say how dear you are,
    Or ask you if you hold me dear,
Or trouble you with things for you
    The way I did last year.

So still the orchard, Lancelot,
    So very still the lake shall be,
You could not guess—though you should guess—
    What is become of me.

So wide shall be the garden-walk,
    The garden-seat so very wide,
You needs must think—if you should think—
    The lily maid had died.

Save that, a little way away,
    I'd watch you for a little while,
To see you speak, the way you speak,
    And smile,—if you should smile.

Guinevere at Her Fireside

DOROTHY PARKER

A nobler king had never breath—
    I say it now, and said it then.
Who weds with such is wed till death
    And wedded stays in Heaven. Amen.

(And oh, the shirts of linen-lawn,
    And all the armor, tagged and tied,
And church on Sundays, dusk and dawn,
    And bed a thing to kneel beside!)

The bravest one stood tall above
    The rest, and watched me as a light.
I heard and heard them talk of love;
    I'd naught to do but think, at night.

The bravest man has littlest brains;
    That chalky fool from Astolat
With all her dying and her pains!—
    Thank God, I helped him over that.

I found him not unfair to see—
    I like a man with peppered hair!
And thus it came about. Ah, me,
    Tristram was busied otherwhere. . . .

A nobler king had never breath—
I say it now, and said it then.
Who weds with such is wed till death
And wedded stays in Heaven. Amen.

Iseult of Brittany

DOROTHY PARKER

So delicate my hands, and long,
　　They might have been my pride.
And there were those to make them song
　　Who for their touch had died.

Too frail to cup a heart within,
　　Too soft to hold the free—
How long these lovely hands have been
　　A bitterness to me!

Launcelot

SINCLAIR LEWIS

"Oft Launcelot grieves that he loveth the Queen
But oftener far that she cruel hath been."

Blow, weary wind,
The golden rod scarce chiding;
Sir Launcelot is riding
By shady wood-paths pleasant
To fields of yellow corn.
He starts a whirring pheasant,
And clearly winds his horn.
The Queen's Tower gleams mid distant hills;
A thought like joyous sunshine thrills,
"My love grows kind."

Blow, weary wind,
O'er lakes, o'er dead swamps crying,
Amid the gray stumps sighing
While slow, and cold, and sullen,
The waves splash on the shore.
O'er wastes of bush and mullen,
Dull crows flap, evermore.
The Autumn day is chill and drear
As you knight, thinking Guenevere
Proves almost unkind.

Ballad of Launcelot and Elaine

EDGAR LEE MASTERS

It was a hermit on Whitsunday
That came to the Table Round.
"King Arthur, wit ye by what Knight
May the Holy Grail be found?"

"By never a Knight that liveth now;
By none that feasteth here."
King Arthur marvelled when he said,
"He shall be got this year."

Then uprose brave Sir Launcelot
And there did mount his steed,
And hastened to a pleasant town
That stood in knightly need.

Where many people him acclaimed,
He passed the Corbin pounte,
And there he saw a fairer tower
Than ever was his wont.

And in that tower for many years
A dolorous lady lay,
Whom Queen Northgalis had bewitched,
And also Queen le Fay.

And Launcelot loosed her from those pains,
And there a dragon slew.
Then came King Pelles out and said,
"Your name, brave Knight and true?"

"My name is Pelles, wit ye well,
And King of the far country;
And I, Sir Knight, am cousin nigh
To Joseph of Armathie."

"I am Sir Launcelot du Lake."
And then they clung them fast;
And yede into the castle hall
To take the king's repast.

Anon there cometh in a dove
By the window's open fold,
And in her mouth was a rich censer,
That shone like Ophir gold.

And therewithal was such savor
As bloweth over sea
From a land of many colored flowers
And trees of spicery.

And therewithal was meat and drink,
And a damsel passing fair,
Betwixt her hands of tulip-white,
A golden cup did bear.

"O, Jesu," said Sir Launcelot,
"What may this marvel mean?"
"That is," said Pelles, "richest thing
That any man hath seen."

"O, Jesu," said Sir Launcelot,
"What may this sight avail?"
"Now wit ye well," said King Pelles,
"That was the Holy Grail."

Then by this sign King Pelles knew
Elaine his fair daughter

Should lie with Launcelot that night,
And Launcelot with her.

And that this twain should get a child
Before the night should fail,
Who would be named Sir Galahad,
And find the Holy Grail.

Then cometh one hight Dame Brisen
With Pelles to confer,
"Now, wit ye well, Sir Launcelot
Loveth but Guinevere."

"But if ye keep him well in hand,
The while I work my charms,
The maid Elaine, ere spring of morn,
Shall lie within his arms."

Dame Brisen was the subtlest witch
That was that time in life;
She was as if Beelzebub
Had taken her to wife.

Then did she cause one known of face
To Launcelot to bring,
As if it came from Guinevere,
Her wonted signet ring.

"By Holy Rood, thou comest true,
For well I know thy face.
Where is my lady?" asked the Knight,
"There in the Castle Case?"

"'Tis five leagues scarcely from this hall,"
Up spoke that man of guile.
"I go this hour," said Launcelot,
"Though it were fifty mile."

Then sped Dame Brisen to the king
And whispered, "An we thrive,
Elaine must reach the Castle Case
Ere Launcelot arrive."

Elaine stole forth with twenty knights
And a goodly company.
Sir Launcelot rode fast behind,
Queen Guinevere to see.

Anon he reached the castle door.
Oh! fond and well deceived.
And there it seemed the queen's own train
Sir Launcelot received.

"Where is the queen?" quoth Launcelot,
"For I am sore bestead,"
"Have not such haste," said Dame Brisen,
"The queen is now in bed."

"Then lead me thither," saith he,
"And cease this jape of thine."
"Now sit thee down," said Dame Brisen,
"And have a cup of wine."

"For wit ye not that many eyes
Upon you here have stared;
Now have a cup of wine until
All things may be prepared."

Elaine lay in a fair chamber,
'Twixt linen sweet and clene.
Dame Brisen all the windows stopped,
That no day might be seen.

Dame Brisen fetched a cup of wine
And Launcelot drank thereof.
"No more of flagons," saith he,
"For I am mad for love."

Dame Brisen took Sir Launcelot
Where lay the maid Elaine.
Sir Launcelot entered the bed chamber
The queen's love for to gain.

Sir Launcelot kissed the maid Elaine,
And her cheeks and brows did burn;

And then they lay in other's arms
Until the morn's underne.

Anon Sir Launcelot arose
And toward the window groped,
And then he saw the maid Elaine
When he the window oped.

"Ah, traitoress," saith Launcelot,
And then he gat his sword,
"That I should live so long and now
Become a knight abhorred."

"False traitoress," saith Launcelot,
And then he shook the steel.
Elaine skipped naked from the bed
And 'fore the knight did kneel.

"I am King Pelles own daughter
And thou art Launcelot,
The greatest knight of all the world.
This hour we have begot."

"Oh, traitoress Brisen," cried the knight,
"Oh, charmed cup of wine;
That I this treasonous thing should do
For treasures such as thine."

"Have mercy," saith maid Elaine,
"Thy child is in my womb."
Thereat the morning's silvern light
Flooded the bridal room.

That light it was a benison;
It seemed a holy boon,
As when behind a wrack of cloud
Shineth the summer moon.

And in the eyes of maid Elaine
Looked forth so sweet a faith,
Sir Launcelot took his glittering sword,
And thrust it in the sheath.

"So God me help, I spare thy life,
But I am wretch and thrall,
If any let my sword to make
Dame Brisen's head to fall."

"So have thy will of her," she said,
"But do to me but good;
For thou hast had my fairest flower,
Which is my maidenhood."

"And we have done the will of God,
And the will of God is best."
Sir Launcelot lifted the maid Elaine
And hid her on his breast.

Anon there cometh in a dove,
By the window's open fold,
And in her mouth was a rich censer
That shone like beaten gold.

And therewithal was such savor,
As bloweth over sea,
From a land of many colored flowers,
And trees of spicery.

And therewithal was meat and drink,
And a damsel passing fair,
Betwixt her hands of silver white
A golden cup did bear.

"O Jesu," said Sir Launcelot,
"What may this marvel mean?"
"That is," she said, "the richest thing
That any man hath seen."

"O Jesu," said Sir Launcelot,
"What may this sight avail?"
"Now wit ye well," said maid Elaine,
"This is the Holy Grail."

And then a nimbus light hung o'er
Her brow so fair and meek;

And turned to orient pearls the tears
That glistered down her cheek.

And a sound of music passing sweet
Went in and out again.
Sir Launcelot made the sign of the cross,
And knelt to maid Elaine.

"Name him whatever name thou wilt,
But be his sword and mail
Thrice tempered 'gainst a wayward world,
That lost the Holy Grail."

Sir Launcelot sadly took his leave
And rode against the morn.
And when the time was fully come
Sir Galahad was born.

Also he was from Jesu Christ,
Our Lord, the eighth degree;
Likewise the greatest knight this world
May ever hope to see.

The Death of Sir Launcelot

EDGAR LEE MASTERS

Sir Launcelot had fled to France
For the peace of Guinevere,
And many a noble knight was slain,
And Arthur lay on his bier.

Sir Launcelot took ship from France
And sailed across the sea.
He rode seven days through fair England
Till he came to Almesbury.

Then spake Sir Bors to Launcelot:
The old time is at end;
You have no more in England's realm
In east nor west a friend.

You have no friend in all England
Sith Mordred's war hath been,
And Queen Guinevere became a nun
To heal her soul of sin.

Sir Launcelot answered never a word
But rode to the west countree
Until through the forest he saw a light
That shone from a nunnery.

Sir Launcelot entered the cloister,
And the queen fell down in a swoon.
Oh blessed Jesu, saith the queen,
For thy mother's love, a boon.

Go hence, Sir Launcelot, saith the queen,
And let me win God's grace.
My heavy heart serves me no more
To look upon thy face.

Through you was wrought King Arthur's death,
Through you great war and wrake.
Leave me alone, let me bleed,
Pass by for Jesu's sake.

Then fare you well, saith Launcelot,
Sweet Madam, fare you well.
And sythen you have left the world
No more in the world I dwell.

Then up rose sad Sir Launcelot
And rode by wold and mere
Until he came to a hermitage
Where bode Sir Bedivere.

And there he put a habit on
And there did pray and fast.
And when Sir Bedivere told him all
His heart for sorrow brast.

How that Sir Mordred, traitorous knight
Betrayed his King and sire;
And how King Arthur wounded, died
Broken in heart's desire.

And so Sir Launcelot penance made,
And worked at servile toil;
And prayed the Bishop of Canterbury
His sins for to assoil.

His shield went clattering on the wall
To a dolorous wail of wind;

His casque was rust, his mantle dust
With spider webs entwined.

His listless horses left alone
Went cropping where they would,
To see the noblest knight of the world
Upon his sorrow brood.

Anon a Vision came in his sleep,
And thrice the Vision saith:
Go thou to Almesbury for thy sin,
Where lieth the queen in death.

Sir Launcelot cometh to Almesbury
And knelt by the dead queen's bier;
Oh none may know, moaned Launcelot,
What sorrow lieth here.

What love, what honor, what defeat
What hope of the Holy Grail.
The moon looked through the latticed glass
On the queen's face cold and pale.

Sir Launcelot kissed the ceréd cloth,
And none could stay his woe,
Her hair lay back from the oval brow,
And her nose was clear as snow.

They wrapped her body in cloth of Raines,
They put her in webs of lead.
They coffined her in white marble,
And sang a mass for the dead.

Sir Launcelot and seven knights
Bore torches around the bier.
They scattered myrrh and frankincense
On the corpse of Guinevere.

They put her in earth by King Arthur
To the chant of a doleful tune.
They heaped the earth on Guinevere
And Launcelot fell in a swoon.

Sir Launcelot went to the hermitage
Some Grace of God to find;
But never he ate, and never he drank
And there he sickened and dwined.

Sir Launcelot lay in a painful bed,
And spake with a dreary steven;
Sir Bishop, I pray you shrive my soul
And make it clean for heaven.

The Bishop houseled Sir Launcelot,
The Bishop kept watch and ward.
Bury me, saith Sir Launcelot,
In the earth of Joyous Guard.

Three candles burned the whole night through
Till the red dawn looked in the room.
And the white, white soul of Launcelot
Strove with a black, black doom.

I see the old witch Dame Brisen,
And Elaine so straight and tall—
Nay, saith the Bishop of Canterbury,
The shadows dance on the wall.

I see long hands of dead women,
They clutch for my soul eftsoon;
Nay, saith the Bishop of Canterbury,
'Tis the drifting light of the moon.

I see three angels, saith he,
Before a silver urn.
Nay, saith the Bishop of Canterbury,
The candles do but burn.

I see a cloth of red samite
O'er the holy vessels spread.
Nay, saith the Bishop of Canterbury,
The great dawn groweth red.

I see all the torches of the world
Shine in the room so clear.

Nay, saith the bishop of Canterbury,
The white dawn draweth near.

Sweet lady, I behold the face
Of thy dear son, our Lord,
Nay, saith the Bishop of Canterbury,
The sun shines on your sword.

Sir Galahad outstretcheth hands
And taketh me ere I fail—
Sir Launcelot's body lay in death
As his soul found the Holy Grail.

They laid his body in the quire
Upon a purple pall.
He was the meekest, gentlest knight
That ever ate in hall.

He was the kingliest, goodliest knight
That ever England roved,
The truest lover of sinful man
That ever woman loved.

I pray you all, fair gentlemen,
Pray for his soul and mine.
He lived to lose the heart he loved
And drink but bitter wine.

He wrought a woe he knew not of,
He failed his fondest quest,
Now sing a psalter, read a prayer
May all souls find their rest.
                    Amen.

Merlin

THOMAS CALDECOT CHUBB

A lonely man, his head among the stars
Walks on the clean sand white beside the sea,—
Merlin, the lonely man of Camelot,
Who left King Arthur and the tournaments
And decorous garlands and the sight of man
Dear to him, yea! the knights and pageantry
To walk beside the waves that curl in foam
And sparkling splendor round him.

                   This because
His vague mysterious power—alchemy
Of mind, by which to purest testable gold
The baser man he strove to elevate
Through curious kabala, muttered words
And formulae, and fiery distillation
Of the elixirs red and white (for this
The allegorists hold to be the sum
And substance of the prime materia,—
Soul-purifier, leaving earth to rest
As 't was)—him lifted flaming far and far
Through unimagined distances of thought
And dream, by pathways metaphysical
To God's own face. And he had seen the face
Of glorious God. And God had looked upon
His eyes.

So now he walks beside the sea
Alone. And nightly chants he: "I have seen
The Moon, and far beyond her. I have seen
The ringèd planets curve around the Sun,
And the great Sun himself, and far beyond
Strewn stars and stars and filmy nebulae.
Past them across the night, too, have I seen
And known that unapproachable face of God.
And now I walk alone lest man should see
Divinity reflected from mine eyes
Which I am granted only to behold."
Thus Merlin. And the waves around his feet
Break in a fiery phosphorescence, while
The stars above are flaked in fire around,
And the moon floats among them like a barge
Of whitest silver on the unrippled mere.

ir Mordred the traitor:-

From *The Story of The Grail and the Passing of Arthur,*
written and illustrated by Howard Pyle.
New York: Scribner's, 1910.

Modred

A Fragment

EDWIN ARLINGTON ROBINSON

                    Time and the dark
Had come, but not alone. The southern gate
That had been open wide for Lancelot
Made now an entrance for three other men,
Who strode along the gravel or the grass,
Careless of who should hear them. When they came
To the great oak and the two empty chairs,
One paused, and held the others with a tongue
That sang an evil music while it spoke:
"Sit here, my admirable Colgrevance,
And you, my gentle Agravaine, sit here.
For me, well I have had enough of sitting;
And I have heard enough and seen enough
To blast a kingdom into kingdom come,
Had I so fierce a mind—which happily
I have not, for the king here is my father.
There's been a comment and a criticism
Abounding, I believe, in Camelot
For some time at my undeserved expense,
But God forbid that I should make my father
Less happy than he will be when he knows
What I shall have to tell him presently;

And that will only be what he has known
Since Merlin, or the ghost of Merlin, came
Two years ago to warn him. Though he sees,
One thing he will not see; and this must end.
We must have no blind kings in Camelot,
Or we shall have no land worth harrowing,
And our last harvest will be food for strangers.
My father, as you know, has gone a-hunting."

"We know about the king," said Agravaine,
"And you know more than any about the queen.
We are still waiting, Modred. Colgrevance
And I are waiting."

                Modred laughed at him
Indulgently: "Did I say more than any?
If so, then inadvertently I erred;
For there is one man here, one Lancelot,
Who knows, I fancy, a deal more than I do,
And I know much. Yes, I know more than much.
Yet who shall snuff the light of what he knows
To blind the king he serves? No, Agravaine,
A wick like that would smoke and smell of treason."

"Your words are mostly smoke, if I may say so,"
Said Colgrevance: "What is it you have seen,
And what are we to do? I wish no ill
To Lancelot. I know no evil of him,
Or of the queen; and I'll hear none of either,
Save what you, on your oath, may tell me now.
I look yet for the trail of your dark fancy
To blur your testament."

              "No, Colgrevance,
There are no blurs or fancies exercising
Tonight where I am. Lancelot will ascend
Anon, betimes, and with no drums or shawms
To sound the appointed progress of his feet;
And he will not be lost along the way,
For there are landmarks and he knows them all.
No, Colgrevance, there are no blurs or fancies
Unless it be that your determination

Has made them for your purpose what they seem.
But here I beg your pardon, Colgrevance.
We reticent ones are given to say too much,
With our tongues once in action. Pray forgive.
Your place tonight will be a shadowed alcove,
Where you may see this knight without a stain
While he goes in where no man save the king
Has dared before to follow. Agravaine
And I will meet you on the floor below,
Having already beheld this paragon-Joseph
Go by us for your clinching observation.
Then we, with a dozen or so for strength, will act;
And there shall be no more of Lancelot."

"Modred, I wish no ill to Lancelot,
And I know none of him," said Colgrevance.
"My dream is of a sturdier way than this
For me to serve my king. Give someone else
That alcove, and let me be of the twelve.
I swear it irks the marrow of my soul
To shadow Lancelot—though I may fight him,
If so it is to be. Furthermore, Modred,
You gave me not an inkling of the part
That you have read off now so pleasantly
For me to play. No, Modred, by the God
Who knows the right way and the wrong, I'll be
This night no poisonous inhabitant
Of alcoves in your play, not even for you.
No man were more the vassal of his friend
Than I am, but I'm damned if I'll be owned."

In a becoming darkness Modred smiled
Away the first accession of his anger.
"Say not like that," he answered, musically.
"Be temperate, Colgrevance. Remember always
Your knighthood and your birth. Remember, too,
That I may hold him only as my friend
Who loves me for myself, not for my station.
We're born for what we're born for, Colgrevance;
And you and I and Agravaine are born
To serve our king. It's all for the same end,
Whether we serve in alcoves, or behind

A velvet arras on another floor.
What matters it, if we be loyal men—
With only one defection?"

               "Which is—what?"
Said Agravaine, who breathed hard and said little,
Albeit he had no fame abroad for silence.

"Delay—procrastination—overcaution—
Or what word now assimilates itself
The best with your inquiring mood, my brother.
These operations that engage us now
Were planned and executed long ago,
Had I but acted then on what was written
No less indelibly than at this hour,
Though maybe not so scorchingly on me.
'If there were only Modred in the way,'—
I heard her saying it—'would you come tonight?'
Saint Brandan! How she nuzzled and smothered him!
Forgive me, Colgrevance, when I say more
Than my raw vanity may reconcile
With afterthought. But that was what she said
To Lancelot, and that was what I heard.
And what I saw was of an even bias
With all she told him here. God, what a woman!
She floats about the court so like a lily,
That even I'd be fooled were I the king,
Seeing with his eyes what I would not see.
But now the stars are crying in their courses
For this to end, and we are men to end it.
Meanwhile, for the king's hunting and his health,
We have tonight a sort of wassailing;
Wherefore we may as well address ourselves,
Against our imminent activities,
To something in the way of trencher service—
Which also is a service to the king.
For they who serve must eat. God save the King!"

They took the way of Lancelot along
The darkened hedges to the palace lights,
With Modred humming lowly to himself
A chant of satisfaction. Colgrevance,

264

Not healed of an essential injury,
Nor given the will to cancel his new pledge
To Modred, made with neither knowing why,
Passed in without a word, leaving his two
Companions hesitating on the steps
Outside, one scowling and the other smiling.

"Modred, you may have gone an inch too far
With Colgrevance tonight. Why set a trap
For trouble? We've enough with no additions.
His fame is that of one among the faithful,
Without a fear, and fearless without guile."

"And that is why we need him, Agravaine,"
Said Modred, with another singing laugh.
"He'll go as was appointed by his fate
For my necessity. A man to achieve
High deeds must have a Colgrevance or two
Around him for unused emergencies,
And for the daily sweat. Your Colgrevance
May curse himself till he be violet,
Yet he will do your work. There is none else,
Apparently, that God will let him do."

"Not always all of it," said Agravaine.
But Modred answered with another laugh
And led the way in to the wassailing,
Where Dagonet was trolling a new song
To Lancelot, who smiled—as if in pain
To see so many friends and enemies,
All cheering him, all drinking, and all gay.

Sir Lancelot du Lake

CHRISTOPHER WARD

In good King Arthur's famous court were knights of every mien and
          sort, some fat, some thin, some tall, some short.
The stoutest man in all that clan,
    So says Sir Thomas Malory,
Was hight Sir Lancelot du Lake, a guy of mighty mold and make, who
          never gave his foe a break,
Who never failed and never quailed
    And always earned his salary.

No other man was in his class. His thews and sinews were of brass. His
          head was bone, a solid mass.
In tilt or fight no other knight
    Could overcome this Paladin.
With curling lip and haughty sneer, he'd stick them through with
          lance or spear, he'd cut their throats from ear to
          ear,
With sword as keen as ever seen
    By Lion Heart or Saladin.

The ladies all with one accord this lusty warrior adored, though he
          their proffered love ignored,
Pursued him dressed in Sunday best,
    In satins, silks, and miniver.

But he disdained them all and each. For he adored a perfect peach
        upon a limb high out of reach.
By that I mean King Arthur's queen,
    The lovely Lady Guenever.

She knew her duty to her spouse, the sanctity of marriage-vows.
        Though his desire she'd arouse
By gentle wiles and tender smiles
    And glances, that she fed him on,
And let him kiss her lily hand, but nothing else, you understand, all
        other dalliance she banned,
Her lips withheld and oft repelled
    His ardor, while she led him on.

Now any knight, who meets rebuff from any chosen bit of fluff and
        doesn't promptly strut his stuff
To show the fair he doesn't care,
    Is lacking in sagacity.
So, when he saw he had no chance, he sharpened up his sword and
        lance, put on his iron shirt and pants,
His steed bestrode and took the road
    To prove his great audacity.

He hadn't very far to go before he met a worthy foe, full six feet six
        from top to toe,
A man of might, Sir Turquine hight.
    The other knights all dreaded him.
But Lancelot no fear had he. He drew his vorpal snickersnee. They
        fought from noon till half-past three,
Then, with a stroke would fell an oak,
    Sir Lancelot beheaded him.

Obliged by knighthood's high noblesse to rescue damsels in duress
        or otherwise in sore distress,
Where'er he went his days were spent
    In chivalrous phlebotomy.
And hardly did a single night descend upon this sturdy wight ere he
        had won some parlous fight
And finished off some other toff
    By skillful tracheotomy.

For years he wandered far and wide, engaged from morn to eventide
in derring do and homicide
And saving girls with golden curls,
With whom he used to dance a lot.
But news now passed from lip to lip that he had made one little slip
while on a philanthropic trip,
With fair Elaine, a lovely jane,
And Gwen lit into Lancelot.

Said he, "Now listen to me, Gwen. You know how 'tis with traveling
men. I swear it shan't occur again.
Though we're apart, my lonesome heart
Will e'er be true to Guenever."
So that was that, but, sad to say, she caught Elaine in negligee with
Lancelot in amorous play.
She saw him kiss that lovely miss,
Who really was worth ten of her.

So then she jumped on him for fair. "False traitor to the oath you
sware, you're banished, fired! Go take the air!
You're bounced, expelled! Get out!" she yelled
Like an avenging Nemesis.
Whereat he lost what sense he had. In fact, he went completely mad
and, though most incompletely clad,
Without a word this crazy bird
Rushed headlong from the premises.

But now the Queen her loss bewails. She sends Sir Perceval de Gales
to search the forests, hills, and dales,
With Sir Gawaine and Sir Uwaine
And others of that fancy lot.
But, though they followed all the trails, searched lunatic-asylums,
jails, and finger-printed all the males,
No whorl or loop of all that group
Resembled those of Lancelot.

A man with matted beard and locks, with nothing on but shirt and
socks, was meanwhile living like a fox
In cave or hole, and not a soul
Suspected he was Lancelot.

It's sad to be misunderstood and cut by all the neighborhood and
        never have a thing that's good
To eat or drink. And one would think
    He must have missed his pants a lot.

No wonder, then, this troglodyte was rendered peevish by his plight
        and never missed a chance to fight
With men or brutes, till his disputes
    Aroused the whole community.
They chased him far with sticks and stones, like any cur that no one
        owns, and kenneled him and fed him bones
And scraps of meat not fit to eat,
    And teased him with impunity.

At last one day by chance there came Elaine the Fair, that faithful
        dame, and cried aloud, "I know his name!
It's Lancelot whom you have got
    Impounded like a tarrier!"
She took him from his loathly jail and set by him the Holy Grail
        whereat (believe or not the tale)
His crazy brain was, presto, sane.
    Then did that rascal marry her?

He did not. Never ask me why. For any one with half an eye could see,
        what no one could deny,
That lollipop was sure the Top!
    There is no good excuse for him,
So let him go his knightly way, bestride his steed and fight and slay
        and sigh for Guenever. I say
Good-bye to Lance. He missed his chance
    And I have no more use for him.

King Arthur

CHRISTOPHER WARD

When Uther Pendragon was monarch of Britain,
He had never a chick or a child—of his own.
So when by the Angel of Death he was smitten,
There was no legal heir to succeed to the throne.

And, that being so, every baron and markis,
Each duke, earl and viscount, assembled in town
To assist in entombing his majesty's carcase,
Was plotting to capture the scepter and crown.

But one Merlin, a learned and crafty old wizard,
Concocted a scheme to throw sand in their gears.
When his plans were perfected from A down to Izzard,
He called a convention of all of the peers.

They gathered in force at the place of the meeting,
All looking suspiciously each upon each,
And after a most ceremonious greeting,
Old Merlin, as toastmaster, made them a speech.

"My lords, you can see in this old iron anvil
There is firmly imbedded the point of a sword.
I'll name as committee Sir Kay and Sir Granville
To assure you there's nothing concealed or ignored.

"Now, whoe'er can withdraw from this anvil that saber
Is heaven-sent King of this tight little isle.
There is nothing to pay, no expense but your labor.
So one at a time, gents. It's quite worth your while."

Then the peers, great and small, in the order appointed,
Had a try at the test, but the sword wouldn't budge.
So it seemed pretty plain that the Lord's Own Anointed
Wasn't one of that group, if the anvil could judge.

So then, having disposed of these noble prospectors,
Mister Merlin produced what he had up his sleeve.
It was Arthur, a boy, foster-son of Sir Ector's,
And the lad pulled the sword out with one mighty heave.

I may add that this wasn't so very surprising,
Considering the part the old conjuror played.
By pressing a button his hand was disguising,
He freed from the anvil the magical blade.

When a rumor ran 'round the assembly that Ector
Had adopted the boy at King Uther's request,
And that Uther had sworn him a faithful protector
Of the lad in his childhood, they hoped for the best.

Then, when some one recalled that the Duke of Tintagil
Had a wife whom King Uther had loved, named Igraine,
That the lady was frail or, to rhyme it, say fragile,
With this and with that then, their duty seemed plain.

So they crowned him the monarch of Britain instanter.
Rewarding the man who had put it across,
He proclaimed James A. Merlin Official Enchanter,
His Postmaster General and Patronage Boss.

Then he looked for a Queen and with Guenever mated,
He got the Round Table along with his wife.
'Twas antique and unique and 'twas much celebrated,
But that was the saddest mistake of his life.

Without doubt 'twas indeed a preposterous table.
'Twas a hundred yards round and a hundred feet wide.

271

And a hundred and fifty stout fighters were able
To sit down around it at once side by side.

Then, in order that none of the seats should be empty,
King Arthur endeavored to gather a clan
Of the lustiest knights he could find, an attempt he
Was sorry indeed that he ever began.

That this project was always a bone of contention
'Twixt the King and his consort was plain to be seen.
So that hardly a meal ever passed without mention
Of the difficult task it imposed on the Queen.

"For," said Gwenny, "how can I be saving and thrifty,
As you're always insisting is part of my job,
When we sit down to dinner a hundred and fifty?
I don't call that a dinner. I call it a mob.

"I really don't see why you took the old table.
It was always a bugbear to mother, I know.
Oh, of course, 'twill be famous in romance and fable,
But that don't pay the butcher the bills that we owe.

"And we haven't got near enough silver to set it.
It looks like the devil when furnished this way.
Oh, it's all right to say it's antique, but I bet it
Could hardly be sold for ten dollars today."

Because of the thundering width of the Table,
For a proper rejoinder the King's at a loss.
Though he knows what he should do, he's really not able
To throw a decanter or plate clear across.

These disputes so disrupted their cordial relations,
That when Lancelot came home from the road he would find
Her more willing to list to his fond supplications
And constantly more in his favor inclined.

Their behavior became a notorious scandal,
And, the King being seemingly blind to their loves,
A few of his cronies conspired to handle
This delicate matter without any gloves.

So Sir Mordred, Sir Agravaine, Knights of the Table,
And a full dozen others concerted a scheme
To produce such strong evidence as would enable
Them to prove to the King their belief was no dream.

They besieged the usurper in Gwenny's apartment,
While the King was away from his house for the night.
But he showed the first man what a sword through the heart meant,
And he fought through the rest and took refuge in flight.

When King Arthur returned they all told him about it.
"Oh, my!" said the King. "What a horrible bore!
But isn't it possible yet for to doubt it?
Are ye sure that he'll never come back any more?"

"We were thinking," said they, "of the Queen's evil doing."
"Oh, that!" said the King. "She shall burn at the stake.
There are wives quite enough to be had for the wooing.
But where's there a knight like Sir Lancelot du Lake?"

So the lady's condemned to be burned to a cinder,
And, as Lancelot's side-kicks have all gone away,
It seems likely that none will endeavor to hinder
The successful event of this *auto-da-fé.*

She is brought to the place where the stake is erected.
She is shriven, anointed, made ready for death.
She is chained to the stake and the crowd there collected,
Standing tiptoe, expectant, is holding its breath.

Then suddenly's heard such a deep-throated shouting,
"Stick 'em up! Stick 'em up! Have at them, my men!"
It is Lancelot's voice, and he's charging and routing
The guards that surround his immaculate Gwen.

He is backed by a gang of his faithful adherents.
There's a riot all over the whole market square.
The policemen, surprised by his sudden appearance,
Are soon beaten back, and she's snatched from the chair.

Then he's off with his gal on a pillion behind him,
And his gang follows after, a pack in full cry.

And it's dollars to buttons the King will not find him,
And it's very unlikely that he'll even try.

So that was the end of the famous Round Table.
For Lancelot's buddies were some of its best
And, though Art did his darnedest, he never was able
To stage a presentable show with the rest.

Sir Gawaine and the Green Knight

YVOR WINTERS

Reptilian green the wrinkled throat,
Green as a bough of yew the beard;
He bent his head, and so I smote;
Then for a thought my vision cleared.

The head dropped clean; he rose and walked;
He fixed his fingers in the hair;
The head was unabashed and talked;
I understood what I must dare.

His flesh, cut down, arose and grew.
He bade me wait the season's round,
And then, when he had strength anew,
To meet him on his native ground.

The year declined; and in his keep
I passed in joy a thriving yule;
And whether waking or in sleep,
I lived in riot like a fool.

He beat the woods to bring me meat.
His lady, like a forest vine,
Grew in my arms; the growth was sweet;
And yet what thoughtless force was mine!

From *Sir Gawain and the Green Knight,*
by Ernest J. B. Kirtlan, decorated by Frederic Lawrence.
London: Charles H. Kelly, 1912.

By practice and conviction formed,
With ancient stubbornness ingrained,
Although her body clung and swarmed,
My own identity remained.

Her beauty, lithe, unholy, pure,
Took shapes that I had never known;
And had I once been insecure,
Had grafted laurel in my bone.

And then, since I had kept the trust,
Had loved the lady, yet was true,
The knight withheld his giant thrust
And let me go with what I knew.

I left the green bark and the shade,
Where growth was rapid, thick, and still;
I found a road that men had made
And rested on a drying hill.

The Holy Grail

JACK SPICER

THE BOOK OF GAWAIN

1

Tony
To be casual and have the wish to heal
Gawain, I think,
Had that when he saw the sick king squirming around like a half-
        cooked eel on a platter asking a riddle maybe only
        ghostmen could answer
His riddled body. Heal it how?
Gawain no ghostman, guest who could not gather
Anything
There was an easy grail.
Later shot a green knight
In a dead forest
That was an easy answer
No king
No riddle.

2

In some kind of castle some kind of knight played chess with an
invisible chessplayer
A maiden, naturally.
You can hear the sound of wood on the board and some kind of
knight breathing
It was another spoiled quest. George
Said to me that the only thing he thought was important in chess was
killing the other king. I had accused him of lack of
imagination.
I talked of fun and imagination but I wondered about the nature of
poetry since there was some kind of knight and an
invisible chessplayer and they had been playing
chess in the Grail Castle.

3

The grail is the opposite of poetry
Fills us up instead of using us as a cup the dead drink from.
The grail the cup Christ bled into and the cup of plenty in Irish
mythology
The poem. Opposite. Us. Unfullfilled.
These worlds make the friendliness of human to human seem close
as cup to lip.
Savage in their pride the beasts pound around the forest perilous.

4

Everyone is impressed with courage and when he fought him he won
Who won?
I'm not sure but one was wearing red armor and one black armor
I'm not sure about the colors but they were looking for a cup or a
poem
Everyone in each of the worlds is impressed with courage and I'm not
sure if either of them were human or that what they
were looking for could be described as a cup or a
poem or why either of them fought
They made a loud noise in the forest and the ravens gathered in trees
and you were almost sure they were ravens.

5

On the sea
(There is never an ocean in all Grail legend)
There is a boat.
There is always one lone person on it sailing
Widdershins.
His name is Kate or Bob or Mike or Dora and his sex is almost as
        obscure as his history.
Yet he will be met by a ship of singing women who will embalm him
        with nard and spice and all of the hallows
As the ocean
In the far distance.

6

They are still looking for it
Poetry and magic see the world from opposite ends
One cock-forward and the other ass-forward
All over Britain (but what a relief it would be to give all this up and
        find surcease in somebodyelse's soul and body)
Thus said Merlin
Unwillingly
Who saw through time.

7

Perverse
Turned against the light
The grail they said
Is achieved by steady compromise.
An unending
The prize is there at the bottom of the rainbow—follow the invisible
        markings processwise
I, Gawain, who am no longer human but a legend followed the
        markings
Did
More or less what they asked
My name is now a symbol for shame
I, Gawain, who once was a knight of the Grail in a dark forest.
           END OF BOOK OF GAWAIN

1

Fool-
Killer lurks between the branches of every tree
Bird-language.
Fooled by nature, I
Accepted the quest gracefully
Played the fool. Fool-
Killer in the branches waiting.
Left home. Fool-killer left home too. Followed me.
Fool-
Killer thinks that just before the moment I will find the grail he will
            catch me. Poor
Little boy in the forest
Dancing.

2

Even the forest felt deserted when he left it. What nonsense!
The enormous trees. The lakes with carp in them. The wolves and
            badgers. They
Should feel deserted for a punk kid who has left them?
Even the forest felt deserted. There were no leaves dropping or
            sounds anybody could hear.
The wind met resistance but no noise, the sky
Could not be heard through the water.
Percival
Fool, like badger, pinetree, broken water,
Gone.

3

"Ship of fools," the wise man said to me.
"I used to work in Chicago in a department store," I said to the wise
            man never knowing that there would be a ship
Whose tiny sails, grail bearing
Would have to support me
All the loves of my life
Each impossible choice I had been making. Wave
Upon wave.

"Fool," I could hear them shouting for we were becalmed in some
                impossible harbor
The grail and me
And in impossible armor
The spooks that bent the ship
Forwards and backwards.

4

If someone doesn't fight me I'll have to wear this armor
All of my life. I look like the Tin Woodsman in the Oz Books.
Rusted beyond recognition.
I am, sir, a knight. Puzzled
By the way things go toward me and in back of me. And finally into
                my mouth and head and red blood
O, damn these things that try to maim me
This armor
Fooled
Alive in its
Self.

5

The hermit said dance and I danced
I was always meeting hermits on the road
Who said what I was to do and I did it or got angry and didn't
Knowing always what was not expected of me.
She electrocuted herself with her own bathwater
I pulled the plug
And there was darkness (the Hermit said)
Deeper than any hallow.

6

It was not searching the grail or finding it that prompted me
It was playing the fool (Fool-killer along at my back
Playing the fool.)
I knew that the cup or the dish or the knights I fought didn't have
                anything to do with it
Fool-killer and I were fishing in the same ocean
"And at the end of whose line?" I asked him once when I met him in
                my shadow.

282

"You ask the wrong questions" and at that my shadow jumped up and
            beat itself against a rock, "or rather the wrong
            questions to the wrong person"
At the end of whose line
I now lie
Hanging.

7

No visible means of support
The Grail hung there like june-berries in October or something I
            had felt and forgotten.
This was a palace and an ocean I was in
A ship that cast its water on the tide
A grail, a real grail. Snark-hungry.
The Grail hung there with the seagulls circling round it and the pain
            of my existence soothed
"Fool," they sang in voices more like angels watching
"Fool."

END OF BOOK OF PERCIVAL

THE BOOK OF LANCELOT

1

Tony (another Tony)
All the deer in all the forests of Britain could not pay for the price of
            this dish
Lancelot took a chance on this, heard the adulterous sparrows
            murmuring in the adulterous woods
Willing to pay the price of this with his son or his own body.
More simply, your heavy hands (and all the deer of Britain) a grail-
            searcher has need.

2

Walking on the beach and you both hear the sound the ocean makes.
The sailors at Tarawa, Java, burning oil at their backs
Swimming for dear life.
You say, and he says and meaningless says the beach's ocean
Grail at point 029.
In the slick of the thing music
Waves brushing past the beach as if they wanted to be human
The sailors screaming.

283

Walking on the beach, fondly or not fondly, they hear the sound the
Ocean makes.

3

Nobody's stranger than the stranger coming to the dinner
He can imitate anything or anybody.
"When they start climbing up the back of the old flash" the runner
                    who had simply hit a single almost had passed him
                    "It is time to quit. I'll never play again."
Almost saw the cup, Lancelot, his eyes so filled with tears.

4

Love cannot exist between people
Trial balloons. How fated the whole thing is.
It is as if there exists a large beach with no one on it.
Eaches calling each on the paths. Essentially ocean.
You do know Graham how I love you and you love me
But nothing can stop the roar of the tide. The grail, not there,
                    becomes a light which is not able to be there like a
                    lighthouse or spindrift
No, Graham, neither of us can stop the pulse and beat of it
The roar.

5

Lancelot fucked Gwenivere only four times.
He fucked Elaine twenty times
At least. She had a child and died from it.
Hero Lancelot feared the question "what is the holy grail?" which
                    nobody asked him.
All the snow on the mountain
It was
For a time
His question to answer.

6

The Irish have only invented three useful things:
Boston, The Holy Grail, and fairies.
This is not to imply that Boston, The Holy Grail and fairies do not
                    exist.
They do and are to be proved in time as much as the package of Lucky

284

Strike cigarettes you smoke or the village your
grandmother came from.
Jack, jokes aside, is very much like entering that forest
Perilous
No place for Lancelot, who has killed more men
Than you I-
Rish will ever see.

7

He has all the sense of fun of an orange, Gawain once explained to
a trusted friend.
His sense of honor is too much barely to carry his body
The horse he rides on (Dada) will never go anywhere. Sharp, in the
palace, he wanders alone among intellectual ser-
vants
He sings a song to himself as he goes out to look for the thing.
The Grail will not be his
Obviously.

END OF BOOK OF LANCELOT

THE BOOK OF GWENIVERE

1

Lance, lets figure out where we stand
On the beach of some inland sea which cannot be called an ocean
The river in back of us is green.
The river is wet. Down it floats what is not the grail-mistress, several
magicians and dead seagulls. Harp
On the same theme. Play the wild chorus over and over again—the
music magic
Lady of the Lake I hate you; cannot stand your casual
Way the wind blows. Listen,
I am Gwenivere.

2

The question is pretty simple. I would never have been admitted to
the Grail Castle but if I had been I would have asked
it: "Why
Did you admit me to the Grail Castle?" That would have stopped him.
I am sick of the invisible world and all its efforts to be visible
What eyes

(Yours or mine)
Are worth seeing it
Or, Lance, what eyes (mine and yours) when, looking at each other
              we forget the Grail Castle for a moment at least
Make it worth seeing it?

3

Good Friday now. They are saying mass in the Grail Castle
The dumb old king
Awaits
The scourge, the vinegar, the lance, for the umptiumpth time
Not Christ, but a substitute for Christ as Christ was a substitute.
You knights go out to tear him from the cross like he was a fairy
              princess turned into a toad
The cup that keeps the blood shed, bled into
Is a hoax, a hole
I see it dis-
Appear.

4

What you don't understand are depths and shadows
They grow, Lance, though the sun covers them in a single day.
Grails here, grails there, grails tomorrow
A trick of light.
A trick of light streaming from the cup
You say, knowing only the unbent rock
The shells
That have somehow survived their maker.
The depths and shadows are beside all of this, somehow
Returning
Each man to what of him is not bone and skin and mortal
The moon
Which is beautiful and shell of the earth
Streaming.

5

Sometimes I wonder what you are looking for. The Monday
After Christ died the women came to his tomb and the angel said
              "What are you looking for?"
A sensible question.
The bloody lance that pierced his side, the scourge, the vinegar had

all turned into relics
Why beat a dead horse?
The women, who were no better than they should be, hadn't seen
        him
If there really was a Christ only
This will happen in the Grail Castle

6

Boo! I tell you all
Scape-ghosts and half-ghosts
You do not know what is going to appear.
Is going to appear at the proper place like you, Lance
Salt Lake City, New York, Jerusalem, Hell, The Celestial City
Winking and changing like a light in some dark harbor. Damn
The ghosts of the unbent flame, the pixies, the kobalds, the dwarves
                eating jewels underground, the lives that seem to
                have nothing to do except to make you have
Adventures.
Naked
I lie in this bed. The spooks
Around me animate themselves.
Boo! Hello!
Lance, the cup is heavy. Drop the cup!

7

This teacup Christ bled into. You are so polite, Lance
All your heros are so polite
They would make a cat scream.
I dreamed last night that your body had become a gigantic adven-
                ture. Wild horses
Could not tear it away from itself.
I
Was the whole earth you were traveling over
Rock, sand, and water.
Christ, and this little teacup
Were always between us.
I was a witch, Lance. My body was not the earth, yours not wild horses
                or what wild horses could not tear
Politely, your body woke me up
And I saw the bent morning
END OF BOOK OF GWENIVERE

287

1

"Go to jail. Go directly to jail. Do not pass Go. Do not collect
     $200.00."
The naked sound of a body sounds like a trumpet through all this
     horseshit.
You do not go to jail. You stay there unmoved at what any physical
     or metaphysical policemen do.
You behave like Gandhi. Your
Magic will be better than their magic. You await that time with
     hunger.
Strike
Against the real things. The colonial Hengest and Horsa
The invasion of Britain was an invasion of the spirit.

2

Wohin auf das Auge blicket
Moor und Heide rings herum
Vogelsang uns nicht erquicket
Eichen stehen kahl und krumm.
Lost in the peril of their own adventure
Grail-searchers im Konzentrationslage
A Jew stole the grail the first time
And a jew died into it
That is the history of Britain.
The politics of the world of spooks is as random as that of a
     Mesopotamian kingdom
Merlin (who saw two ways at the least of the river, the bed of the river.)
     Maer-
Chen ausgeschlossen.

3

The tower he built himself
From some kind of shell that came from his hide
He pretended that he was a radio station and listened to grail-music
     all day and all night every day and every night.
Shut up there by a treachery that was not quite his own (he could not
     remember whose treachery it was) he predicted the
     future of Britain.

The land is hollow, he said, it consists of caves and holes so
         immense that eagles or nightingales could not fly in
         them
Love,
The Grail, he said,
No matter what happened.

4

Otherwise everything was brilliant
Flags loose in the wind. A tournament
For live people. Disengagement as from the throat to the loin or the
         sand to the ocean.
The flags
Of another country.
Flags hover in the breeze
Mary Baker Eddy alone in her attempt
To slake Thursdays. Sereda,
Oh, how chill the hill
Is with the snow on it
What a semblance of
Flags.

5

Then the thought of Merlin became more than imprisoned Merlin
A jail-castle
Was built on these grounds.
Sacco and Vanzetti and Lion-Hearted Richard and Dillinger who
         somehow almost lost the Grail. Political prisoners
Political prisoners. Willing to rise from their graves.
"The enemy is in your own country," he wrote that when Gawain and
         Percival and almost everybody else was stumbling
         around after phantoms
There was a Grail but he did not know that
Jailed.

6

That's it Clyde, better hit the road farewell
That's it Clyde better hit the road
You're not a frog you're a horny toad. Goodbye, farewell, adios.
The beach reaching its ultimate instant. A path over the sand.

And the toadfrog growing enormous in the shadow of fogged-in
              waters. The Lady of the Lakes. Monstrous.
This is not the end because like a distant bullet
A ship comes up. I don't see anybody on it. I am Merlin imprisoned
              in a branch of the Grail Castle.

7

"Heimat du bist wieder mein"
Heimat. Heimat ohne Ferne
You are called to the phone.
You are called to the phone to predict what will happen to Britain.
              The great silver towers she gave you. What you are
              in among
You are called to predict the exact island that your ancestors came
              from
Carefully now will there be a Grail or a Bomb which tears the heart
              out of things?
I say there will be no fruit in Britain for seven years unless something
              happens.

END OF BOOK OF MERLIN

THE BOOK OF GALAHAD

1

Backyards and barnlots
If he only could have stopped talking for a minute he could have
              understood the prairies of American
Whitman, I mean, not Galahad who were both born with the same
              message in their throats
Contemplating America from Long Island Sound or the Grail from
              purity is foolish, not in a bad sense but fool-ish as if
              words or poetry could save you.
The Indians who still walked around the Plains were dead and the
              Grail-searchers were dead and neither of them
              knew it.
Innocent in the wind, the sound of a real bird's voice
In-vented.

2

Galahad was invented by American spies. There is no reason to think
              he existed.

290

There are agents in the world to whom true and false are laughable.
    Galahad laughed
When he was born because his mother's womb had been so funny.
    He laughed at the feel of being a hero.
Pure. For as he laughed the flesh fell off him
And the Grail appeared before him like a flashlight.
Whatever was to be seen
Underneath.

3

"We're off to see the Wizard, the wonderful Wizard of Oz,"
Damned Austrailians marching into Greece on a fool's errand.
The cup said "Drink me" so we drank
Shrinking or rising in size depending how the bullets hit us
Galahad had a clearer vision. Was an SS officer in that war or a
    nervous officer (Albanian, say), trying to outline
    the cup through his glasses.
The Grail lives and hovers
Like bees
Around the camp and their love, their corpses. Honey-makers
Damned Austrailians marching into Greece on a fool's errand.

4

To drink that hard liquor from the cold bitter cup.
I'll tell you the story. Galahad, bastard son of Elaine
Was the only one allowed to find it. Found it in such a way that the
    dead stayed dead, the waste land stayed a waste
    land. There were no shoots from the briers or elm
    trees.
I'll teach you to love the Ranger Command
To hold a six-shooter and never to run
The brier and elm, not being human endure
The long walk down somebody's half-dream. Terrible.

5

Transformation then. Becoming not a fool of the grail like the
    others were but an arrow, ground-fog that rose up
    and down marshes, loosing whatever soul he had in
    the shadows
Tears of ivy. The whole lost land coming out to meet this soldier
Sole dier in a land of those who had to stay alive,

291

Cheat of dream
Monster
Casually, ghostlessly
Leaving the story
And the land was the same
The story the same
No hand
Creeping out of the shadows.

6

The Grail was merely a cannibal pot
Where some were served and some were not
This Galahad thinks.

The Grail was mainly the upper air
Where men don't fuck and women don't stare
This Galahad thinks.

The Grail's alive as a starling at dawn
That shatters the earth with her noisy song
This Galahad thinks.

But the Grail is there. Like a red balloon
It carries him with it up past the moon
Poor Galahad thinks.

Blood in the stars and food on the ground
The only connection that ever was found
Is what rich Galahad thinks.

7

The Grail is as common as rats or seaweed
Not lost but misplaced.
Someone searching for a letter that he knows is around the house
And finding it, no better for the letter.
The grail-country damp now from a heavy rain
And growing pumpkins or artichokes or cabbage or whatever they
                used to grow before they started worrying about the
                weather. Man
Has finally no place to go but upward: Galahad's
Testament.

ENDOF BOOK OF GALAHAD

1

"He who sells what isn't hisn
Must pay it back or go to prison,"
Jay Gould, Cornelius Vanderbilt, or some other imaginary American
            millionaire
—Selling short.
The heart
Is short too
Beats at one and a quarter beats a second or something like that.
            Fools everyone.
I am king
Of a grey city in the history books called Camelot
The door, by no human hand,
Open.

2

Marilyn Monroe being attacked by a bottle of sleeping pills
Like a bottle of angry hornets
Lance me, she said
Lance her, I did
I don't work there anymore.
The answer-question always the same. I cannot remember when I
            was not a king. The sword in the rock is like a
            children's story told by my mother.
He took her life. And when she floated in on the barge or joined the
            nunnery or appeared dead in all the newspapers it
            was his shame not mine
I was king.

3

In the episode of le damoissele cacheresse, for example, one stag,
            one brachet, and one fay, all of which properly
            belong together as the essentials for the adventures
            of a single hero, by a judicious arrangement supply
            three knights with difficult tasks, and the maiden
            herself wanders off with a different lover.
So here, by means of one hunt and one fairy ship, three heros are
            transported to three different places. When they
            awake the magic ship has vanished and sorry adven-
            tures await them all. Not one of them is borne by

the boat, as we should naturally expect, to the love
of a fay
Plainly we are dealing with materials distorted from their
original form.

4

The faint call of drums, the little signals
Folks half-true and half-false in a different way than we are half-true
and half-false
A meal for us there lasts a century.
Out to greet me. I, Arthur
Rex quondam et futurus with a banjo on my knee.
I, Arthur, shouting to my bastard son "It is me you are trying to
murder!"
Listening to them, they who have problems too
The faint call of   them.   The faint call of
(They would stay in Camelot for a hundred years) The faint call of
Me.

5

I have forgotten why the grail was important
Why somebody wants to reach it like a window you throw open.
Thrown open
What would it mean? What knight would fight the gorms and
cobblies to touch it?
I can remember a lot about the kingdom. The peace I was going to
establish. The wrong notes, the wrong notes, Merlin
told me, were going to kill me.
Dead on arrival. Avalon has
Supermarkets—where the dead trade bones with the dead. Where
the heros
Asking nothing

6

The blackness remains. It remains even after the rich fisherman has
done what he can do to protect home and mother.
It is there like the sun.
Not lost battles or even defeated people
But blackness alive with itself
At the sides of our fires.
At home with us
And a monstrous anti-grail none of those knights could have met or
invented

294

As real as tomorrow.

Not the threat of death. They could have conquered that. Not even
        bad magic.

It is a simple hole running from one thing to another. No kingdom
        will be saved.

No rest-

Titution.

7

A noise in the head of the prince. A noise that travels a long ways

Past chances, broken pieces of lumber,

"Time future," the golden head said,

"Time present. Time past."

And the slumbering apprentice never dared to tell the master. A
        noise.

It annoys me to look at this country. Dead branches. Leaves unable
        even to grimly seize their rightful place in the tree
        of the heart

Annoys me

Arthur, king and future king

A noise in the head of the prince. Something in God-language. In
        spite of all this horseshit, this uncomfortable music.

END OF BOOK OF THE DEATH OF ARTHUR

Launcelot in Hell

JOHN CIARDI

That noon we banged like tubs in a blast from Hell's mouth.
Axes donged on casques, and the dead steamed through their
          armor,
their wounds frying. Horses screamed like cats, and men
ran through their own dust like darks howling. My country
went up in flames to the last rick and roof, and the smoke
was my own breath in me scorching the world bare.

We fought. May the clerk eat his own hand in fire forever
who wrote I would not face Arthur. Iron sparks iron.
We fought as we had been made, iron to iron. Who takes
a field from me tastes his own blood on it.
Three times I knocked him from the saddle. What's a king?—
he'd had the best mare ever danced on turf

and couldn't sit *that* saddle. Well, I rode her:
king's mount from bell to cockcrow while bed, castle and country
shook under us, and he snored holiness to a sleeping sword
from the fairies. Excalibur's ex-horseman. Yes, I fought him:
I took my damnation as it came and would have hacked
a thousand Arthurs small to mount her again.

He did better by a warhorse. That saddle, at least, he knew
how to climb into. Iron to iron he charged, and could have knocked
a castle over. But still a fool, too pure for a feint
or sidestep. Three times I dumped him with his ribs stove
and could have finished him backhand, but reined and waited
with my own head split and a puddle of blood in my pants.

The fourth, he hove dead already into the saddle and came on.
But even a king won't work with no blood in him:
his point dropped till it grounded, and poled him
over his horse's rump. And I did not rein but took him
clean in air, though I broke my arm to do it. And there he lay:
my two horns on his head, my third through his back.

What can a clerk know of the day of dead kings and dead countries?
I blew and no one answered. The men were dead
and scarcely boys enough left to carry a king's bones
to the smoke of the burned chapel. What other burial
was done that day was done by crows and gypsies. And in my heart:
where would I find another worth damnation?

I never turned back and I never looked back. My country
burned behind me and a king lay skewered on a charred altar,
his sword in blood at my feet. I took it up and flung it
into a swamp. He had bled into it: why hold back his sword?
No fairy arm reached out of the muck to catch it. That
was another life and spent, and what was there left to save?

Except the mare! Even bled down to dust and my bones shivered,
my veins pumped at the thought of her. Why else
had I cracked king, castle, and my own head? I rode,
and mended as I rode—mended enough—enough to be still alive—
or half alive—when I found her. And when I had waited
a cool two hours at her door, what came to meet me?

A nun! Eight thousand men dead and the best iron in England
black in the burned stones of a burned shire, and my own bones
stitched in by nothing but scars, and there she stood,
black as the day we had made of the world, and gave me
—a litany of tears! A whore of heaven wailing
from a black cassock as if she stood naked in a hollow tree!

With her eyes turned in unseeing: as if to Heaven:
as if there were no world and we had not dared it
beyond damnation! That was the death of all:
she dared not even look at what we were! And for *this*
I had fed the best meat in England to carrion crows
and left a crown in mud for a gypsy's picking.

I did not turn back and I did not look back.
I had left a king and country dead without turning.
Should I turn now for a mare? Let Heaven ride her spavined:
I had the heat of her once, and I'd sooner
have turned Saracen and ripped the crosses from Europe
than deny my blood spilled into his in the field that made us.

Once of a world she danced like flame, and the man who would not
die to be scorched there was dead already. Dead as the clerk
who rhymed us to a moral. There is no moral. I was. He was. She
           was.
Blood is a war. I broke my bones on his, iron to iron.
And would again. Without her. Stroke for stroke. For his own sake.
Because no other iron dared me whole.

Merlin Enthralled

RICHARD WILBUR

In a while they rose and went out aimlessly riding,
Leaving their drained cups on the table round.
Merlin, Merlin, their hearts cried, where are you hiding?
In all the world was no unnatural sound.

Mystery watched them riding glade by glade;
They saw it darkle from under leafy brows;
But leaves were all its voice, and squirrels made
An alien fracas in the ancient boughs.

Once by a lake-edge something made them stop.
Yet what they found was the thumping of a frog,
Bugs skating on the shut water-top,
Some hairlike algae bleaching on a log.

Gawen thought for a moment that he heard
A whitethorn breathe *Niniane.* That Siren's daughter
Rose in a fort of dreams and spoke the word
Sleep, her voice like dark diving water;

And Merlin slept, who had imagined her
Of water-sounds and the deep unsoundable swell
A creature to bewitch a sorcerer,
And lay there now within her towering spell.

Slowly the shapes of searching men and horses
Escaped him as he dreamt on that high bed:
History died; he gathered in its forces;
The mists of time condensed in the still head

Until his mind, as clear as mountain water,
Went raveling toward the deep transparent dream
Who bade him sleep. And then the Siren's daughter
Received him as the sea receives a stream.

Fate would be fated; dreams desire to sleep.
This the forsaken will not understand.
Arthur upon the road began to weep
And said to Gawen *Remember when this hand*

Once haled a sword from stone; now no less strong
It cannot dream of such a thing to do.
Their mail grew quainter as they clopped along.
The sky became a still and woven blue.

WITHDRAWN